Exorbitance

THE LEWIS HENRY MORGAN LECTURES

Kathryn Mariner and Llerena Searle, Co-Directors

EXORBITANCE

A SPECULATIVE ETHNOGRAPHY OF INHERITANCE

Deborah A. Thomas

DUKE UNIVERSITY PRESS | *DURHAM AND LONDON* | 2025

Project Editor: Lisa Lawley

Designed by Dave Rainey

Typeset in Arno Pro and Malaga by Westchester Publishing Services

Library of Congress Cataloging-in-Publication Data

Names: Thomas, Deborah A., [date] author

Title: Exorbitance : a speculative ethnography of inheritance /
Deborah A. Thomas.

Other titles: Lewis Henry Morgan lectures

Description: Durham : Duke University Press, 2025. | Series: The Lewis
Henry Morgan lectures | Includes bibliographical references and index.

Identifiers: LCCN 2025009636 (print)

LCCN 2025009637 (ebook)

ISBN 9781478032595 paperback

ISBN 9781478029236 hardcover

ISBN 9781478061441 ebook

Subjects: LCSH: Sovereignty | Postcolonialism—Caribbean Area |
Anthropology and history—Caribbean Area

Classification: LCC JC327 .T52 2025 (print) | LCC JC327 (ebook) |
DDC 320.1/509729—dcundefined

LC record available at https://lccn.loc.gov/2025009636

LC ebook record available at https://lccn.loc.gov/2025009637

Cover art: Leniqueca A. Welcome, *Unbounded*, 2025. Mixed media
collage.

For the ancestors, dead and living

Contents

Foreword

Deborah A. Thomas delivered her Lewis Henry Morgan Lecture in October 2023. The public talk, "Bodies, Knowledge, and Modes of Repair," was followed by a workshop in which invited scholars and faculty at the University of Rochester provided feedback on the manuscript for this book. Formal discussants included Faith Smith (Brandeis University), Maya J. Berry (UNC–Chapel Hill), and Kristin Doughty (University of Rochester).

Thomas's lecture continued the tradition of the oldest and longest-running anthropology lecture series in North America. The Lewis Henry Morgan lectures were conceived in 1961 by Bernard Cohen, Chair of the Department of Anthropology and Sociology at the University of Rochester, and supported by gifts from the families of Joseph C. and Joseph R. Wilson. Meyer Fortes gave the first lecture in 1963. The lectures have been organized and edited over the years by Alfred Harris, Anthony T. Carter, Thomas Gibson, Robert Foster, and Daniel R. Reichman. The Lewis Henry Morgan Lectures include pathbreaking contributions to the discipline, constituting an archive of ethnographic and theoretical innovation. Thomas's lecture—and this book—contribute to this legacy, providing an inheritance for future scholars.

Exorbitance is a speculative ethnography—risky, invested, innovative—that seeks forms of sovereignty that exceed the state and its juridical power. Thomas retools terms and practices freighted with racist, colonial legacies—sovereignty and possession, for example—looking to Caribbean, African, and indigenous antecedents to theorize sovereignty not premised on control over violence and possession not understood as territorial dominion. In centering relational, embodied performances—for example the myal possession of Jamaican *kumina* dancers or the spiritual testimonies of Coptic brethren—she finds alternate inheritances, in forms of evidence, archives, and modes of thought that elude frames of reference tethered to Western modernity.

The Morgan Lectures are themselves freighted with the kinds of inheritances with which Thomas grapples. The lectures honor the complex legacy of Lewis Henry Morgan, the attorney, businessman, and ethnologist who collaborated with Caroline Parker and Ely S. Parker, members of the Tonawanda Seneca Nation, to write one of the earliest examples of systematic ethnography, *League of the Ho-dé-no-sau-nee, or Iroquois,* published in 1851. Even as he worked closely with the Parkers, Morgan favored Native assimilation into white society and saw the role of anthropologists as documenting vanishing ways of life. His subsequent writings have been foundational to kinship studies, anthropology, and Marxist thought. In *Ancient Society* (1877), Morgan links technology to intellectual and social development, creating a model of cultural evolution with direct links to the race science that Thomas critiques in chapter 1. Rather than ignore or disavow this legacy, Thomas engages it, analyzing the 1929 study *Race Crossing in Jamaica* to excavate alternative forms of embodiment and autonomy that were illegible to its authors' anthropometric methods.

The rituals, practices, and exclusions of academia are also an inheritance with which we, as editors of the Morgan Lectures, and Thomas, in *Exorbitance,* wrestle. Thomas argues that "particular bodies in particular moments in particular contexts are exorbitant to European philosophical categories of Being and action"—and, we would add, to European ideologies about who *can* philosophize. The very embodiment Thomas seeks to recuperate has been seen as inimical to thought and used as an alibi for excluding women and people of color from the Academy and ignoring their contributions. We see this in the history of the Morgan Lecture itself: The first eleven lectures were delivered by men. Two women were honored in the 1970s and four in the 1980s before the lectures achieved a rough gender balance in the 1990s. As a record of anthropology as a discipline, the lectures thus chart slow changes in scholarly institutions. Deborah Thomas—whose scholarship, filmmaking, teaching, and institutional leadership have done so much to bring Black anthropology to the center of the discipline—has helped anthropologists and this lecture series to recognize and celebrate other inheritances.

Fieldwork, lectures, books, and academic workshops are some of the inherited practices of academic anthropology. In her lecture and workshop, however, Thomas performed the exorbitance of Black feminist praxis she describes in the book, creating new legacies within and beyond the old forms. With the poise of a dancer, Thomas performed her talk rather than reading it. She transformed the dull lecture hall with music and carefully framed video clips from Tambufest, the *kumina* dance festival she co-organized in Jamaica, that suggested her care for and with her interlocutors. She refused the impulse to analyze Tambufest in expected ways—to catalog and frame it. Rather, she described a process of contributing to events that would "cooperatively active the conditions for the relational space of *myal*," modeling collaboration, possession, bodily engagement, and surrender as a modes of anthropological praxis. The talk was like a beacon: "I didn't understand everything, but I got this overwhelming inspiring feeling that's what anthropology could be," one of my students told me afterward. It was, in the best way possible, speculative: a risky and optimistic investment in the future of our discipline.

Similarly, Thomas and her invited discussants transformed the lecture's workshop into a generous unfolding. By evoking evidentiary modes that included personal experiences and memories, the discussants' comments helped to build a mode of relationality with Thomas that exceeded their formal roles as discussants and author. Thomas was humble, vulnerable, curious. The tenor of the discussion was collaborative and open-ended: What could the manuscript be/become/do? Now, as a book, *Exorbitance* alerts us to forms of embodied knowledge in relation with others that enable *sovereign-ing*: creating new possibilities within old and harmful structures.

LLERENA GUIU SEARLE
KATHRYN MARINER

COEDITORS, LEWIS HENRY MORGAN LECTURE SERIES
DEPARTMENT OF ANTHROPOLOGY
UNIVERSITY OF ROCHESTER
FEBRUARY 2025

INTRODUCTION

SOVEREIGN-ING
The Body as Method

For as long as I can remember, I have had what would now be called an embodied practice. I was seven when we moved to the United States from Jamaica, and because one starts school earlier in the British system than in America, I was often at least a year younger than the other students. This meant that I was also less physically developed, and my lack of coordination plagued me in gym class, where I was regularly brutalized in dodgeball. After several tearful outbursts, my parents enrolled me in a gymnastics class. I took to it immediately and soon was flipping in circles around my classmates. I competed for various club teams as we moved from place to place, and then for my high school team (we won the state championships twice!), and then for Brown University. After my freshman year in college, I tired of turning tricks four feet in the air on a four-inch-wide piece of wood, and I started to wonder what other people did in the afternoons, evenings, and on weekends. So I quit.

To stay in shape, I tagged along with a roommate one day to a jazz dance class, and I fell in love instantly. I invited the teacher to lunch—that was Joe Bowie, then a junior at Brown, who would go on to dance professionally with Paul Taylor and Mark Morris—and I asked him to tell me everything: What other classes could I take? Who were his favorite teachers? How could I catch up, given I was starting so late? What did I need to know to change my gymnast body into a dancer body? He told me, and I followed his lead. I took three classes a day (ballet, modern, jazz, African, improv—whatever was on offer), I read incessantly, I learned dance history, and I started performing, first with student groups and then with a company in Providence. I moved to New York to do the Alvin Ailey Scholarship program, but I ended up working in theater. After a year in Bahia, Brazil—performing with contemporary dance companies that were incorporating the rhythms and dances of candomblé into their movement vocabularies—I came back to New York, and through a series of serendipitous surprises, I became a member of the Urban Bush Women (UBW), a company founded in 1984 by Jawole Zollar to use performance as a means of addressing issues of social justice and encouraging civic engagement, and to bring the untold stories of disenfranchised people to light through dance from a woman-centered perspective and as members of the African Diaspora community.

At the time, the company was touring about thirty-five weeks out of the year, and seeing the world through dance, in my twenties, was a huge gift. So was being salaried, but that is another story. Although it would later become common for companies to integrate dancers' vocalization and percussion with choreography, this practice was something that Jawole innovated (and something that likely emerged in part because of her training with Dianne McIntyre's Sounds in Motion). Jawole's process of making work through research, through improvisation, and through collaboration with musicians, artists, and writers generated moments of brilliance and laughter, struggle and tears, joy and recognition. Touring meant that we connected with audiences across the country (and around the world) and that we listened to new stories and encountered new motivations for the work she continually developed, work that broadened the space to hear, acknowledge, and value Black women. Dancing with the company thus became a kind of ongoing and processual conversation, between Jawole and us, among ourselves, and between the company as a whole and our audiences and interlocutors. The work of UBW drew from my body language, from the dance repertoires with which I was familiar or in which I had trained; indeed, it drew from the languages of all who passed through the company to develop something unique, something powerful, something that was always growing, something that valorized our stories, and something that nurtured these stories into spaces where we could live and laugh together.

Certain movement sequences from the company's repertoire—the "lanes" in "Shelter," the clump in "Bitter Tongue"—are forever lodged in my body because they required a particular kind of attention to our one-ness. Even now, having not rehearsed them in decades, I know that if I heard the drum break or the verbal cue, my body would automatically fall in line. On stage or in the rehearsal studio, when we were particularly attuned to the music and to one another, those sequences could feel transcendent, and in that state, we were one organism, one breathing body, one relational chorus. We would dance it and, afterward, not remember exactly how or when we got offstage. Those sequences are part of my corporeal and affective memory, and they inform how I walk in the world.

While I was in the company, we began a program of work that we then called Community Engagement Projects, which has since developed into the UBW Summer Institute and the other aspects of collaborative engagement in which the company is involved. Over the course of a year, we began learning from popular education leaders, from experts on embodied work with grassroots groups, and from community leaders in order to develop longer-term residencies through which we would collaboratively build skills and consciousness through movement and music. Our first residency was in New Orleans over twelve weeks in 1992; there, we worked with a community bookstore, a teen pregnancy prevention center, a welfare rights organization, a basketball team that needed math tutoring, and others. I was stationed with two other company members at a puppet theater organization in the Ninth Ward whose project was to host a block party to which they would invite a rival neighborhood group with the intention of enjoying an afternoon together without incident. Over six weeks, we worked with them on improvisation, on relaxation techniques, on expression and de-escalation, and the party went off without a hitch. Jawole and I also met regularly with a group of young women to talk about Black women's health and wellness issues, and after we left, this group went on to become a chapter of the National Black Women's Health Project. These community engagement projects transformed the company, individually and collectively. For me, this transformation ultimately meant leaving the company for graduate school to learn more about how artists have been involved in political and social change movements elsewhere in the diaspora, but this mode of working also grew and developed into an incubator for broader interventions that would reach far beyond what individual company members themselves were doing.

Why am I telling you all of this? In part, I am telling you because for years I have avoided writing about dance except insofar as it has been a portal into broader political questions. Although I read it, I was not interested in *writing* what was then called dance ethnography. I saw people like Katherine Dunham, Pearl Primus, and Yvonne Daniel as fellow travelers, as models of what it could mean to be a Black woman who was both performer and scholar and who was committed to and embedded in the communities with which they were conducting research. But as a graduate student, I was also inspired by those mid-twentieth-century anthropologists in the Manchester school who provided examples for thinking political life through performative, embodied rituals. I wanted to learn about the infrastructures that dancers were trying to create, the changes they were catalyzing, the impact they were having as they tried to transform the world. The *feeling* of dance I would leave to memory, or to Saturday nights in the club. But in fall 2022, after two decades out of the dance studio, I went back to dance class. Because of the ways I have been thinking about what sovereignty feels like, I needed to remember—and try to consciously experience—what it means to know through the body. I needed to make explicit what I had learned to take for granted, to exteriorize what had always felt normative to me. It took a few weeks, but after the muscle soreness subsided, and after I reacclimated to anticipating where the teacher's movement vocabulary would lead us in a sequence, I remembered how it *felt* to be in relation with the music and with others.

After presenting an early iteration of these thoughts at the University of Texas at Austin, one of my former graduate students, who now teaches there, squealed with delight: "It took you three books but finally you're getting back to dance!" This is true, in a way. But it is also true that dance has never really left me. It has always, perhaps subconsciously, informed my approach to problem-solving, to entering space, to editing films. And it certainly has informed my understanding of what a kind of exorbitant sovereignty could feel like. This book seeks to explore this exorbitance and, with it, the interplay between the feeling of bodily freedom and the intensities of political sovereignty. It asks what sovereignty might look like, and feel like, if we approached it not exclusively in terms of its foundational violences (conquest, imperialism, settler colonialism, capitalist extraction, and so on) but through the embodied forms of autonomy and relation we create in the realm of everyday life.

It was this interplay that Allen Feldman (1991) interrogated long ago in his ethnographic and oral historical account of political conflict in Northern Ireland between 1969 and 1981, an interrogation he called a "genetic history" of violence, "a genealogical analysis of the symbolic forms, material practices, and narrative strategies through which certain types of political agency are constructed" (1).

His interest, in that project, was to destabilize European philosophical equivalencies between the formation of the body and the formation of the political subject, instead showing how the body is a site of material and symbolic discourse through which history is culturally constructed over time. The body, Feldman argued, "accumulates political biographies, a multiplicity of subject positions, as it passes in and out of various political technologies of commensuration" (9). It is, as such, a potent site for political engagement, one that, he argued, intensifies in agency as the space for political action in the public sphere shrinks. Although the language of agency reflects the theoretical constellation of the late 1980s and early 1990s, it is Feldman's probing of the relationship between the body and political subjectivity (and subjugation) that I find useful. On one hand, it raises the question of who properly possesses a body and, therefore, the potential for meaningful political action. On another, it asks us to think about the ways particular bodies in particular moments in particular contexts are exorbitant to European philosophical categories of Being and action. And finally, it encourages us to explore the dynamic ways we express and engage our inheritances.

Like many others, I have long been interested in the proliferating and palimpsestic histories of dispossession and in the assertions of humanness that have emerged alongside, against, and across these histories. Within the Caribbean, the range of instantiations of self-determination that are legible in relation to classic iterations of political life include *marronage,* revolution, and anticolonial struggle. In and through each of these, however, we can also read their obverse— the continued incursion of the entities and projects to which they are opposed. In this book, I am interested in the ways thinking through the frame of *inheritance* might discombobulate this recursive feedback loop. If we read sovereignty through a phenomenological notion of inheritance—one that is not strictly concerned with genealogy or cause and effect but is instead experiential and indeterminate though historically embedded—we understand it not as a state of being grounded in instrumental rationality but as a mode, and a mode of being with, that I want to read not through Heidegger but through Édouard Glissant and his notion of *donner avec,* or "giving-on-and-with" (1997), a refusal of Hegelian recognition, an engagement with difference that seeks neither domination nor assimilation but respects autonomy, a reciprocity grounded not in knowing (transparency, extraction, exploitation) but in relational opacity. This reorientation would attune us to the modes of autonomy and interdependence that either circulate through or refuse these classic sovereign statements, and thus to the relations and forms of exorbitance that can produce a sovereignty beyond utility.[1] It would propel us toward practice-based and durational articulations of self-determination that are processual, performative, and grounded in the everyday intimacies of living together, and it would allow us to attune ourselves toward questions about how what we inherit can evidence modes of world-building that exceed classic political frames.

Exorbitance thus builds on my earlier interrogations of sovereignty to propose a different lexicon through which we might envision a political present and future rooted in relational and speculative Black feminist praxis. This lexicon, for me, is grounded in the body and thus will require a certain amount of what Bonaventure Soh Bejeng Ndikung (2022) has called corpoliteracy, "an effort to contextualise the body as a platform, stage, site and medium of learning, a structure or organ that acquires, stores and disseminates knowledge" (14). My argument is that, first, we are heir not only to colonial logics but also to the means to refuse or retool them, and that both of these inheritances are inscribed in and on the body.[2] Second, I assert that our understanding of the relation between inheritance and embodiment directs our attention to particular forms of evidence over others. By foregrounding embodied methods and embodied insights, I am also seeking to embrace quieter experiments with what a more radically humanist anthropology could look like, one that eschews Western Enlightenment modes of recognizing, categorizing, and collecting difference, one that moves beyond binary conceptualizations of the relationship between body and mind, self and other, and one that refuses linear teleologies, themselves the inheritances of liberal constructions of the transparent, knowable, and governable subject, constructions possible only through the violent policing of the category of the human. My interrogations are thus as much about the process and practice of anthropology as they are about the ins and outs of any specific interrogation of political life in Jamaica. By the end of this book, I hope I will have convinced you that to be in the world exorbitantly—however ephemerally and in whatever dimension—is to sovereign.

THE PROBLEM WITH SOVEREIGNTY

Within both critical Black and Indigenous studies, sovereignty has been a vexed topic. This is because having been defined as universal reason and absolute perspectivity, sovereignty constitutes the interior humanity of the rational European self against which all Others are compared and measured (and found wanting). Because violence is the constitutive force of conquest, colonialism, and slavery, and because in classic formulations of political philosophy, control over violence defines and legitimizes the sovereign, sovereignty is grounded in historical-ideological and onto-epistemological phenomena that benefit its architects and their progeny, producing whiteness, maleness, and Europeanness as the apex of humanity, the epitome of transparency, universality, determination, and causality (Ferreira da Silva 2007; Wynter 2003; Moreton-Robinson 2015; Kauanui 2008; Sturm 2002). Sovereignty operates by solidifying boundaries, controlling movement, demanding a singularity of life out of a vast multiplicity, creating and then naturalizing hierarchies that function through dehumanization, dispossession, and exclusion. These processes proceed through the ongoing and simultaneous recognition and elimination of Indigenous populations, through the constitution of Black people as dispossessed and therefore depoliticized subjects, and through the standardization of dominant settler reckonings of time and relationship to place.[3] How, then, can one engage sovereignty as self-making when new forms of dispossession are continuously rewritten over earlier removals and displacements, what Shanya Cordis (2019, 20) would call the "settler ascription of sovereign in/capacity"? How can sovereignty be a language through which to call attention to alternative ontologies, modes of governance, accountability, community, and ceremony when the logic of recognition has been a way to reiterate colonial rule through the perpetuation of the tropes of Black and Indigenous cultural and temporal difference (Coulthard 2014; Alfred 1999; Moreton-Robinson 2017; A. Simpson 2014)? Find another word, my friends have begged me. While this book in part represents an attempt to "find another word," we should also remember that all of our words for freedom, liberation, and self-determination—not merely *sovereignty*—are corrupted by and seemingly trapped within juridical etymological and geopolitical lineages that render Blackness external to life and being human. My endeavor here is not to recuperate sovereignty as a claim to or for the power of the state (and therefore subjectivity) but to explore why it remains such an important term for many around the world and how it might be conceptualized and experienced as exorbitant to these lineages.

There are, of course, other words. "Autonomy" is an obvious candidate, in part because it has already been resignified by both Marxists and feminists. Whereas for Kant, autonomy was the foundation of a moral philosophy in which being autonomous meant having the capacity to be self-determined, to govern oneself through impartial and rational awareness unconstrained by either internal or external forces, John Stuart Mill mobilized it in the service of a political liberalism concerned with individual freedoms and rights. Both were grounded in an understanding of moral or political rights as universal, untainted by specific cultural commitments or racial regimes, or any other particularities of Being or history or experience. It is this universalism that feminists have rejected, advocating on one hand for an analysis of capitalism that extended the Marxist concept of labor through the whole society, thereby advancing women's unwaged housework as falling within the capitalist wage-labor relation (Federici 1975; S. James [1974] 2012, 2021; Weeks 2011), and, on the other, for an understanding of self-determination rooted not in independence and noninterference but in relation and nondomination (Pettit 1997). This kind of self-determination is what Iris Marion Young (2001), drawing from Indigenous refusals of the grounding of liberal sovereignty in private property, called "relational autonomy" (34). Young's argument is that the presumption of noninterference does not fully capture the ways people are constituted through relationships, making the notion of ontological freedom a fallacy. Relational autonomy, on the other hand, "entails recognizing that agents are related in many ways they have not chosen, by virtue of kinship, history, proximity, or the unintended consequences of action. In these relationships, agents are able either to thwart or to support one another" (34). In this framing, autonomy becomes a capacity for "regulating and negotiating relationships so that all persons are able to be secure in the knowledge that their interests, opinions, and desires for action are taken into account" (Young 2001, 35; see also Boggs 2012). This approach helps to contextualize the observations of someone like the feminist anthropologist Eleanor "Happy" Leacock (1978), who found that women in Montagnais-Naskapi communities seemed interested not in equality but in the ability to make independent decisions about their own lives, individually and collectively, even in the face of a leadership that was predominantly male.[4] It also helps us to understand, as Jessica Cattelino (2008) has argued, that settler states like the US exist in a relation of interdependency with Indigenous peoples.

Feminisms across Latin America and the Caribbean have also been central to conceptual reformulations of autonomy, as they have understood theory and knowledge as being made and remade through activism and the celebration of different forms of sociality, and because they have conjoined antiracism, anticapitalism, and anti-imperialism with decolonial struggles toward Indigenous thriving.[5] For these feminists, a relational framing of autonomy is particularly necessary in contexts where the patriarchal cultures of organized party politics has marginalized women's interests and erased their participation in revolutionary struggles throughout the region, and where significant power inequalities among women have also obtained.[6] Autonomy, in these contexts, is perhaps most usefully understood as a *method* of working against these power disparities, encapsulated by the question the Red Thread Organization in Guyana has posed as a mode of reflection and organization: "How are we related to each other and what have I not understood about my situation when I didn't understand hers?" (Trotz 2007, 74; see also S. James [1974] 2012, 2021). In this way, relational autonomy disrupts the Enlightenment imagination of legitimacy through rationally chosen and unconstrained authority, in the sense of juridical authorship.

Another critical approach to autonomy has addressed its discursive roots in settledness. Charles Carnegie (2002), for example, has asked us to consider an ethos of *marronage* as a counterpoint to a version of autonomy that is grounded in the state or in the capacity for self-determination or self-governance. For Carnegie, *marronage* extends far beyond "settled communities of runaways" (119) into a wider dynamic of transfrontier mobility and fugitivity. In his trenchant critique of sovereignty, *Postnationalism Prefigured*, we are confronted with Black sailors and interisland traders who exploit the various vulnerabilities of planters, colonial officials, and nationalist policymakers who are constantly trying to constrict the mobility of those on whose movement they nonetheless depend. We come to apprehend the modernity of control and containment as continually one or two steps behind the countermodernity—a kind of fugitive autonomy— of subalterns. For Carnegie, these subalterns create a "loosely articulated infrastructure," an "institutional complex" as much urban as rural and grounded in actual and potential relationships, a complex "whose recognition significantly alters present-day political perspectives tied to fixed notions of race and territory" (136). He shows us, in other words, that the plot constantly exceeds the space and time of the plantation, and that autonomy is rooted not in the race-nation-territory triad but in the everyday movements within and across it. Like others, he sees *marronage* as orienting us away from a view of sovereignty in which control of the state is the site of aspiration and potential social change, and toward one that is grounded instead in accountability, spiritual practice, and nonlinear and nonteleological relations with others, including nonhuman others (Bonilla 2015; N. Roberts 2015; Gross-Wyrtzen and Moulton 2023; Lewis 2023).

The term *possession* is another plausible substitute for *sovereignty*, and this too is a term that both aligns with and disrupts imperialist and nationalist commitments. Like *sovereignty*, *possession* has a juridical and legal etymology that emerged in intimate relationship with modern processes of conquest and imperialism, processes for which the English are *arrivants*, coming on the scene in the early seventeenth century, centuries after the Treaty of Tordesillas (1494) divided the lands of non-Christians between Spain (Castile) and Portugal. In a context in which the right to absolute and independent rule (imperium) was based on the right to possess and rule territory (dominium), the British had to promulgate new understandings of land ownership grounded in both Roman law and post-Reformation understandings of Genesis and Psalms that placed a premium on the actual, physical occupation and improvement of territory (terra incognita or terra nullius) (MacMillan 2006). Territorial possession of lands thought to be "unimproved" thus paved the way not only to the evisceration of Indigenous claims to land but also to the recognition of English claims to sovereignty supranationally. These maneuvers were supported by emergent theories of property and ownership (by political philosophers such as Thomas Hobbes and John Locke) and by cartographic practices (by geographers such as John Dee). In this conceptual tracking, possession shares with sovereignty the violences of modern juridical orders and the institutions of the state, as well as the post-Enlightenment view of the rational, agential, accountable, and self-determined individual as the proper subject of liberal governance.[7]

There is a second sense of *possession*, however, that emerges from the realm of spiritual practice, and this sense allows us some inroads into the modalities through which juridical dominium could be unsettled. In tracking this parallel etymology, anthropologist Brent Crosson (2019a) has demonstrated that by the early modern period, possession not only applied to territorial dominion but also "to the inhabitation of humans by spirits or demons" (546). Given that attention to this kind of possession emerged at the same moment when post-Enlightenment political philosophy began to position the rational, "self-possessed" individual as the proper subject of liberal governance, Crosson argues that spirit possession was foundational to Western modernity insofar as it became a kind of "constitutive other" for Western personhood (see also Johnson 2011, 2014a, 2014b, 2019). Unsurprisingly, possession thus also came to be a key focus of study for anthropologists and other ethnographers who were interested in non-Western (and particularly African and African diasporic) spiritual practices.

If dispossession (of land, of oneself, of one's "body-lands," to quote Ana-Maurine Lara) constitutes nonpersonhood, then possession requires "spiritual and bodily reclamation and healing" (Cordis 2019, 12; Alexander 2005; Lara 2020). In this sense, possession is embodied practice, process, and dialogue; it is ephemeral, performative, affective. It indexes that altered ordering of consciousness, time, and space caused by the inhabitation of humans by gods, spirits, and ancestors (both eventfully and in the everyday), the moments in which one is claimed by and in dialogue with a network of spirits and co-presences (Beliso-De Jesús 2015; Berry 2021). It is an embodied phenomenon that can both produce and transform power through cultural memory and everyday performance,[8] and by *performance* here I mean to invoke Diana Taylor's (2003) notion of repertoire as set of embodied practices that also constitutes a system of knowledge production and transmission (26). Possession thus marks the nonlinear and unexpected ways something that feels like relation circulates and is transmitted from one to another, today, yesterday, and maybe tomorrow. It constitutes knowing without determination (Ferreira da Silva 2017a, 2022) and reaches toward a reorientation of colonial recognition (see, for example, Lamming, interviewed in Scott 2002; Matory 2018).

If possession (by spirits or ancestors) undoes the certainties of coloniality and liberal possessive individualism, it does so only if we surrender to it. While *surrender*, like *sovereignty* and *possession*, has etymological roots in law, militarism, and territorial expansion, it also indexes a yielding, a giving up of something to the power of another. This "giving up" not only refers to property or, in the case of war, territorial authority but also to giving "oneself over to something," which potentially makes surrender into something less juridical than relational (Glissant's "giving-on-and-with"), something that requires embodied attunement to what the body knows and how it knows, and how we come to appreciate the evidence it generates. In her examination of moments of military surrender, sociologist Robin Wagner-Pacifici (2005) tells us that surrender is "an event on the threshold" (24–25). Coming from the Old French *sur rendre* (to give back) and the Latin *rendere* (to repeat, to recite), the term suggests not only a prior claim but also repetition and some form of translation.

But *surrender* as a term is itself indeterminate, and that is perhaps best seen when we attempt to translate it. In Spanish, for example, to surrender could be translated as *rendirse, entregar, renunciar, capitular, abandoner, cesar,* or *dar.* Or in modern French, it could also mean *se librer.* Each of these words carries different affective resonances and thus has different implications for thinking about self-determination and agency. In some cases, we read intentional action, as in *renunciar* or *abandoner*; in others, we infer that a struggle has led to an involuntary surrender, as with *capitular.*[9] But we also know that capitulation in one moment can be turned into something that feels like freedom in another, which means that in all cases we are being asked to think through the broader contingencies and contexts—historical, spatial, and affective—in which the action of surrender is occurring. For Wagner-Pacifici (2005), it is the French reflexive verb *se rendre* that most clearly suggests in surrender "an implicit return of the self to its true sovereign . . . a sense of a recovery of an original state that either is true in its essence or is made true by the work of witnesses" (19). The presence of an audience suggests that surrender, like possession, generates archives that are in one way or another public, archives that might allow insights into what surrender means for those experiencing or bearing witness to it.

Other scholars have worked from locally relevant terms to describe something that looks and feels like sovereign-ing. I'm thinking here about how Thomas Cousins (2023) uses the isiZulu term *amandla* in his ethnography of repair in South Africa. For the timber plantation workers among whom Cousins conducted research, the elaboration of disalienation in contexts of extreme exploitation was not generated through a refusal to work but through the "ordinary scenes around the plantations," through "mutual incompleteness, becoming with others, and a relational effort to absorb, without effacing, the wounding effects of colonial displacement" (4). Timber workers enacted these efforts by, for example, engaging in forms of marriage play or by distributing traditional medical remedies. Cousins sees these daily practices as the work of repair, the development of capacity and strength, which he identifies as *amandla*, a term that resonates historically as "power" but that here indexes ethical life in a post-Apartheid labor regime.

I'm also thinking about Khaled Furani's (2022) offering of *khalifah*—"an ideal through which the Muslim tradition formulates the human telos as inherently transient" (483)—as a way to disturb secular understandings of sovereignty grounded in its purported indivisibility. Furani argues that within Abrahamic religious traditions, indivisibility is the province of God alone, and its transmutation to secular governance creates individuals who are, under the governing sovereign, conscripted in "enslavement projects that masquerade as freedom" (483). For Furani, a conception of sovereignty as finite and incomplete (rather than universal and indivisible)—and here he is drawing from Hobbes's framing of the state as a mortal god—opens the door to a valorization of transience and fragility. The gap created between the body of the king and the body politic, or the "God otherwise" who refuses "her own utterance" (McAllister and Napolitano 2020, 4) produces a vulnerability to the appearance and endurance of other ontologies of sovereignty (see also Rutherford 2012, 2018). Furani's (2022) claim is that Qur'anic *khalīfah* is not coterminous with rule but instead evokes replacement, transmission, succession, and inheritance, all terms that evoke an ethos of trusteeship (of each other, of land) rather than of the ownership so central to liberal conceptions of citizenship.[10] "To uphold a khalifal ideal for an ethically oriented life, then, is to handle finitude with care," he writes, "to treat as a trust (*amānah*) the earth that we receive upon entry and leave upon departure" (500).

Just as there are other words that strive toward enactments of sovereignty through this kind of ethical accountability, there are other genealogies of and referents for the term itself. Building on her classic articulation of refusal in *Mohawk Interruptus* (2014), Audra Simpson (2020), for example, has attempted to distinguish sovereignty as a Western form of exceptionalism and dominance from "sovereignty as Indigenous belonging, dignity, and justice" (686). In the latter context, the language of sovereignty has been central to Indigenous claims for self-governance, whether these claims are being presented to other Indigenous nations, to other governments (such as the US or Canadian), or to international tribunals. Sovereignty matters, therefore, because it is a way to talk about an ontology that makes land and water central to personhood, safety, and integrity; indeed, possession in this context dissolves the border between body and land.[11] This connection also holds within the Australian context, as Aileen Moreton-Robinson (2007b, 2) has argued: "Our sovereignty is embodied, it is ontological (our being) and epistemological (our way of knowing), and it is grounded within complex relations derived from the intersubstantiation of ancestral beings, humans and land. In this sense, *our sovereignty is carried by the body* and differs from Western constructions of sovereignty, which are predicated on the social contract model, the idea of a unified supreme authority, territorial integrity and individual rights" (emphasis mine). In these ontological recalibrations, where easy spatial and temporal binaries and Western hierarchies of being are refused, sovereignty becomes a mode of relationality rather than an instrument of exclusion and violence.

Similarly, Nishnaabeg scholar and writer Leanne Simpson (2017) discusses Indigenous governing structures as processual and emergent, systems of leadership that reflect the local landscape. The idea of nationhood that emerges from this relationality of context, land, and people reflects what she calls an "ecology of intimacy" (8), one grounded in connection, relationship, reciprocity, respect, and self-determination (see also Maynard and Simpson 2022). For Simpson, as for others, sovereignty cannot be rooted in recognition by the political form of the nation-state because it is inherent and unceded. Instead, Indigenous scholars note, sovereignty emerges from the kind of "grounded normativity" that Glen Coulthard (2014) has argued grows through resurgent political and cultural practices. These are what Laura Harjo (2019) identifies as "practices of futurity" (13)—everyday community-based practices through which people recognize their own power to act and to self-determine—practices that bring a "radical sovereignty" into being. Conscious efforts to revitalize languages are among the ways to elaborate this kind of sovereignty, one that can also redound to new forms of economic autonomy (Cattelino 2008; Davis 2018). So are documentations of oral tradition, such as *The Mohawk Warrior Society: A Handbook on Sovereignty and Survival* (Hall 2023) and the more eventful moments of protest and the enactment of self-rule, such as NoDAPL (the protests against the Dakota Access Pipeline), moments David Myer Temin calls "earthmaking" (2023, 15), practices of care and responsibility toward human and other-than-human beings. In these contexts, sovereignty resonates as decoloniality, a world-making project that defies the state's claim to unilateral and indivisible power, instead privileging care, accountability, relation, and interdependence.[12]

The Caribbean context too—where, as Michelle Stephens (2013) has argued, the very concept of *island-ness* fits the Caribbean region into the "geopolitical imagination of early modern Europe" (14)—offers genealogies of political philosophy that privilege relation and interdependence rather than linearity, teleology, and hierarchy. Europeans' understandings of islands as "early visual tropes of the utopic, insular features of the sovereign state," Stephens argues, tamed what she defines as the region's "archipelagic relationality" (14, 12), a relationality rooted not in the landmasses that dot the Caribbean Sea and Atlantic Ocean but in these bodies of water themselves. This relationality is what would have grounded Kamau Brathwaite's (1975) famous assertion that "the unity" of the Caribbean region "is submarine" (1),[13] as well as his rejection of the dialectic and his proposal of the "tidalectic" (Brathwaite 1999) as a way to read political theory through quotidian Caribbean life. The old woman sweeping sand from her yard every morning, her constant reiteration of a seemingly futile ritual, stands for Brathwaite as a constant reference to the Middle Passage, which brought her from Africa to Jamaica, and to travel that might in the future take her to another land mass, maybe a continent, maybe an island, "perhaps creative chaos" (Brathwaite 1999, 34). The "tidalectic" is a back-and-forth rather than a repetition (which is, on the other hand, what he calls "the Sisyphean statement"); it is a nonlinear phenomenon of cyclical, rhythmic fluctuation with unpredictable and complex results. This rejection of fixity and embrace of a rhizomatic relation with others is also what constitutes Glissant's (1997) poetics of relation, already discussed briefly. In relation, truths are neither grasped nor proselytized, and identity is not rooted in a past or in a territory but is emergent, indeterminate, and interdependent. This earlier generation of Caribbean scholars embraced particle physics and chaos theory because they already knew that the contradictions facing people around the world would not be transcended by aspiring to control of the state.[14] Their iterations of sovereign-ing were thus grounded in nonteleological and fractal phenomena that also regularly appear as elements of Caribbean landscapes.[15]

More recent Caribbeanist scholarship has asked us to reconsider *marronage*, to think anew about Afro-Indigenous relations in the region, and to consider the forms of solidarity and relation that are forged through spiritual practice. Take, for example, Ronald Cummings's (2018) positioning of *marronage* as an assemblage, not merely a bid for freedom through flight from the plantation but also "a remaking of structures and possibilities of community and a renegotiation of relationships to space, land, and territoriality in response to ongoing structures of colonial violence and the forging of a range of practices for making Maroon life" (49). Such a positioning reflects a processual understanding of sovereignty as something that repeats, not just spatially throughout "Plantation America"—the term developed in 1957 by anthropologist Charles Wagley—but also temporally (see, for example, R. Price 1972, 2011; Besson 2016; Bilby 2006; Freitas 1978). It brings into view the struggles over the boundaries of sovereign maroon territory and how those struggles have continued beyond the abolition of slavery (the immediate context of their establishment, in Jamaica, through the 1739 treaty between the British government and both Leeward and Windward branches of maroons)[16] to the contemporary moment, when negotiations regarding land and access (to clean water, clean air) involve the independent Jamaican nation-state and the Chinese companies now involved in bauxite mining in the Cockpit Country. While the Maroon Wars in Jamaica may have eventfully occurred during the decade before the signing of the treaty, their articulation of terms of struggle and their conflicting visions of sovereignty continue to wash ashore, "in terms of recurring arcs and experiences of vulnerability and insecurity" (Cummings 2018, 49), at different levels of scale and through different modalities of articulation.

This approach to *marronage* also requires a more nuanced understanding of the ways maroons have come to embody "resistance" within the nationalist (and "post"-nationalist) imagination. Indeed, scholars and commentators have for years demanded a public reconsideration of the historical role of maroons in quelling rebellions, given that their own juridical sovereignty depended on the return of those who had escaped from plantations or who otherwise threatened the viability of the plantation system. Consider the following story. In spring 2022, Jamaica's governor-general announced that April 8 would be known as National Chief Takyi (Tacky) Day. Chief Takyi led the longest insurrection of enslaved people in Jamaica, from 1760 to 1761. While the insurrection was inspired by the First Maroon War (1728–40), it was maroons who ultimately captured and beheaded Tacky, thereby ending the revolt. Intrinsic to attention to actually existing *marronage*, then, is also a reconsideration of the presumed solidarities on which our notions of collectivity are built.

It should not be seen as incidental that Afro-Indigenous relations, as Sylvia Wynter (n.d.) surmised in her epic work "Black Metamorphosis," may also have been grounded in sixteenth-century solidarities generated by *marronage*, solidarities that have largely been erased in the Caribbeanist canon (Newton 2013). Melanie Newton (2022) has argued that European imperial ethnocartography both created and reproduced this erasure through Janus-faced legal instruments distinguishing between an Indigenous continent and non-Indigenous islands. These distinctions persisted even as the Lesser Antilles resembled the continent demographically well into the eighteenth century, even as Afro-Indigenous populations consistently stymied British administrators' attempts to reinforce boundaries, and even as resistance to British colonial rule persisted and was militarily effective. The effect of this erasure is the reproduction of a dominant colonial narrative of Indigenous absence in the face of the ur-modernity of plantation-based monocultural, protocapitalist sugar production for export.

Engaging these relations has been the project of recent scholarship across critical Indigenous and critical Africana studies (see, for example, S. Jackson 2012; Cordis 2019; Byrd 2011; Maynard and Simpson 2022; King 2019). Ana-Maurine Lara's (2020) work with criollo traditionalists and feminist and LGBT activists in the Dominican Republic, for example, led her to argue for the elaboration of a "zambo consciousness," one that shifts analytic frames from *mestizaje* and "toward Afro-Indigenous solidarities manifest through the erotic, desires, sex, faith, friendships, and through embodied and spiritual struggles for queer freedom : Black sovereignty" (21). This is a freedom, needless to say, that exists beyond the state and instead emerges from knowledges, experiences, and spiritual practices that

Lara calls "criollo traditions," traditions that rupture the expectations and certainties of Christian colonial sovereignty: "Criollo traditions could reorient our beings toward other possibilities: the figure of the sovereign disappears and, in its place, emerge the *misterios*, the ancestors and the spirits that preside over the shifting relationships expressed through community; body-lands are not the object of conquest, the reflection of authority or power, but rather the material through which life forces are enabled" (125). Attending to the realm of the spiritual also requires an engagement with other inheritances and with the generations of transnational Black feminists who have long argued that freedom is realized as an everyday practice that conjoins the political, the spiritual, and the erotic.[17] This engagement necessarily alters not only our conceptualizations of the space-time of sovereign claims making but also our sense of the modalities through which something that might feel like sovereign-ing appears, flows, and recedes. If imperialism and slavery have afterlives in the context of the still-colonial present, then the modes and embodiments generated by refusals of the constrictions and constraints posed by these structures continue to circulate in unpredictable, though contingent, ways.

Our surrender to these modes and embodiments is necessarily guided by spirit, and this surrender requires not only an acknowledgment of the multiplicity and ongoing-ness of processes of dispossession, of the ways "violently dislocating transregional processes (conquest, colonialism, migraiton, war, wage labor) are rendered internal, are (literally) incorporated into people and their social and cultural practice" (Shaw 2002, 5). Surrender also requires faith, what Ajay Skaria (2022), in a brilliant essay on the figure of the "minor" in the work of Qadri Ismail and other contemporary subaltern studies scholars, defines as the "equality of vulnerability" (290). In tracing the difference between faith and belief (drawing from Ambedkar and Gandhi), Skaria argues that "at work in faith is a reverential equality with the sacred itself." He writes: "Precisely because we are acutely aware here that faith is groundless, we cannot subordinate ourselves to the sacred. Cannot. even as we surrender to the sacred, we are thrown back into ourselves in our freedom and equality to what we surrender to. As such, faith always intimates (even if it does not usually accomplish) a surrender without subordination, a vulnerable freedom with the sacred" (290). In the Jamaican context, we might think of this as the Rastafari I-and-I, a shared common essence with the divine, and indeed this is how Sylvia Wynter (1977) (following Hans Jonas) explores the implications of the Gnostic heresies. Understanding one's oneness with the divine produces a worldly transformation, a rejection of dominant systems and a reconstitution of the self in relation to others. Faith, as outlined here, is a practice of knowing that is oriented toward a "messianic impossibility," a "striving to realize the impossible in the here and now" (Skaria 2022, 293), a cultivation of authority through a practice of unbounded love rather than violence.

What I am arguing is that we must be open to articulations of sovereignty that are not tethered to the state or the parameters of its institutions but are instead offered as practices, performances, and processes that refuse law and dominion and draw attention to alternative inheritances of governance, community, and ceremony. I do not stand alone in this approach; other Caribbeanists have made similar claims in their own attempts to understand the affective and performative ways leaders articulate sovereignty and generate authority, ways that engage with but sometimes stand in tense relation to more normative forms of legitimacy (Kivland 2020; Jaffe 2024). The genealogies of scholarship I have rendered here show us that we can, and must, attribute to gestures toward sovereign-ing the quotidian enactment of process rather than sweeping project, safety rather than security, affect and performance rather than law and dominion, by reading it through a phenomenological notion of inheritance, and the forms of "implicancy"— what Denise Ferreira da Silva (2017b) has understood as quantum-level entanglements that exceed the limits of space and time—that redound from this. Further, I am entreating us to appreciate these gestures—moments of what Kevin Quashie (2021) has called "aliveness"—while also resisting the impulse to "scale up," as it were, refusing to turn local (and sometimes ephemeral) practices of sovereign-ing into modalities for reforming liberal structures of governance, which is impossible in any case. If sovereignty is historically contingent, if it is neither unitary nor universal but is instead messy, interdependent, nested, and entangled,[18] then it can be, and often is, unhinged (Thomas and Masco 2023). If we can imagine surrender without subordination, as Skaria (2022) has articulated, then perhaps we can also imagine autonomy without authority, and sovereignty without stability. My argument is that we can do this if we reflect and invite vulnerability and intimacy, theoretically and methodologically—modes of experience that demand attunement to the corporeal.

Bodies matter here because they are integral not only to the elaboration and management of liberal promises of inclusion and citizenship but also to the refusal of dehumanizing ascriptions—as property, as non- or not-quite-human, as traffic-able, or as socially and politically dead (Patterson 1982; Wynter 2003). The Caribbean, unsurprisingly, was central to the development of imperial and colonial knowledge about the body, not only during the early modern period of Spanish empire but also throughout the height of mercantilist colonialism throughout the British and French West Indies (Gómez 2017; Hogarth 2017, 2021). At the same time, transplanted Africans also developed a science of the body within New World plantation contexts, a science that was often advanced through such relational and embodied technologies as divination and possession (Palmié 2002; Gómez 2017). Stephan Palmié (2002) understands these technologies as providing a "record of the reflections of people on the moral texture of the world in which they conduct their daily business of being humans in the face of danger" (76), a co-constituted body of knowledge that emerged from and within the violent elaboration of modernity and one that was accessible analytically only through embodied attunement. The Black body is thus what Vanessa Agard-Jones (2013) has called a "scalar intertext" (184); it both indexes and reproduces local, regional, and global forms of power,[19] and it has the capacity to unsettle these both perceptibly and intangibly (Ferreira da Silva 2021).

Just as there are multiple genealogies of sovereignty, there are also multiple conceptualizations of the body and, therefore, of heritability and what it means to be a person.[20] I am interested in how we encounter and read those genealogies, and in what they might tell us about the modes of collective world-building that exist outside of but in relation to the juridical structures of sovereignty that govern modern Western political and social life. We know that Western political theory has been "profoundly somatophobic" (Threadcraft 2015, 208), an effect of Kantian critiques in which reason, interiority, and universality are located in the rational mind. For Cartesians, the mind-soul was trapped in (and therefore inseparable from) the body, whose subordination to the mind-soul also organized other subordinations—of non-Europeans to Europeans, of women to men, of colonized to colonizers (Covington-Ward and Jouili 2021). Moreover, the body was to be transparently apprehended (and controlled) through reason as an object among all other objects. In its purest elaboration, this process of apprehension led, analytically, to the forms of scientific racism and eugenics I discuss in chapter 1. During the period of conquest and throughout the transatlantic slave trade, however, what this process meant pragmatically was that Europeans were afforded interiority and subjectivity. Their closed bodies were not subject to violations by others, and also were not breached by spirits, and this condition is what purportedly allowed for the flourishing of mind. Black and Indigenous bodies, on the other hand, could never attain such interiority; their fleshiness—the conditions of possibility for

European interiority—was too penetrable.[21] Porous Black bodies thus became fungible flesh, whereas dispossessed Indigenous bodies became carnal, both lacking the interiority that would have made them legible as persons to imperialist adventurers.[22] While Cartesian dualisms have persisted across various philosophical lineages and developmentalist pragmatics, the emergence of phenomenology allowed us inroads that would move us beyond these Eurocentric binaries.[23]

The phenomenological lineage regarding embodiment in which I am most interested here is the one that moves from Husserl and Heidegger toward an understanding of the relationships between the body and conceptualizations of experience, both individually and communally, and this is a lineage that (within anthropology) begins with Marcel Mauss. Mauss's (1935) interventions regarding embodied habitus—that the ways we move are neither physiologically nor individually determined—provided inroads to thinking about bodily capacity, and therefore bodily perspectivity, as historical and social. If Mauss taught us that the body is not natural and universal, then Maurice Merleau-Ponty (1962) taught us that it is perceptual, where perception is indeterminate and preobjective (though not precultural). For Merleau-Ponty, the body is not an object to be known by the mind but is instead the grounds for knowing, where the mind becomes instead the site of objectification.[24] As Thomas Csordas (1994) has put it, "Embodiment is the existential condition of possibility for culture and self" (12), and gleaning insights into the latter requires what he has called "somatic modes of attention," "culturally elaborated ways of attending to and with one's body in surroundings that include the embodied presence of others" (Csordas 1993, 138). These phenomenologists have seen the body as both a physiological and a social relation among bodies (T. Turner 1994)[25] and as a site of "perceptual processes that *end* in objectification" (Csordas 1994, 7); it is thus medium and mode of intersubjectivity (G. Weiss 1999). Within this formulation, the body is not an isolated object but is actively engaged in world-making. As the essential condition of being in the world (Heidegger's Da-sein), the entangled and emplaced relational body brings "History" and "Society" in dialogue with the day-to-day embodied practices of individuals and communities.

While this lineage is compelling, it has also produced certain analytic problems. A body that is perceptual and that is part of making a world must be a body that properly exists for itself, not as "flesh" (Spillers 1987), not as property, not as the grounds for modernity, but as self-possessed interiority. Rizvana Bradley (2023) has argued that the limit of phenomenology is constituted through its refusal to "engage blackness as a serious theoretical problematic for 'moving beyond' the proper body" (82). "Black people," Bradley observes, "do not properly have bodies, insofar as such 'having' is in fact a linguistic concealment of a terrible claim: both to the presumptive ontic status of normative personhood and to the regimes of property and propriety to which the metaphysics of individuation are inextricably bound . . . flesh constitutes the body's very condition of (im)possibility" (87). The body is, for Bradley, a "racial apparatus" (83) that renders Black bodily sovereignty impossible; it is an entity that only indexes the ongoing violences of racial modernity, the conditions of possibility for Euro-American interiority. Bradley goes on to argue that "flesh is before the body in that it is everywhere subject to the body as racial machinery, violently placed at the disposal of those who would claim the body as property" (86). As a result, she states, "Phenomenology cannot furnish the conceptual tools for apprehending either the 'lived experience of the black' or the experiments in form which emerge from that experience, because black people have never had (which is to say, had the capacity to lay claim to) bodies in the sense presumed by phenomenology" (89). In a way, this is an important claim that serves the purpose of unsettling what she sees as overly celebratory anthropological investigations of corporeality that position bodies as "porous, affectable, malleable, or experimental" (82). However, for me, it is also a claim that presupposes a kind of historical boundedness that allows for no antecedent to the moment when racial terminology becomes tethered to civilizational hierarchies and notions of being human, the moment when we are conscripted within modernity (Scott 2004).

It is important to be attuned to alternative concepts of "bodiliness" (T. Turner 1994), to alternative modes of being and becoming such as the "pluriverse" (de la Cadena and Blaser 2018; Escobar 2020; Stengers 2010) or the kind of "anachoreography" that Fahima Ife has proposed as a "recursive practice of refusal" (2021, ix),[26] and to the coexistences and copresences that accompany bodies (Beliso-De Jesús 2015; de la Cadena 2015) not in order to descend into the realm of ethnographic particularity but to more properly understand how various challenges to the temporal teleologies of imperial philosophy and politics and their associated representational violences are articulated through the body. Moreover, this attunement allows us to pay attention to ways the body is not only "a means of passing on memory and history, it is also a means of *challenging, creating, and redefining* memory and history" (Covington-Ward 2016, 16). Inheritances, like bodies, are not stable.

My own feeling is that reading sovereignty through a phenomenological notion of inheritance helps us transit between flesh and body, moves us in and out of the world of totalizing ascription and toward potentiality and indeterminacy, toward the possibility of an interiority that honors other inheritances in which we are not engulfed by Enlightenment philosophical conceptualizations of space and time, form, and matter(ing) (see Ferreira da Silva 2017a, 2017b). Analytically, this releases us from the totalizing realms of colonial, poststructuralist, and Afropessimist discourse and toward an appreciation of performance and improvisation[27]—modes of practice, we will remember, that have also been central to Caribbean formulations of "giving-on-and-with." Everyday forms of bodily reverberation, for Brathwaite and Glissant as well as for us today, are modes through which to glean insights into sovereign-ing that are exorbitant, that in not being legible to liberal Enlightenment conceptions of value, or of space and time, or of transparency, also evade capture by its juridical norms. The Black body, then, is an archive not only of modernity's violences but also of its antecedents and its iterations yet to come.[28]

Finally, we return to the question of the body as an index of political community. Within ancient legal and philosophical formulations, this is the *corpus politicum*—echoing Plato's early formulation of human society as a collective body—itself derived from *corpus mysticum*, the Christian doctrine of the church as the mystical body of Christ. Hobbes's notion of the fictive body of the state had its roots in ancient Greek and Roman formulations of the sovereign as the head of the body and therefore its mind-soul, and in imperial Roman legal concepts of the corporation (*universitas*). It was Baldus de Ubaldis, however, who connected the theory of corporation to the ancient political and biological concept of the body politic, in which the whole body of a people forms a *populus* ruled by government, just as an individual is ruled by its soul. The soul, thus, persists as the mind-force of governance whose (consensual) authority over the individual was absolute. This would have been the position advanced by Hobbes; as Shatema Threadcraft (2015) has argued, "The state is but an artificial body for Hobbes; sovereignty, its vaunted soul" (208). Yet, if bodies don't everywhere conform to Cartesian notions of the mind-soul–body divide, if the soul can exist and act independently of the body, and if we perceive (ourselves, others, broader social collectivities and capacities) through our bodies, then paying attention to collective practices of embodiment can offer us insights into inheritances that locate the sovereign impulse outside of, but in relation to, European juridical norms.

If there is an argument for the need to find another word to identify the sovereign impulse, it emerges from this proposition, and if I had to choose one, it would be myal, which is, as I elaborate in chapter 3, a state in which the body is released—if only ephemerally and vibrationally—from the juridical realm altogether. What I hope to convince you of here, however, is that it is the *doing* and not the *naming* of sovereignty that is key to separating Western juridical notions of sovereignty from iterations of sovereign-ing grounded in exorbitant embodiment, in spiritual practice, in quotidian life, and in relation.

Let me suggest that our attempts to chart these terrains of sovereign-ing (and the modes through which we chart them) are perhaps best understood as forms of speculation, "the forming of a theory or conjecture without firm evidence" (Oxford English Dictionary), or the "investment in stocks, property, or other ventures in the hope of gain but with the risk of loss." The questions that are raised here have to do with evidence (What exactly is firm evidence?), and risk (How risky is too risky?). Speculation, therefore, invites questions of faith, but it is also the driver of conspiracy, itself an attempt to relationally read bodies of circumstantial evidence in order to draw conclusions about things we "know" happened but have no firm proof of. Evidence itself resonates multiply, and it is often not self-evident despite the word's etymological roots in notions of visibility and legibility. If we imagine evidence as something that can establish a truth claim, then we are privileging a positivist and juridical vision for ethnographic inquiry, one with roots in liberal, Enlightenment ideas encouraging reasonable deduction on the basis of evidence over "'slavish' and hidebound" obedience to authority (Kuipers 2013, 400). Evidence here becomes a question of science and law, institutional spaces in which a body could move "seamlessly from being viewed as person to property to evidence" (Crossland 2009, 71).[29]

But if we understand evidence to pertain not just to facts—objects and events that are somehow seen to exist outside a research relation—but also to affects and experiences, which inevitably include the ethnographer,[30] then we must understand evidence, as Kirsten Hastrup (2004, 461) has argued, as "enfolded within the relational nature of anthropological knowledge that—epistemologically—precludes the use of evidence as an independent measure of validity" (see also Strathern 2008). When we ask epistemological questions about what evidence is, how it is recognized, for whom it is legible or sensible, and how it is valued, we are thinking about evidence as a problem of the possibility of representation and narration. We are questioning the limits of legibility, and bringing into being the grounds for nonteleological relation on post-but-still-colonial terrain. We are attuning ourselves to how people make sense of their experiences in the world and how, in doing so, they potentially refute the inscriptions, categorical or temporal, that shape others' assessments of their being in the world. And we are enacting what Ana-Maurine Lara (2020) has called speculative anthropology, "an anthropology that eschews positivism's imperatives and instead attends to the poetics of being" (24).

Each chapter of *Exorbitance* takes as a point of departure an evidentiary mode, asking what these modes tell us (or what they are designed to tell us) about bodily inheritance and knowing, and speculating about the forms of sovereign-ing this knowing generates. In the first chapter, I explore the concept of trace evidence through an analysis of an early eugenics study conducted in Jamaica. The second chapter mobilizes testimonial evidence in its exploration of the Ethiopian Zion Coptic Church, and the third considers embodied evidence in relation to the performed ritual of *kumina*, a Congolese-based ancestral practice in eastern Jamaica. While the common assumptions undergirding the eugenics study in chapter 1 are that Black people in the New World were unable to inherit the gifts of the West, and while chapter 3 shows scholars and practitioners alike making claims to a history of Being that is not tethered to New World inheritances, chapter 2 limns a bimodal attempt to create practices and ontologies that extend beyond the state but also take advantage of the state system. This is an issue that has resurfaced now as the Jamaican government has opened an avenue for the legal cultivation of ganja for sale on medicinal markets. As I have already stated, my aim is to read the embodiments and articulations of sovereignty as emergent, ephemeral, processual, and—ultimately—relational. But I am also charting a story about the pasts and presents (and maybe the futures) of anthropology, one that moves from an obsession with measuring and collecting to cooperative praxis, in order to explore what it could mean to put our bodies on the line and to acknowledge that our bodies are always—unequally—on the line (Berry et al. 2017).

The mode of investigation that undergirds this book is critical now as we grapple with how to organize political life in a global context in which the violence that (re)produces racial inequalities and insecurity globally have only deepened. Today, the neoliberal dynamics that prioritize American, and recently Chinese, political and economic interests have further entrenched a condition in which the commonly cited benefits of citizenship are not being provided by the state but instead must be sought in and through other forms of community (including those that are transnational and diasporic). Attending to these forms releases us from the grip of the nation-state and attunes us to what has been disavowed, misrecognized, and destroyed through the global historical transformations glossed as "modernity"—specifically, the Black and Indigenous knowledges, experiences, and spiritual practices that undermine spatiotemporal teleologies and boundaries between self and other, human and nonhuman.

Throughout *Exorbitance*, I hope to demonstrate that the Caribbean region, foundational to the initial violent elaboration of Western modernity, can now teach us something about its unsettling. It can teach us that moving beyond liberal commitments to self-determination to embrace the forms of world-making that have always existed alongside and in relation to modern dispossessions might generate the conditions for sovereign-ing, a sovereign-ing that is rooted—at least in part—in collective, nonteleological, and boundless embodied practice toward a relational, iterative mode of being, however ephemeral. I also hope to enact an analytic process that responds to the questions confronting contemporary anthropologists: What would twenty-first-century anthropological scholarship look like if it invited vulnerability, if it surrendered to a praxis of cooperation, an openness to new archives, and a sweeping interrogation of the relationships between discipline and method? And, finally, I hope to give one account of what dance can do for the world,[31] of what is produced when we are attuned to, and engaging, each other's kinespheres.

1

TRACES

It is sometimes difficult to accept that during the late nineteenth and early twentieth centuries, there was a scientific consensus—both among those whom we celebrate as pathbreakers within anthropology, genetics, and zoology, and those whom we now label racist pseudoscientists—that the measuring of bones, facial angles, arm spans, height, cranial capacity, and myriad other bodily features could generate critical contributions to the study of something called race. Of course, for anyone familiar with the long history of how assumptions about innate racial difference justified the regimes of imperialism, slavery, and extractive capitalism, the elaboration of measures to solidify these assumptions, to ground them in empirical "objective" science, would come as no surprise. Today, this consensus is both lamented and disavowed. It is understood to be emblematic of a racist social scientific imagination that has been roundly condemned and superseded. However, as William Faulkner famously wrote in his 1951 theatrical novel *Requiem for a Nun*, "The past is never dead. It's not even past." That Faulkner himself opposed integration and advocated for a return to slavery—a system, he thought, of "benevolent autocracy" (Cep 2020; Kindley 2020)—should inform our understanding of his reflections on temporality. I am interested in this chapter in excavating a moment in this not-past past in order to reflect on one way early-twentieth-century physical anthropologists understood the relationship between inheritance and embodiment.

During the 1920s, the Carnegie Institution of Washington supported a program of study centered on "the problem of race crossing" in countries containing "mixed" populations. Charles Davenport, a prominent eugenicist and director of the Department of Genetics at the institution, was tasked with supervising the research of Morris Steggerda, then a graduate student in the University of Illinois's Department of Zoology, toward this end. For two years, Steggerda conducted anthropometric, developmental, and psychological tests with at least fifty men and fifty women in Jamaica of each racial "group"—"pure-blooded negro, mulatto and White"—from similar class positions in the society (categorizations in the original brief for the study). He also measured more than twelve hundred schoolchildren. The purpose of this research, published in 1929 as *Race Crossing in Jamaica* (Davenport and Steggerda 1929), was to identify evidence of innate genetic traits and their variability along racial lines, and to discover the extent to which this variability redounded to differences in mental capacity. They were, in other words, mobilizing "trace evidence," which, in its juridical sense, can be defined as material that is transferred in conditions of contact, invisible to the eye and requiring specific tools and techniques to unearth. For Davenport and Steggerda, the arsenal of their evidence demonstrated that while racial "groups" may not constitute different species, differences in achievement were due not to environment but to a fundamental inferiority of the mental capacity of "Gold Coast Negroes" as compared to Europeans.

The copy of *Race Crossing* that I own today, purchased from an online bookseller, is one that had been decommissioned from the Fisk University library. It seems to have been borrowed only by two individuals, once in 1957 and twice in 1969 (these last two times by a math major who went on to work for the National Aeronautics and Space Administration [NASA]). I first encountered *Race Crossing*, however, in the New York University library as a graduate student. As I paged through the book, I recognized the name of one of the families for which there is an extensive genealogical profile. The Kamekas, in *Race Crossing*, were one of the Seaford Town families Steggerda measured, representatives of white agriculturalists descended from German farmers who migrated to Jamaica after the abolition of slavery. The matriarch of one of the families with whom I was close during my dissertation fieldwork had been named Kameka before she married, and we examined together the many plates of the white side of her family that appeared at the end of the book.[1] Revisiting the text now, in the context of intensified protest against ethnographic museums' holdings of remains of Native American and African American ancestors in so-called bone rooms (Redman 2016; Fabian 2010; Coombes 1994, 109–60; Conklin 2013, 19–58), and with state governments and university systems mandating that inventories be done of all human remains in these institutional settings—and of course, in the ongoing aftermath of the discovery that the remains of children who were killed in 1985 when the City of Philadelphia dropped bombs on the MOVE compound had been held in the Penn Museum without consent and were used for teaching and research—provides other vantage points for reflection.

A close analysis of this text offers many rabbit holes to explore. One could follow the money, in which case we would learn about the genesis of the Pioneer Fund and the links between Wilhelm Frick, minister of the interior of Nazi Germany, and the American eugenics movement. We would even learn about the contemporary scholars who, as recently as 2018, continued to receive financial support from the foundation established by the patron of *Race Crossing*. One could follow the local networks that facilitated this project, in which case we would learn about the Jamaica Hookworm Commission and its connections with the Rockefeller Foundation as new imperial arrangements were coming into view through global public health interventions. One could also take a deep dive into Davenport and Steggerda's mobilization of statistics, and especially the error measure, but not being a statistician, I am not equipped to do this. Suffice it to say that the error measurement often means that their physical evidence does not correspond to the genetic arguments they are trying to make, but I will say more about that later. There are side stories to follow as well, such as that of the relationship between Steggerda and Davenport while the former was trying to finish his PhD and obtain a job at the Carnegie Institute, or of Steggerda's attempt to get other people interested in the anthropometrics of his own hometown of Holland, Michigan, populated by Dutch immigrants, and his trip to the Netherlands for comparative research.

While I will touch on many of these stories here, what I am most interested in following has to do with the common assumptions that grounded Davenport and Steggerda's methods, the ways they discussed their research process, and the effect of the mountains of data produced by this study (eight thousand sheets, we are triumphantly told in the introduction!). What does such an excess of data do, especially when it doesn't unequivocally prove the hypotheses with which they began and, therefore, doesn't support the broader objective of finding a scientific rationale for segregation? And to what extent might we glean some insights into the experience of Jamaicans who participated in the study? In her discussion of bodily evidence in relation to the ways racial identity was adjudicated throughout the long nineteenth century and beyond in the United States, Sarah Chinn (2000) argues that there were "moments in which the information that bodies could be expected to provide about themselves became unclear, ambiguous, or contradictory. Alternately, [there] were times in which modes of registering the body shifted, and evidentiary arguments (medical, legal, gendered, raced) had to be reconfigured to shore up the equilibrium of power." Limning the ways skin, blood, and DNA have been positioned as means to solidify the boundaries of citizenship, Chinn notes that "bodies—both individual bodies and groups of people—resisted being recast as 'the body,'" holding on to other modes of identity "to render their bodies actual rather than abstract" (7). Similar processes are afoot in this case, and in asking these questions in this chapter, I am interrogating the ways Mendelian genetics was mobilized to develop a kind of anthropological racial folklore.

It is not inconsequential that this orientation toward data also characterized the work of other anthropologists who were amassing bodies of "folk" knowledge through their collection of songs, stories, and religious "superstitions" (about which I have more to say in chapter 3). Probing the relationships between these two branches of early-twentieth-century anthropology, and the intellectual and sociopolitical contexts in which they emerged and sought to intervene, helps us to interrogate modes of evidentiary analysis across the anthropological landscape. Here, I hope to show that, though anthropometric research has long been discredited, the impulses toward classification, categorization, isolation, and transparency continue to undergird social scientific imaginations of difference, even as researchers are constantly confronted with research participants who refuse, reject, rescript, and reinscribe these imaginations, releasing us from the hegemony of juridical teleologies and indexing practices of relational autonomy.

READING INNATE RACIAL DIFFERENCE ON THE BODY

Here is one way to tell the story of the elaboration of racial difference and the emergence of models of human evolution: As Europe emerged from the medieval period and into its "Age of Enlightenment," explorers (and, later, merchants, missionaries, and government officials) traveled the world, returning to Europe with reports of and objects from people who seemed to them to be exotic Others, the missing links—they supposed—between rational humans and irrational animals. These early travelers, encountering the diversity of human existence, wondered about the people who seemed so different from them, and equipped with biblical reasoning, they defined them against a Western (Christian) self. They elaborated hierarchies of practices and beliefs that they eventually correlated to "stages" of development from "savage" to "primitive" to "modern," stages that were ultimately also racialized. Race would thus become a modern classificatory principle and mechanism of domination, and ideas about racial difference would allow Europeans (and, later, Americans) to disregard and erase Indigenous forms of knowledge and to justify slavery. Race would also become the mechanism through which Others could now be studied and known through the emergent discipline of anthropology. Sylvia Wynter (2003) tells this story far more compellingly than I, helping us to understand the material, spatial, and ideological processes by which contemporary racial and class inequalities were developed and are perpetuated through the supersession of a theocentric paradigm with a secular political one, grounded in science and propelled by and through imperialism.

Other scholars caution us against seeing this supersession as complete. Terence Keel (2018), for example, has sought to demonstrate that "universal narratives of human becoming created by modern science are derived from Christian European traditions of thought and belief that conceal their parochial foundations" (2). He urges us to see secularization not as a complete break from the past "but instead as a transference of religious forms into nonreligious spaces of thought and practice" (15). On one hand, this leads us toward an interrogation of the ways forces (whether God or Nature)—rather than random natural selection—are seen as the basis of human evolution and racial difference. On the other, it asks us to reckon with the fact that Christianity, while proclaiming itself to be a universalist and inclusive doctrine, is in fact invested in drawing divisions and distinctions among social groups. Christendom is first positioned in opposition to Jews, Greeks, and Romans, Keel argues, and then "subsequently against racial and religious others" (9).

Throughout the Enlightenment, naturalists and racial scientists such as Johann Friedrich Blumenbach in the eighteenth century mobilized the creation narrative to "articulate biological theories about the origins of human life and the biospiritual bond shared across the races" (Keel 2018, 25). These theories, of course, were grounded in concrete material and sociopolitical realities. In Blumenbach's case, these realities had to do with emergent ideas about a unified German nationhood undergirded by the marginalization of Jews, but for American ethnologists in the nineteenth century, they would revolve around the abolition of slavery (first in the British colonies and later in the US), Reconstruction and crown colony rule, and the intensification of migration—both from Europe and from South to North in the early-twentieth-century United States.

Early polygenists—like the Jamaican planter Edward Long, who argued for the separate development of races in his 1774 *History of Jamaica*—also maintained elements of Christian causality in their theories of race. In the early nineteenth century, a few decades before Charles Darwin would argue for the antiquity of humans and their derivation from animals, Josiah Clark Nott developed his own theory of polygenesis on the shoulders of Samuel G. Morton's work. Morton, a physician trained at the University of Pennsylvania School of Medicine and later at the University of Edinburgh, was the founder of the so-called American School of racial science. His 1839 *Crania Americana* built on the cranial racial science of the German and Dutch physicians and naturalists who developed the measuring techniques for facial angles and cranial capacities in the late eighteenth century, and who amassed large collections of skulls toward that end (Mitchell 2022; Stocking 1968). Morton understood his measurements to demonstrate that different racial groups globally exhibited consistent differences in facial angles and skull capacities, a finding he would then use to argue that racial traits were fixed and thus untethered to environment or climate. The logical conclusion of this argument was that each group descended from different ancestors. In other words, the observation that the Christian timeline for human creation could not accommodate the evolutionary development of different races from a common ancestor propelled nineteenth-century American ethnologists to posit a scientific accounting of race that was tethered to stages of development (Keel 2018).

This accounting would be buttressed by its own technologies of anthropometry and biometric statistics, the latter having been pioneered by Sir Francis Galton (Charles Darwin's cousin and the founder of modern eugenics) and then introduced to biologists by Charles Davenport. Nott, Morgan, and others, including Charles Caldwell, Samuel Cartwright, George Gliddon, and Louis Agassiz, took it upon themselves to obtain crania from around the world in order to provide evidence for hereditary, immutable physical differences. The skull became the "privileged object for constructing racial categories and inscribing racial difference in the body" (Mitchell 2022, 49; see also M'charek 2020), thereby literally hardening the notion of absolute racial difference. These physician-scholars believed that cranial "traits" and other phenotypic differences like skin color and hair texture, differences that could be measured empirically, also reflected intellectual and moral dispositions that were passed down from originary ancestors of present-day races (Stocking 1968; Keel 2018; Hogarth 2017).

Craniometry thus emerged as the principal method for linking biology to sociology, morality, and psychology (Blakey 1987). Here was a vision of the world that was ordered and stable, not random and dynamic as Darwin would propose. By this reasoning, cultural differences evolved from physical differences that were reckoned racially, and these differences were primordial. This reckoning meant, on one hand, that the condition of those who occupied "lower" rungs on the evolutionary ladder could not be improved through social and political channels. Emancipated slaves would *not*, therefore, thrive as free people, and Indigenous groups would *not* adapt to the white civilization that was being spread through imperialism and settler colonialism. In other words, as Denise Ferreira da Silva has elaborated, "Both the anthropological and sociological versions of racial knowledge transform the consequences of hundreds of years of colonial expropriation into the effects of efficient causes (the laws of nature) as they operate through human forms (bodies and societies)" (Ferreira da Silva 2017a). As a result, Blackness, as a category of racial knowledge, does the work of obscuring the juridical forms of colonial violence that bring it into being in the first place.

Physical anthropologists and physicians across the imperial universe were elaborating these hierarchies through anthropometric technologies, and they were circulating their findings visually. For Morton, this meant drawing, but later and elsewhere we see the proliferation of photographic archives that have become emblematic visual representations of colonial categorizing.[2] These scholars reified "colonial categories as racial categories" (Mak 2020, 331), and they believed that it was possible to reconstruct racial "types" that could represent racial groups writ large (Stocking 1968; Blakey 1987). Many physical anthropologists would maintain this proposition into the mid-twentieth century, and the legacies of believing that intellectual and moral difference was sedimented in the body is evident in contemporary approaches to DNA (Abu El-Haj 2007; Fullwiley 2007; Goodman, Heath, and Lindee 2003; M'charek 2014; Nelkin and Lindee 2004; Nelson 2016; D. Roberts 2011), and in the kinds of craniofacial reconstruction and facial composite sketching done within criminal investigations (M'charek 2013, 2020).

THE PROBLEM WITH HYBRIDITY

If racial differences were essential, the only process that could change a race would be mixture or, as polygenists would put it, "race crossing." Josiah Nott was convinced that dire consequences would proceed from the breaking of what he understood to be natural law. "Death and extinction could ensue," he wrote, "if racial groups were taken out of their habitat or if they mixed with one another" (quoted in Keel 2018, 71). Racial demographer Joseph Arthur de Gobineau, for his part, believed that "the fall of cultures was not caused by sociocultural events, but by degeneration" (quoted in Teo Thomas 2004, 85). These and other scholars and propagandists were observing animals and asking whether they could tell us anything about human hybridity. Would hybrids be sterile? Would they produce disharmony? Were they degenerate and unstable?

The problem of racial hybridity was not just theoretical. It also had practical significance to pro-slavery polygenists, and it was a problem of colonial management, though differently so in each imperial setting. In Hawai'i, the quick inauguration of anthropometric studies conducted by Boasians at the beginning of the twentieth century was oriented toward refuting "facile Mendelian defamations" (Anderson 2012, 597). And in New Zealand, racial crossing would come to be understood as a *strategy* of British colonialism rather than as a challenge to it (Salesa 2011). Nevertheless, the fears that accompanied the abolition of slavery and the influx of southern and eastern European migrants at the turn of the twentieth century spurred American polygenists preoccupied with racial hybridity to argue that "mulattos" were physically weak and short-lived, that they would die out or revert to a so-called dominant type, and that they were mentally, morally, or physically inferior to either parent group (Stocking 1968). These arguments were, however, based largely on anecdotal evidence and thus begged for systematic and scientific study. Charles Davenport would be in the right place at the right time, and his own work would build on the physical anthropology that emerged from the American School of Nott, Morton, and George Gliddon.

Charles Davenport was born on his father's farm near Stamford, Connecticut, on June 1, 1866, and he grew up between that farm and his father's real estate business, located in Brooklyn. In fact, because he worked on the farm, Davenport did not formally attend school until age fourteen, yet he ended up at Harvard, where he received his bachelor's degree in 1889 and his PhD in 1892. Davenport became director of the summer school of the biological laboratory of the Brooklyn

Institute of Arts and Sciences in Cold Spring Harbor, New York, and in September 1899 he accepted an assistant professorship at the University of Chicago. He resigned from this position in 1904 to become director of genetics at the Carnegie Institute's newly established Station for Experimental Evolution in Cold Spring Harbor. There, he began a series of breeding experiments with mice, snails, bugs, cats, canaries, and chickens that led to some publications. As Davenport proceeded to develop human applications for Mendelian genetics, he solicited funds for the establishment of the Eugenics Record Office at Cold Spring Harbor from Mary Williamson Harriman (the wife of railroad executive E. H. Harriman) in 1910, and work there was maintained until 1940 (Riddle 1947).

Like other researchers at the time, Davenport held that racial hybrids would be maladapted to their environment. His views on race derived from the polygenist forerunners who placed the emergence of racial groups in the distant past. As they understood the matter, racial mixture and environmental modifications served to obscure "underlying racial categories," and so the role of the anthropologist was to get "to the core of hereditary racial essence by an analysis of the distribution of stature, pigmentation, and especially headform" (Stocking 1968, 63). What Davenport added to this postulate was an embrace of both the Mendelian genetics of the time and the biometric statistical models that had been developed by Galton. It was this approach to race and heredity, one that required the particular tools of anthropometry and statistics in order to trace the evidence of racial traits that was believed to exist within the genetic material of individuals and groups, that shaped Davenport and Steggerda's (1929) study.

When Wickliffe Preston Draper agreed to put US$10,000 toward research into racial hybridity in Jamaica, Davenport jumped at the chance. Draper was born in Hopedale, Massachusetts, a company town built by his father, who had become a wealthy textile machinery manufacturer. His mother was Jessie Fremont Preston, daughter of Confederate brigadier general William Preston III. After graduation from Harvard in 1913,[3] Draper joined the British Army, transferring to the US Army after the US declared war on Germany in 1917. He returned home after he was injured in battle, and when his father died in 1923, he inherited the family wealth. For a time, Draper lived in England and studied archaeology and anthropology at the University of London, funding (and participating in) missions such as the one that excavated the fossil of Asselar Man, a late Stone Age skeleton discovered in northern Mali. Elected as a fellow of the Royal Geographical Society, Draper became interested in eugenics and began making substantial donations to the American Eugenics Society. Charles Davenport became the first scientist to benefit from Draper's deep pockets (W. Tucker 2002).

In his summary article that appeared in *Scientific Monthly* just before the publication of the study's results, Davenport (1928) defined race as "a group of individuals constituting a subdivision of the species characterized by the possession of some one distinctive hereditary trait" (225). For Davenport, the lack of population isolation globally—the result, for him, of "rapid transportation to all parts of the globe" (225) and markedly *not* imperialism, settler colonialism, or the transatlantic slave trade—meant that one was hard-pressed to find "pure" representatives of any race, as these "standard races" were "rapidly disintegrating" (225). This "racial intermingling" would present a problem to those convinced that "a population of hybrids will be a population carrying an excessively large number of intellectually incompetent persons" (238). Luckily, Davenport wrote, there was a way to answer the question of whether "hybridization, such as is going on even among the races of Europe, leads to an inferiority of the offspring" (225), and that way was genetic research.

Davenport was convinced that emergent genetic studies of heredity helped scientists understand how racial traits would be distributed in successive generations following a racial crossing. In his exposition of these studies, he noted that the principal contributions of this work had to do with the degree of variability in hybrids (whether the issue of racial crossings showed "traits" that were blended or more fully approximated one parent or the other in trait expression) and the extent to which hybrids exhibited "vigor" (whether racially crossed individuals would be fertile and productive, materially and otherwise). Complex statistical equations were mobilized to measure these processes, and thus comparisons with other groups around the world were deemed possible. He reported that the results of the Jamaica race crossing study showed that variability was widespread among the first generation, especially with respect to intellectual performance. A society of hybrids between Blacks and whites, he argued, would be intellectually daft, though potentially "better endowed in appreciation of music and in simple arithmetical or mental computations, as well as more resistant to certain groups of diseases, than a pure white population" (Davenport 1928, 238).

Here, Davenport appears to be offering a balanced view of the positives and negatives associated with race crossing, but his real end game of racial improvement is revealed toward the end of the essay: "If only society had the force to eliminate the lower half of a hybrid population, then the remaining upper half of the hybrid population might be a clear advantage to the population as a whole" (Davenport 1928, 238). Unfortunately for Davenport, as he himself lamented, the inability to control "human matings"—even despite what he argued was a "strong instinct for homogeneity" among whites—prevented the possibility of selectively breeding out undesired traits, which for him was the only way to bring into being "a commonwealth characterized by peace and unity of ideals" (Davenport 1928, 238). Nevertheless, continued research on hybridization was warranted on the basis that it could scientifically support the political project of eugenics.

Steggerda and Davenport first traveled together to Jamaica in September 1926, where they were introduced to Jamaican officials by the US consul, José de Olivares, a veteran of the Spanish-American War and longtime member of the American Foreign Service. After several weeks, Davenport traveled back to the United States, leaving Steggerda to continue data collection until that December, when he returned to Cold Spring Harbor. Steggerda went again to Jamaica in early January 1927 and stayed until October of that year, at which point the two began data analysis and writing. In Jamaica, the pair was aided by a variety of individuals who represented a diverse swath of institutions, which is to say that this eugenics project created a network of local leaders in education, medicine, religion, the police force, and folklore, along with representatives of the colonial government and international organizations such as the Rockefeller Foundation (whose International Health Board supported the Jamaica Hookworm Commission, about which I say more below).[4] They also hired Sydney Rhoden, "a sixteen year old brown boy," who acted as assistant and recorder.[5]

Initially, the study design for what they called the Draper Fund Project supported the collection of data "for 50 adults of each sex of the three groups: pure-blooded negro, mulatto and White, of as nearly as possible the same social level" (Davenport and Steggerda 1929, 4). Of course, a scientific study such as theirs would need to provide a rationale for these categorical designations, which they did as follows, with some attention to emic meaning: "Black denotes an individual whose genetic constitution, so far as it is possible to ascertain, is that of a pure African Negro. The term is thus applied in Jamaica. Brown indicates a hybrid—sambo, mulatto, quadroon, or more complex cross. This term is sometimes thus applied in Jamaica. Whites have a genetic constitution of a European as nearly as can be ascertained. Since Black, Brown and White are here used as proper names (names of groups) they are in this report printed with capital letters" (20). It is important to highlight the doubt introduced in their definition of racial classificatory terms—"so far as it is possible to ascertain," "as nearly as can be ascertained"—since this doubt resurfaces in different ways throughout their analysis of the data. The anxiety this doubt produces, especially in relation to the constitution of whiteness, is compounded when we remember that Wickliffe Draper was later involved in funding research into the development of a mechanism to identify the "Blackness" in those passing for white. Davenport and Steggerda also pay some lip service to how "Black" and "Brown" are "applied in Jamaica," but tellingly not "White."[6] This distinction introduces the question of how local cultural and class logics also figured into the racial classifications Davenport and Steggerda mobilized, especially since their own apprehension of race was supplemented by subjects' self-identification, genealogical records (in an attempt to define "the racial constitution of the grandparents"), and "gathered opinions from reliable persons concerning the color of the measured person" (22). That several of these "reliable persons" recorded other terms on the test sheets—"sambo," "quadroon," "yellow," and most often, "coloured"—is neither mentioned nor analyzed in the text.[7]

Even given this triaging of assessments, there were cases "where the evidence of pedigrees, or of older members of the community, was not full or concordant" (Davenport and Steggerda 22). In other words, there was local disagreement about the racial placement of one or another research subject. In these cases, they turned "cautiously" to "physical evidence" to make a final determination (observations about hair curl, nose breadth, arm span, and cephalic index, which in any case wouldn't have been obtained until after the individuals were measured). What "cautiously" could mean in this exposition is unclear, but what Davenport and Steggerda were trying to establish here was that while their "judgment is not considered perfect . . . the error certainly is not large" (22).

The question of choosing research subjects at "the same social level" is also explained in a footnote, which elaborates the problems raised by this decision:

[I]t was decided that all three groups should belong to the prevailing agricultural class and that the Whites of the governing class and the white merchants of Kingston should be excluded. A difficulty arises in this, that just those Whites who are satisfied to live as agriculturalists in the midst of the island are hardly as representative of the more ambitious and intellectually endowed Whites as the agricultural Blacks are of the run of the Black population. It is possible that in choosing non-urban Whites we have selected farther below the average of Whites than in selecting non-urban negroes we have selected below the average of negroes. (Davenport and Steggerda 1929, 4)

We should remember that this study was conducted before the massive urbanization of the 1950s, when 85 percent of Jamaicans still lived rurally, and when there were still many white people living on the island prior to the great exodus following independence in 1962. This purported focus on rural agriculturalists also reflects a preoccupation of eugenics studies at the time with differences between rural and urban dwellers. The research subjects with whom Steggerda spent the most time and had the most ongoing interaction, however, were male students at Mico College, the oldest teacher-training institution in the western hemisphere. This focus means that while these men may have grown up rurally, not only were they not, at the time of the study, agriculturalists, but they also were training to take on leadership roles in the early-twentieth-century educational system in Jamaica, an important marker of status privilege at the time. The researchers themselves acknowledge that "the scholastic standard of Mico College might favorably compare with the end of the freshman year of an American college" (Davenport and Steggerda 1929, 10), and that the "third year of Shortwood [the sister institution of Mico] would possibly compare with the first year of American university work" (11). Their sampling, therefore, is inconsistent with their research design, something that was the subject of many contemporary critiques of *Race Crossing*.

The early pages of the book present a table listing where their research subjects were from. Of the 61 men who were measured at Mico, 15 were Black and 46 were Brown. At Shortwood College, 32 Brown women, 4 Black women, and 1 white woman were measured. Already we see a preponderance of Browns in their sample, which would not necessarily elicit surprise due to their focus on the problems of hybridization. Yet Davenport himself acknowledged these sampling issues in the 1928 *Scientific Monthly* article. "Rather more [Browns] than were desirable were studied at the training schools for teachers," he wrote, "for these brought into the statistics a lot of non-agricultural people" (Davenport 1928, 231). His earlier statements that "it was much more difficult to find persons of unmixed white stock living as agriculturalists in an island composed of 98 per cent colored persons," and that "it was fairly easy to find full-blooded Blacks, especially in the so-called Maroon towns, such as Accompong in the West" (231) raise other kinds of questions. One of these has to do with the fact that the majority of their Black research subjects were not from Accompong, and another is that the population breakdown by race published in the book itself does not match his assertion that 98 percent of the population is either Black or Brown. But these inconsistencies are not explained.

In noting that the opportunity to measure individuals in Gordon Town (St. Andrew) and Glengoffe (St. Catherine) arose from the opening of offices of the Jamaica Hookworm Commission in these locations, Davenport and Steggerda betrayed the particular convenience they used in sampling, a convenience that was rooted in the emergent US imperialism after World War I. Hookworm itself was discovered in 1902; it was seen as the "germ of laziness" since it made people anemic and therefore lethargic. In 1904, the US Department of the Army launched an antihookworm campaign in Puerto Rico, and in 1908, the British created a Colonial Office Hookworm Committee (Abel 1995). By 1909, John D. Rockefeller had established the Rockefeller Sanitary Commission for the Eradication of Hookworm Disease to reduce hookworm in the US South through physician training, the establishment of state laboratories, traveling dispensaries, public education, and sanitation facilities (Elman, McGuire, and Wittman 2014). This commission was the precursor to the Rockefeller Foundation's International Health Board, which made its first trip to British Guiana in March 1914 to experiment with these same methods for the treatment of hookworm disease. Shortly thereafter, the Health Board was involved with hookworm programs in six Central American and Caribbean sites.[8] US intervention in these places arose in part as a result of British abandonment of its earliest colonies and the public health crises that were emerging from poor housing and sanitation conditions and a lack of prenatal care. One might also argue, however, that the campaign was also motivated by the need for healthy laborers to work on the plantations of the United Fruit Company, whose growth also began in the early twentieth century. In Jamaica, the hookworm campaign began in May 1919 and continued for ten years (Pemberton 2003). B. E. Washburn, the director of the campaign for Jamaica, stayed on the island until 1937, long after the Health Board's work ended.[9]

Whites were measured in Seaford Town (as descendants of the German migrants tended to "interbreed"), at the fire department in Kingston, and in the homes of Miss Ethel Henderson and Mrs. Althea Bodden, who procured 15 office workers (again, *not* agriculturalists) in Kingston. To measure additional white people, Steggerda also traveled to Grand Cayman (the Cayman Islands, at the time, were administered by the British colonial government through Jamaica).

He also measured 37 mothers in the Kingston Crèche building, half of whom were Blacks and Browns. While not elaborated in the book, Steggerda also conducted his tests with students from Calabar College, Jamaica High School, the Wesley school, Falmouth School, and Alpha Elementary School; with young women (primarily of Indian descent) at the Lyndale Home for Girls in Highgate (known formerly as the Happy Grove Industrial School for East Indian Girls); and with babies at the Jubilee Hospital. With respect to the infants, he sought to measure "Babies of Black parents, Babies of one black and one white parent, Babies of Mulattoe (*sic*) parents (Brown), and Babies of pure white parents (or nearly white) within twenty-four hours of their birth, and again on the ninth day before they leave the hospital." This was in response to a memo he received from Davenport, then already back in New York:

> On the occasion of a visit to the National Museum on December 10th, [I] saw a Boston physician working on pelves in the Division of Physical Anthropology. He said that no studies had been made on the possible lack of harmony between the size of the head of mulatto children and the form of the pelvis of its full black negro mother. He thought from what he had seen that there probably was a certain disharmony. He said that measurement of the form of the children within 24 hours of birth would give some indication of the form of pelvic opening. He suggested, accordingly, a series of measurements of as large a number as possible of full black negro infants, mulatto infants of negro mothers and white infants of white mothers, all within 24 hours of birth. The same heads should be measured at 7 to 10 days after birth in order to get the comparative shapes of the heads of negro, mulatto and white children. This investigation would be of great interest in connection with the general theory of disharmonies in race crosses.[10]

Putting aside the various absurdities underlying this suggestion, notice again the acknowledgment of the difficulty of identifying racial purity.

As Davenport and Steggerda planned to enter new localities, they made arrangements in advance to be introduced to the community by locally influential persons. This might be a pastor, as was the case in the Cascade region of Hanover, where, after presenting a public lecture at the church, "there was no difficulty in securing persons for study" (Davenport and Steggerda 1929, 12). During these introductory lectures, "each person to be measured was promised a good photograph of himself, and mention was made that all were directly benefiting the cause of education and science" (19). The researchers also had to familiarize people with the techniques of measurement that were to be used, but they found that if one industrious and interested person agreed to be the guinea pig, others would follow. In *Race Crossing*, Davenport and Steggerda noted "that if the physical measurements were completed and the subject was allowed to leave with the idea that he was to return later for the psychology tests, he very rarely returned" (19). Here is our first inkling that all may not have gone as smoothly as the researchers might have hoped it would—a point to which I return later.

Research participants were subjected to sixty-three different physical measurements, which are detailed in the book across eleven pages. Here are a few examples:

(3) *Suprasternale height*—This measurement was taken as quickly as possible after the vertex height before the patient has time to slump . . .

(5) *Omphalion height*—The center of the umbilicus was taken; the patient in the military attitude . . .

(9) *Right dactylion height*—The tip of the horizontal arm was placed at the level of the extreme distal end of the middle finger. The hand was in contact with the thigh, to keep it steady . . .

(21) *Transverse diameter of chest*—Using the anthropometer still as calipers. Contact with the ribs was made, as nearly as possible, on each side with the sixth rib. The movable arm was moved back and forth upon the rod during different phases of respiration. Note was taken of the different readings, and a median reading was recorded.

(25) *Trochanter breadth*—Distance between most prominent points of thighs at the level of the great trochanters.

(26) *Horizontal depth of tragion*—The depth measurer was used for all "horizontal depths." The subject was placed standing against a smooth wall with his head in the Frankfort horizontal; occiput in contact with the wall. The horizontal distance of the tragion from the wall is determined. (Davenport and Steggerda 1929, 22–26)

The list continues, and includes the horizontal depth of glabella,[11] of subnasale,[12] of the gnathion;[13] the girths of the chest, upper arm, lower arm, thigh, calf, ankle, and neck; the sagittal and transverse head arches; head height, length, and breadth; the outer and inner angles of the eye; mouth width; length of and breadth of the pinna;[14] the distances from trichion[15] to gnathion, nasion[16] to gnathion, nasion to stomion,[17] and nasion to subnasale, and on and on and on. After some practice, they were able to complete all these measurements within twenty minutes.

Following this series came general observations about the body, which included the drawing of hand and foot, the examination of teeth for decay, the use of a dynamometer (measuring grip strength, which was done mainly with men), and the taking of hair samples (to evaluate the diameter of the curl) and fingerprints, which were later classified by the amount and extent of ridges and whorls and the patterns they contained. These procedures were projected to take another twenty minutes.

The precision with which Davenport and Steggerda described the method for taking hair samples imbues their interrogations with a sense of scientific rigor, not only in terms of the actions taken but in relation to the interpretation and analysis. "A few strands of hair were cut as closely to the head as possible," they wrote. "The hair was then placed in a coin envelope, on which was written the date and the name of the individual. The envelope was then fastened on the anthropometry sheet. . . . Five typical hairs were selected for measurement" (Davenport and Steggerda 1929, 28). We also learn that the determination of hair color itself was not made in the field but in the lab. This brings us back to the relationship the two elaborated between subjective and objective interpretation that we first saw in their discussion of how they identified the race of research participants, where they offered some evidence that their own perception was insufficient to evaluate racial difference in this study. This was true also of eye color: "In the early part of the work personal estimates were made of individual eye color. The person stood facing the light, and his eye color was judged either as Dark Brown, Medium Brown, Light Brown, Hazel, or Blue. Later, however, Dr. Rudolph Martin's Augenfarbentafel was used, which made the work considerably more accurate" (1929, 29). The Augenfarben-Tafel was a metal case holding twenty glass eyeballs of various colors, which we now know was also being used for racial experiments and research geared toward promoting Nazi ideologies regarding racial distinctions.[18] Skin color was also not identified by Steggerda himself, but instead was measured according to the Milton Bradley color top, "using the white, black, yellow and 'red' discs and expressing the result in the percentages that each color makes of the whole" (1929, 32).

Additional observations included general build (whether slender, medium, fleshy, or obese); sex "facies" (whether infantile, juvenile, or adult); color of hair (whether flaxen, light brown, medium brown, dark brown, black; clear light red, clear vivid red, brownish-red, or reddish-brown); form of scale hair (whether straight, wavy, curly, frizzy, woolly, or "pepper corn"); eyebrows (whether narrow, median, or broad); hair on arm (with a special interest in the length of down); bite, palate, uvula, and wrist joint (Davenport and Steggerda 1929, 31).

These observations were followed by a panel of sociological questions, questions that betrayed the common sense of the (white, middle-class, American) researchers, including:

> What is your father's name?
> Have you ever been sick with typhoid fever or pneumonia?
> Do you have malaria very often?
> Have you ever had any operations for appendicitis or tonsils, or other?
> Do you have any birthmarks, moles or anything like them?
> Do you walk fast, slow or moderate?
> What games do you like to play?
> How old were you when you stopped going to school? At what book?
> What study did you like best of all? Which one did you like next best?
> Which one did you hate to do? (Davenport and Steggerda 1929, 32)

While all research subjects were asked these questions, if a research subject was "real bright," they were asked a number of other questions relevant to their educational background. However, if subjects were "dull and ignorant," they were asked the following:

> Do you hate anyone?
> Do you ever faint?
> Have headaches very often?
> [Do you do] carpenter work, mason work or machinery?
> Do you like to teach, preach, and make public speeches?
> Would you like to be a business man or would you rather do the thing you
>   are doing?
> Are you very nervous?
> Do you worry over many things? . . .

Do you walk in your sleep? Talk in your sleep?

Do you like to live in the town or the country?

Do you like to travel? Where have you been?

Do you smoke? Do you use alcohol?

Do you go to church? Which one? (Davenport and Steggerda 1929, 32–33)

After this barrage of questions, research subjects were asked to talk about their families, and some provided genealogies. Autobiographies were also elicited, but only from the Mico men,[19] and while these are not discussed in the *Race Crossing* text, I have more to say about them below. After the sociological questions, the psychological tests began. These were presented as games and puzzles, which, the researchers argued, meant that "most of the subjects were not aware that any of the tests were in progress, so engrossed had they become in solving the separate little problems" (Davenport and Steggerda 1929, 33). For these tests, Steggerda removed all but fifteen of the Brown men from Mico, as there were only fifteen Blacks from the school, and he wanted to make sure the groups were "socially more comparable" (33). This series of tests generally began with the cube imitation test and then continued through tests of musical capacity (which were meant to measure sense of pitch, intensity, time, consonance, rhythm, and tonal memory). These were followed by form discrimination tests (to see whether subjects could tell the difference between two circles) and form substitution tests. Subjects were then asked to copy geometric figures and to draw a man freehand.

Afterward, subjects were asked to listen to a sentence that didn't make sense and to identify the nonsense. For example,

1. An unfortunate man, riding a bicycle, has had his head broken and is dead from the fall; they have taken him to the hospital, and they do not think that he will recover.
2. I have three brothers: Paul, William, and myself.
3. A man said to his friend, "May you live to eat the chickens that scratch sand on your grave."
4. Yesterday there was an accident on the railway. But it was not serious; only 48 people were killed.
5. I received a letter from a friend in which he said, "If you don't get this letter, just let me know and I'll write again." (Davenport and Steggerda 1929, 38)

Research subjects were then asked to repeat a sequence of seven numbers, to identify the design that would emerge if a folded piece of paper were cut and unfolded, and to respond to the ball and field test, in which the subject was presented with a round field and then told that their baseball was lost in the field. Subjects were also told they didn't know what direction the ball came from or the force with which it was hit, and they were asked to mark a path to show the researcher how they would hunt for the ball, beginning at the gate. Perhaps this test proved to be too culturally dissonant for Steggerda's respondents, as he applied it only to a few cases and did not tabulate results related to it. Finally, subjects were asked to do a manikin test (a test designed to measure the ease with which subjects can take apart and put back together a human figure), the Knox Moron Test (a test that requires the subject to place blocks correctly in a form board), and finally, the Army Alpha Test (which was used in US Army psychological examinations during the First World War). The social-data gathering and psychology tests together were to take thirty minutes, and after all this, subjects would be photographed. On average, this meant that each individual gave an hour and ten minutes of their time to the elaboration of race science.

We could pursue many angles to critically analyze this research process. One would be to note the cultural dissonance inherent in the tests and to think about what it meant in relation to the evaluation of research subjects' responses. I have already mentioned the ball and field test, but by using the Army Alpha Test, which had been developed to evaluate US military recruits during World War I, Davenport and Steggerda betrayed their ethnocentric understanding of what knowledge could be held in common, and then punished Jamaicans for not necessarily knowing who Christy Mathewson, Alfred Noyes, or Becky Sharp were; what a "Rhode Island Red" is; what the "Brooklyn Nationals" were called; when General Lee surrendered; whether the game "Five Hundred" was played with rackets, pins, cards, or dice; what the primary industry of Gloucester was; whether the advertisement called "There's a reason" was for a drink, a revolver, flour, or a cleanser; or where the "Pierce Arrow car" was made. On the other hand, most of the research subjects, whether urban or rural, educated or uneducated, were in the main able to identify the nonsense in the sentences above, which leads one to wonder whether they identified the whole process as nonsense.

Another line of critical interrogation would have to do with Davenport and Steggerda's assumptions about who they were encountering in each of the locations where they conducted measurements. I have already mentioned that, though they sought to focus on "agriculturalists" (whom they perhaps believed would be more isolated than city dwellers), their sample comprised very few agriculturalists (the majority living in Gordon Town, and some in Hanover). And while they may have imagined rural Jamaicans to be parochial and of limited intelligence, in reality they were meeting a fairly worldly group, for whom Cuba, Costa Rica, Panama, and, to a degree, the United States would have been part of their experience.[20] Looking at the rich collection of ninety oral history interviews Erna Brodber and her research team conducted during the mid-1970s with people born around the turn of the twentieth century makes this abundantly apparent. The single most consistent pattern that emerges in the interviews conducted by Brodber's team was, in fact, the experience of migration during the first two decades of the twentieth century. Their interviewees had worked in the Panama Canal Zone; they had cut cane on American-owned farms and worked in American mills; they had cultivated bananas in Costa Rica and sugar in Cuba; they were tradesmen, seamstresses, drivers, and domestics. One even worked at the US Naval Station in Guantánamo Bay. Of course, they also had children overseas and they circulated ideas, money, and family members.[21] Had Davenport and Steggerda paid more attention to their interlocutors' self-reporting of birthplace on either the music test form or on the Army Alpha Test booklet, they would have noticed that several were born in Panama, a couple in Cuba, a few in Costa Rica, one or two in the "Turks Islands," one in Trinidad, one in Nicaragua, one in Nigeria (where his missionary father was stationed), and one in Haiti (who, incidentally, listed their race as "Palestinian").[22]

Like the Brodber team's interviewees, many of Davenport and Steggerda's interlocutors would also have been exposed to various strands of pan-Africanism, Black nationalism, and internationalism that were in circulation at the time, an exposure not unrelated to the high levels of intraregional migration. Marcus Garvey's Universal Negro Improvement Association, having been established in Harlem in 1914, was building chapters throughout the Atlantic world in the 1920s (Lewis and Bryan 1991). Even earlier, Dr. Robert Love, the medical doctor, minister, and politician born in the Bahamas, lived for decades in the United States and later for eight years in Haiti, eventually settling in Jamaica, mobilized racial consciousness and pan-Africanism through his establishment of the *Jamaica Advocate* newspaper, his reinvigoration of Emancipation Day celebrations, and his political agitation as a member of the Legislative Council of Jamaica and chairman of the St. Andrew Parochial Board (Lumsden 1987). And Alexander Bedward, heir to the Native Baptist Revival movement, mobilized anticolonial sentiment and Black pride among his August Town congregation and other groups (St. Aubyn Gosse 2022). At the center of these early-twentieth-century racial projects was the reclamation of dignity.

It is within this context that the following sentences—a series of details blithely reported in relation to Steggerda's conditions of measurement—were so shocking to me. "All Mico men were measured and weighed without clothing" (Davenport and Steggerda 1929, 10).[23] And, "The girls were measured in their school uniform which consisted of dress, blouse, stockings and underclothes; the shoes were removed before the examination" (11). In Gordon Town, "The males were measured in their underclothes, and the females removed only their shoes. All these people are hard field laborers, including the females" (11). In Hanover, all those who were measured "wore all their clothing while being measured, with the exception of their shoes" (12). At the police depot, where 11 of the 27 men were Black, ranging from twenty to thirty-five years old, "The men were measured without clothes, in a quiet room. Only the examiner, warden and the subject were in the room during the examination" (18). The Kingston whites "wore the usual tropical clothing which is estimated to be two to three pounds for each sex" (19), and during the examination of the 31 persons who were measured in the General Penitentiary in Kingston, only the guard, recorder, prisoner, and examiner were present. "The men were measured without clothing, whereas the women's clothing weighed approximately four pounds" (18). At the Crèche, women "were measured like the other Jamaican women without shoes, but with the usual clothing, which is estimated to be approximately two and one-half pounds" (19). And then, more generally, "The subject, if a male, was asked to remove his clothing with the exception of his underclothes. Females removed their shoes and often their outer aprons in the case of country women. No one refused this request" (20).

The men were measured and weighed without clothing. What must it have been like to go for a hookworm test and then be asked by a foreign white man to participate in an anthropometry study? To stand as a specimen and be photographed in your underwear? To be asked inane questions and to have to detail (sometimes complicated) genealogical histories? And for the women at the Crèche, how would it have felt to hold your child for the camera? What bodily memories may have been surfaced by these moments? What difference would it make in this context to have been "in a quiet room"? To have a warden in the room during the examination? How do we explain the juxtaposition of male prisoners, who were measured without clothing, to the women's clothes themselves, which "weighed approximately four pounds"? Or the juxtaposition of women in Gordon Town who removed their shoes for measurement to the fact that they were "hard field laborers"? And what do we make of the statement "No one refused this request"?

In fact, it seems that at least some people did refuse. Steggerda wrote in his notes wrote about a Mico student who "did not seem to like the idea of these measurements. He said that he didn't have time to write his family history."[24] Of one woman from Gordon Town he wrote, "This woman was very suspicious of all my measurements. And when I got around to taking a hair sample she put her hands over her head and said No! No! When asked why, she said that it wasn't full moon yet."[25] And of an untalkative gentleman from Darliston, he wrote: "When so few comments are given, it is proof that the individual was very uncooperative. Some keep back many things and will tell very little."[26] Davenport and Steggerda acknowledged these hesitations in a global way in *Race Crossing*.

For example, they mention that "at first," not many firemen wanted to be measured, but "after the usual lecture on nature and heredity, he [Steggerda] measured 12 Brown men and 2 Blacks" (Davenport and Steggerda 1929, 17). Regarding the blood oxidation testing, they write: "At the start the subjects, although desiring to be cooperative, were certainly somewhat apprehensive, and it required not a little ingenuity and diplomacy to adjust them to the novelty of the situation" (284). And, noting that people often did not return for the psychological tests if they left after the physical measurements, the researchers realized that "it was necessary to complete the entire operation at one sitting, and that it should not last much more than one hour" (19). This would account for the fact that there is, in the files, very truncated information for many of the research subjects outside the Mico students, for whom there is more detail, presumably because Steggerda was living for a time on the Mico campus and because the study was endorsed by the principal, who also had staff members provide evaluations of the students to Steggerda, through which we learn something about the men's scholastic ability, athletics, and leadership. We see their teachers assessing the students as "inclined to the original" or "dull and heavy in public," as "pleasing but quiet" or "not impressive but earnest," as "cheerful, quiet, decent" or "phlegmatic" or "mischievous" or "inclined to be irresponsible."[27] While these assessments can never speak to the men's full personhood, they provide glimmers into wide-ranging personality expressions. With respect to other research participants, we cannot know whether people who didn't complete the paper tests chose not to complete them or just ran out of time.

WHAT THE BODY TELLS EUGENICISTS

After this elaboration of research methods, the bulk of *Race Crossing* (Davenport and Steggerda 1929, 43–369) details the anthropometric results and the results of the psychological tests. There is then a chapter on children in schools, followed by one that presents a detailed analysis of two families (one of which is the Kameka family). At the end of the book, we are presented with a general discussion and summary conclusion, followed by a bibliography, twenty-nine image plates, and a genealogical chart of the Kameka family.[28]

One reads the anthropometric analysis, and a feeling of overwhelm descends. We encounter charts upon charts, equations upon equations, an absolute excess of data, compounded by the discussions of standard deviations and error. We are also presented with a recurring comparative discussion that surfaces in relation to most, but not all, measurements. Often there are comparisons with US "negro" troops at demobilization (about whom there was an anthropometric study), and then of "certain peoples of the Gulf of Guinea" (Togos, Ashantis, Fangs) as well as those from French West Africa, Bantus of South Africa, Nile negroes, Soudanese, Niger tribes, Masai, Leibu of Senegambia, Buduma of Lake Chad, Bongio of the Congo, Ba-Teké of the Congo, the Ubanghi of the Belgian Congo, and so on. In part, these discussions are oriented to understanding the ancestral derivation of Jamaican "negroes," whom Davenport and Steggerda suspect did not descend from South Africans, "Nile negroes," or Soudanese, but instead "from the Gulf Coast and the Cameroons country" (Davenport and Steggerda 1929, 48). However, there is also comparison between the Jamaican whites with European groups—Scandinavians and Swiss, for example. And often other groups are mentioned, as with a reference to mid-eastern provinces of China. This kind of comparison reflects the encyclopedic impetus in this kind of study, and indeed within early anthropology in the United States and elsewhere.[29] Global anthropometry was a sort of precursor to the Human Relations Area Files (HRAF) but for measurements,[30] and we might think about the extent to which contemporary genetic mapping stems from the same impetus toward cataloging, classifying, and knowing from the body in a particular kind of way.

Lest we imagine that this statistical reckoning of mountains of data was unique to anthropometric studies conducted using the rubric of eugenics, we need only take a look at Boas's own "Heredity in Anthropometric Traits" (1907), which is a preliminary report on his study of immigrants and head form, meant to determine whether offspring tended toward a blend of both their parents or toward one or another parental "type," the phenomenon that was called "alternating inheritance." This article, published in *American Anthropologist*, presents pages of measurements (those he took of each individual), plotted into complex equations such as the following, the first of many meant to get us to the mean variability of children's cephalic index in relation to their parents:

$$s_n^2 = \frac{1}{n}\sum\left(x - \frac{\sum x}{n}\right)^2 = \frac{1}{n}\left\{\sum x^2 - \left(\frac{\sum x}{n}\right)^2\right\} = \frac{(n-1)\sum x^2 - \sum x_p x_q}{n^2}$$

Here, x is the child; the deviations of the children of a family of n children are x_1, x_2, x_3, and so on until x_n; the coefficient of correlation between children of the same family is r_c; and the variability of children around their mean is s_n^2 (Boas 1907, 457). In this early article, Boas reports that with respect to stature, children do not seem to "revert to the parental types" (462), but that the cephalic index shows "alternating inheritance" with reversion also to ancestors further back than parents (461). Ultimately, he concludes that "more material is required to solve this problem" (462).

With this drive toward precise quantification, it seems odd to encounter interpretive sections in *Race Crossing* like the following, regarding sitting height, after we are shown a table and a figure and given the mode and mean for all groups: "Thus the Blacks have much the shortest trunks relatively; while the Whites have the longest. That is, the female Black tends to be leggy. The variability of the ratio is greatest in the case of the Browns and least in the Whites. Here, again, is evidence of 'hybrid variability'" (Davenport and Steggerda 1929, 54). On one hand, what we are meant to learn is that "mixed-race" groups express more variability than "pure stocks" in relation to the "traits" being measured—here, sitting height. But we also learn that "legginess" is a Black female quality, without having any precise understanding of what it means to be "leggy."

And then there are the many statements like the following, in relation to intercristal breadth among women (which is "the horizontal distance between tangents parallel to the sagittal plane and lying at the maximum distance apart in contact with the pelvic brim" [Davenport and Steggerda 1929, 65]): "It is probably correlated with the size of the lower pelvic opening, and thus, in women, is related to obstetrical problems. . . . Few measurements were obtained of White women; they may be neglected. . . . The means are 26.25 plus or minus 0.19 [for Blacks] and 25.82 plus or minus 0.18 [for Browns]. . . . Thus, of the two groups, the Blacks have the larger and more variable pelvic breadth. But the difference is not certainly significant" (65, 67). Indeed, there are many moments when they write that the differences in their measurements were not statistically significant. For example, with respect to the equation they developed regarding the relationship between chest girth, stature, and body build: "There is little difference in body build in Jamaica between Whites and Blacks. Under like conditions of development the Whites are probably a trace the stouter" (73). Is this an acknowledgment of the importance of environment on physical development? Consider this statement, in a summary of the trunk measurements of Blacks, Browns, and whites:

> A comparison of these three groups of about the same stature reveals that the Blacks have shorter trunks than the Whites. The absolute shoulder breadth is about the same in the two races, although perhaps slightly greater in the Black than the White female. The chest girth of the Blacks is slightly less than that of the Whites (in the male at any rate). . . . While the shoulder breadths of the two races do not differ significantly and the chest girth differs only a trifle, the intercristal breadth differs significantly. The Blacks have, on the average, narrower pelves than the Whites. Though the difference between the races in torso form is slight, the White torso tends more toward a flattened cylinder and the Black torso more toward an inverted cone. *The body build shows no marked racial difference.* (75; emphasis mine)

Or this, regarding arm span:

> The differences between Blacks and Browns are insignificant; but the Whites have distinctly the shortest span. The variability, measured by the standard deviation, of the Whites is greatest . . . as contrasted with Blacks and Browns . . . but the difference is not statistically significant. (83)

We learn here that while Blacks and Browns showed little difference in arm span, Blacks had "significantly" longer arms than Whites (100), and that they had the largest "brachial index," which is the length of the lower arm divided by the length of the upper arm. From these results, Davenport and Steggerda argued for the possibility that "the adult Black is, in this respect, less progressively evolved than the Whites" (105) on the basis of a study of Swiss children that showed that the brachial index tends to diminish as one ages from childhood to young adulthood. What this indicated to the two researchers is that "the high index of the Blacks is a persisting juvenile condition" (105).

Or consider this statement of findings, regarding head and neck height:

> The Blacks have a shorter head-and-neck than the Whites. Since there is no difference, on the average, in head height, the conclusion must be drawn that the Negroes have a significantly shorter neck than the Whites. . . . The suggestion naturally arises that carrying loads on the head may be a cause of the short neck of Blacks. It is chiefly the women who carry such loads, and they have the shorter necks. Against this hypothesis is the fact that the White women likewise have shorter necks than the White men, though neither sex carries weights on the head. The short neck of the Black is probably a constitutional condition. (Davenport and Steggerda 1929, 78)

This leaves readers wondering what the difference is between a "constitutional condition" and a genetic one, and whether again they were making an argument for environmental influence. Regardless, it is a speculative comment that redounds from ethnographic observation rather than the science they are so careful to parse, but one that also signals a kind of neo-Lamarckianism—the suggestion that the practice of carrying heavy loads would lead to an inherited difference—within their own Mendelianism.

Similarly, after twenty pages of charts and discussion of prevalence of loops and whorls in fingerprint patterns, the scientists concluded "that there is a close correlation, in any race, between the slenderness of hand and finger and the fineness of finger pattern" (Davenport and Steggerda 1929, 219) and that "there are marked differences in the palmar configurations of the right and left hands in Blacks and Browns as well as in Whites" (252), but that these are not necessarily genetically based. In other words, the more data they collected, the less racial typology made sense, and the harder they had to work to avoid acknowledging this fact. Davenport and Steggerda would not have been alone in this phenomenon, as it was also confounding Dutch and German physical anthropologists (Mak 2020; Sysling 2016). The truth value of the evidence, in this research mode, does not inhere in what the data might actually prove but in its collection. As Sarah Chinn (2000) has argued regarding the emergent nineteenth-century emphasis on quantification, evidence became "something to be sifted through: columns of figures to be collated, discrete bodily formations to be declared pathological or normal, words to be rendered material or irrelevant." She continues: "Nothing is too minor to be recorded, compared, and evaluated. But evidence is mute unless it speaks the language of rules. The detail is displaced and redefined by the system to which it gives form" (19–20). Evidence, in other words, becomes a fetish detached not only from the person from whom it is extracted but also from the historical context that gives rise to its extraction in the first place (Crossland 2009).

Where Davenport and Steggerda *did* find significant differences, they argued for a genetic basis for that difference. Take, for example, their analysis of the length of hand, for which they find Blacks exceeded whites "by more than three times the square root to the sums of the probable errors" (Davenport and Steggerda 1929, 109). This led them to believe the difference was a "real one" and that it had a genetic basis (109). The same conclusion obtained for the lower extremities, which they found in Blacks "absolutely and relatively" longer than in whites (139), and with interocular distance, which was longer in Blacks than in whites, leading them to argue that these differences reflected the effects of either direct or indirect genetic differentials (166). Finally, the differences between nose height and nose breadth between Blacks and whites were understood to be genetically determined, and comparisons with other anthropometric studies led the pair to conclude that "the Blacks of Jamaica, as selected by us, are a fair representation of uncontaminated Gold Coast negroes" (182). Interestingly, though, when they looked at differences by sex, they saw greatest differentiation among Blacks, which to them suggested that "while in Whites the form of the nose is not a secondary sex character, in Blacks it is. In Browns the activity of the secondary sex character is diluted" (182).

Importantly, their findings regarding cranial capacity seem to upend the historic relationship that had been posited between cranial capacity and brain size and function. Here, they noted no significant difference in head height between Blacks and whites:

> The Blacks have clearly, in both sexes, the longest heads, and since height and breadth are the same for all three groups, it would follow that the Blacks have the largest heads, and, hence, largest cranial capacity. . . . Since the difference between the head length of Blacks and Whites is over four times the probable difference, and since there is no evidence of differential deforming factors of the head in the races of Jamaica, we have probably to do with a genetic differ-

ence between the Black and White races in respect to head length. (Davenport and Steggerda 1929, 148)

With respect to head breadth and frontal breadth (which, we remember, was argued to correlate with intelligence), Blacks and Browns were more variable than Whites (159), but in this case the researchers doubted whether this was the result of distinct genes. Taken together, these measurements suggested to Davenport and Steggerda that while the Blacks have larger crania than Whites, what this reflected was white deviation from European norms, and Black approximation to these same norms, and *not* a superior intelligence among Black Jamaicans:

> Accordingly we find that the height ÷ breadth ratio of Whites and Blacks is very similar. The height ÷ length index of the Black is lower than that of the White, because of the long head of the Black; and for the same reason the width ÷ length index is smaller in Blacks than Whites.
>
> In so far as the brain cavity may be compared to a cylinder, in the two races the cylinders are alike except in antero-posterior length. On the other hand, in most African negroes the brain cavity forms smaller and longer cylinders than in Whites. The cranium of the Jamaican Black seems to have changed from that of his African ancestral type by becoming enlarged on vertical cross-section without change in length. In this vertical section the head of the Jamaican Black has evolved toward the European type. (165)

Davenport and Steggerda (1929) go on to analyze their findings regarding hairiness (arguing that Browns exhibit considerable variability here, but are "nearer to the semi-glabrous Blacks" [265]), tongue furrows (only one-sixth of Blacks and Browns had them, compared to two-sixths of Whites [267]), and wrist laxness (more pronounced in Whites than in Blacks, which "may be influenced by the harder labor of the Blacks; since it is well known that prolonged hard labor tends to stiffen the ligaments" [273]). And when analyzing metabolism, they argue that while Browns exhibit a metabolism slightly "below that of American college students (and this points towards a distinct racial effect), if allowances could scientifically be made for the lower protein intake and for the somewhat higher temperature and humidity, the racial element as such might in large part disappear" (290). Here, they are arguing against the idea that differences in metabolism are environmental, but again we see the introduction of doubt into Davenport and Steggerda's data. Stocking argued that this was inherently a problem with anthropometric methods. "Paradoxically," he wrote, "the more precise and extensive the observation and the measurement of mankind, the more tenuous was the 'reality' of the races they served to define. The natural variability of biological phenomena combined with the laws of particulate inheritance to make it increasingly difficult to maintain in practice the view that race is a phenomenon expressed in the individual human being" (Stocking 1968, 57–58).

Nevertheless, Davenport and Steggerda persevered in their method of argumentation, giving us long sections on correlations between physical traits, which are again littered with equations upon equations and coefficients of correlation (between, for example, sitting vertex height and stature, sitting vertex height and span, cephalic index and span, weight and relative sitting height, arm length and leg length, body weight and foot index, foot index and hand index, nose index and skin color, and on and on). They argued that where there was no relation between particular traits, those dimensions was not correlative, and thus that their "association in the Negro race is apparently due to two independent mutations in the same race" (Davenport and Steggerda 1929, 297).

As we move into their analysis of the psychological tests, it is worth quoting their opening gambit to this section at some length:

> It is often held that, while physical differences between races are beyond dispute, it has never been shown that there is such a thing as a racial differentiation in mentality. Those who look at matters broadly were inclined, on *a priori* grounds, to think such difference in mentality and instincts to be probable. . . . In humans there has seemed to be a nomadic instinct in Gypsies and Bedouins, a trading instinct in Arabs and Jews, an instinct for industry in the Chinese, for tracking in Australian aborigines, for hunting in Indians, and for life on the sea in Norwegians and many English. These differences in behavior have been ascribed by the doubters to tradition, to early training, to opportunity. There has been no satisfactory evidence of innate, constitutional differences.
>
> To test the hypothesis that such constitutional differences in the intellectual and sensory spheres exist, special attention was directed toward psychological tests to be made on our three groups of people from Jamaica. (Davenport and Steggerda 1929, 299)

I won't go into the details of their discussion test by test here. Suffice it to say they found Blacks to have significantly more developed senses of rhythm, time, pitch, and intensity than whites, whose musical record was, for them, "disappointing"

(316). They argued that this proficiency in music among Black Jamaicans could also be observed in their "love of vocal music" but must be attributed to some superior arrangement of "structural elements" in the ear or brain (316). Black adults also performed very well on the number series test, leading the researchers to wonder whether "their success [was] associated with their high sense of rhythm?" (360), a provocation they do not pursue. Blacks also did better than whites and Browns in simple arithmetic, which they explained by arguing that "the more complicated a brain, the more numerous its 'association fibers,' the less satisfactorily it performs the simple numerical problems which a calculating machine does so quickly and accurately" (469). Blacks (and Browns) also exhibited a sharper sense of discrimination among differences in form than whites, but on most other psychological measurements, whites were found to be superior. In a couple of instances, Blacks were stronger when younger but stagnated with increasing age, but Whites improved to and through adulthood, and in their analysis of these cases we see their need to attribute early Black "brightness"—which also emerges among the children at the Kingston Crèche—and subsequent Black "decline" to something genetic rather than environmental.[31]

Browns, while highly variable for the most part, were clearly superior in the criticism of absurd sentences, but again as they reached adulthood, this superiority was seen to decline. Generally, Davenport and Steggerda found (especially in relation to the Army Alpha Test) an excessive number of low scores among Browns (as compared to both Blacks and whites), which indicated to them "that the mixture of Black and White capacities and instincts has produced an excessive proportion of highly ineffective persons (as well as some normally effective persons)" (Davenport and Steggerda 1929, 364). Yet their analysis of "mulatto" twins at the end of the book leads them to argue as follows: "The consideration of these two Mulattoes is chiefly instructive as a warning against drawing final conclusions as to dominance or recessiveness from single matings, no matter with what assurance that the parents belonged to full-blooded Black and White races respectively. Among both Blacks and Whites are many biotypes; and both races carry gametically many genetic possibilities, not expressed phænotypically" (453). Again, doubt intervenes and that last sentence leads one to ask whether if this is the case, why bother with all the measuring at all?

It is worth mentioning here that in insisting on a rubric outlining three "pure" racial categories, Davenport and Steggerda also ignored what many of their research subjects reported about their own genealogical pedigrees. Numerous notes taken by Steggerda (or perhaps Sydney or another assistant) read: "Mother and father pure black but grandfather colored," or "Her mother is black, but not as much as herself. No white blood," or "As far as he knows there is no white blood in his relations. Some of his cousins are fair." Research subjects also not infrequently identified themselves as "pure black" and then mentioned a Scottish grandfather or great-grandfather.[32] On one hand, this seeming confusion reflects a material history. Not long after Admiral William Penn and General Robert Venables seized Jamaica from the Spanish in 1655, Oliver Cromwell banished twelve hundred Scots prisoners-of-war to the new colony, after which point additional Scots immigrants also arrived, some as indentured servants and others as criminals exiled by the British government. Scotland's role in the slave trade to Jamaica during the eighteenth and early nineteenth centuries catapulted its economy from one of the weakest in Europe to one of the most powerful, and Scots made up the majority of overseers on sugar plantations, in addition to their roles as plantation owners, agents, attorneys, merchants, and shopkeepers. By 1817, Scots held almost one-third of the enslaved people in Jamaica, though it is also true that some Jamaicans of Scottish descent were prominent in the struggle to abolish slavery. It is an oft-cited dictum that every Jamaican family has a Scotsman lurking somewhere in its genealogy, something Zora Neale Hurston ([1938] 1990) commented on during her sojourn in Jamaica during the late 1930s. "When a Jamaican is born of a black woman and some English or Scotsman," she wrote, "the black mother is literally and figuratively kept out of sight as far as possible, but no one is allowed to forget that white father, however questionable the circumstances of birth. . . . You get the impression that these virile Englishmen do not require women to reproduce." (8).

However, it is also the case that on the back of the music test form that Davenport and Steggerda used, after questions about musical attainments (personal and family) and general biography (nonmusical) for the research subject and family, there is a prompt for "Nativity of Grandparents," with two questions: native country and province, state, or town, regardless of blood or stock; and racial stock or blood, regardless of where born. In some cases, people responded to these two questions by writing "Jamaica" for native country, and then "Negro" or "Black" or "Coloured" for racial stock. Equally, however, racial stock was listed as "Jamaican" or sometimes "Scottish" or "African." In one case, racial stock was identified as "Eboe, African." And sometimes native country was listed as "Half Scotch" or "Coloured" or even "African Hindu."[33] The point I am making is that the people Davenport and Steggerda were testing and measuring as representatives of three racial groups had enormously varied ways of representing themselves in response to the questions they were asked. There was no universal mode of reckoning or distinguishing race from country from origin. And, frankly, more often than not these questions were left blank.

In addition to the lack of uniformity among both assistants and respondents with respect to racial and national terminology, there were many places where Steggerda and Davenport declined to universally find what they hypothesized—significant variability and, even more important, disharmony among "hybrids." This makes it more than a bit puzzling when, at the end of the book, they finally argued for trait-based genetic differences:

> This high variability is found in our Browns of Jamaica in such traits as interpupillary distance, nasal breadth, ear index, skin color, diameter of hair curl. These are all marked differential characters between the White and the Black.
>
> The fact of this high variability of these traits in the mixed group is excellent evidence that human traits segregate just as those of other animals and of plants do. The evidence of Mendelian inheritance in man is, indeed, so overwhelming and has been so long known that reference to it here might seem unnecessary, were it not that, occasionally, anthropologists arise who appear to be skeptical on the matter. (Davenport and Steggerda 1929, 460)

At the same time, they find Browns to be closer, in general, to Blacks in their various measurements, an affinity they attribute to "repeated back-crossing" (in other words, Browns "mating" with Blacks rather than whites). They also, perhaps relatedly, conclude that there is "no evidence of physical hybrid vigor in the Browns" (464), which diverges from others' findings. The Brown, they argue, "is contrasted unfavorably with the Black who, though he may be stupid and lazy, can at least be depended upon to react in his own way" (469).

It should come as no surprise that Davenport and Steggerda also argued, at the end of the text, for the mental inferiority of Blacks, linking this to the question of polygenesis (which they disclaimed). As geneticist William Provine (1986) put it in his overview of genetics research on race throughout the late nineteenth and twentieth centuries, their arguments were that "Negroes were inferior to whites . . . that Negroes had made no original contribution to world civilization; they had never risen much above barbarism in Africa; they did little better when transplanted to Haiti; they had not achieved white standards in America; and their disease resistance was inferior to that of whites in America" (867). Davenport and Steggerda do not, in fact, mention Haiti in the text itself, but they do argue that while species change over time, "mutations are constantly occurring, and some of them may, under favorable conditions of mating and breeding, come to be the heritage of a considerable population" (Davenport and Steggerda 1929, 467). Again, we see hints here of Lamarckianism filtering into a largely Mendelian argument, but they do conclude that there are a number of genetic differences between negroes and Europeans and that this should prove to "anthropologists who doubt" that "the main races of mankind differ in innate capacity for mental operations" (468).

While the eugenics movement certainly provided the driving ideological context for Davenport and Steggerda's *Race Crossing*, other contemporary eugenicists criticized the study. Karl Pearson, a student of Galton's who became the founding father of statistics, was generally skeptical of Mendelian principles and began his review: "If length of title, weight of names, and number of printed pages can make a great book, this work should certainly be such" (Pearson 1930, 427). He argued that the sample sizes were too small to make relevant comprehensive arguments; indeed, he found incredulous that Steggerda and Davenport had calculated percentages for measurements taken of only a handful of individuals, and sometimes only one. He also argued that there was no possibility for homogeneity within their samples, observing that "Jamaica, with its centuries of racial intermixture is the last place where a study of the relative physical and mental traits of White and Negro can be made" (427). Taking the cephalic index measurements as an example, Pearson noted that the whites were admittedly mixed (German and English), and that the Black Jamaicans would likely have had some "white blood" in them (428) and were, in any case, undoubtedly descended from people who inhabited many regions in Africa. Even the photographs, he argued, were unstandardized, and the statistical tables were arcane. For Pearson, Davenport and Steggerda's data therefore proved nothing. And five years prior to Race Crossing's publication, American zoologist and geneticist Herbert Spencer Jennings (1924) had already issued a more general critique of the unit-character approach—the idea that there was a one-to-one correlation between a phenotypic characteristic and a gene—arguing for greater attention to gene-environment interaction when thinking eugenically through heredity.

Geneticist William Castle (1930) similarly criticized Davenport's emphasis on disharmony, arguing that he and Steggerda overstated the impact of the differences in measurement they found. For example, he noted, if Browns have legs that are one centimeter longer than Whites or Blacks, it doesn't make it harder for them to lean over and pick something up. This led Castle to contend:

> We like to think of the Negro as an inferior. We like to think of Negro-white crosses as a degradation of the white race. We look for evidence in support of the idea and try to persuade ourselves that we have found it even when the resemblance is very slight. The honestly made records of Davenport and Steggerda tell a very different story about hybrid Jamaicans from that which Davenport and Jennings tell about them in broad sweeping statements. The former will never reach the ears of eugenics propagandists and Congressional committees; the latter will be with us as the bogey men of pure-race enthusiasts for the next hundred years. (605–6)

Physical anthropologist Wilson D. Wallis also specifically critiqued the Jamaica study, arguing that, as Garland Allen (2011) has put it, "Davenport should have used the *coefficient of variation* (standard deviation divided by the mean of each population), since the populations under consideration (whites, blacks and browns) all had different means for the traits that were examined" (20). And other critics, including Thomas Hunt Morgan, who eventually left the eugenics movement, "pointed out that social reforms would be a far more quick and effective way to deal with many of the problems eugenicists wanted to solve through genetics" (G. Allen 2011, 21).[34]

Even Wickliffe Draper was disillusioned by the lack of definitive findings in the *Race Crossing* study. He decided not to invest further in the study of hybrids, instead going on to develop and circulate pamphlets to use in congressional lobbying on issues related to the resettlement of African Americans in Africa and the restriction of immigration (W. Tucker 2002). *Race Crossing* seemed to go nowhere, but despite these criticisms, which Davenport tended to slough off, he continued to pursue research on miscegenation. He sought information about the anthropological traits of Brazilians from a fellow Mendelian, the Brazilian scientist Edgard Roquette-Pinto (Sebastião de Souza 2016), and he directed a longitudinal anthropometric study at the Tuskegee Institute from 1932 to 1944 (Lombardo 2016), a study that began the same year as the infamous syphilis study. At Tuskegee, it was again Steggerda, by then based full-time at the Carnegie Institution, who did the measurements, following much the same protocol as the study in Jamaica. Steggerda also continued work on race crossing in the Yucatan with Maya communities, in association with Dr. A. V. Kidder's archaeological studies there.[35]

Critiques of eugenics increased in visibility after 1925 due to nativist debates surrounding immigration restriction and the Supreme Court decision that upheld as constitutional a Virginia statute that allowed forcible sterilization of institutionalized individuals. These critiques intensified during the mid-1930s as more people became aware of the eugenic programs of German National Socialism. In 1930, and again in 1937, a commission of evaluators visited the Eugenics Record Office (ERO). The report of the 1937 commission chastised the ERO: "The records, upon which so much effort and money have been expended, have to date been extremely little used, to judge by the number of publications based upon them. Thus the Office appears to be accumulating large amounts of material, and devoting a disproportionately great amount of time and money to a futile system for indexing it, without certainty, or even good probability, that it will ever be of value" (cited in G. Allen 2011, 9). Davenport's retirement and this report ultimately led to the closure of the ERO when its funding ceased at the end of 1939.

After a brief consideration of how anthropometric research might "fit into a federal defense program,"[36] this methodological approach began to fall out of favor within the scientific community. This waning influence was due in part to postwar shifts in anthropological approaches to race. Although Franz Boas had an early enthusiasm for biometrics, he eventually came to believe that "heritable differences were familial in origin" and that "races, as distinct biological entities, did not exist except as folk taxonomy" (Blakey 1987, 20). As most anthropologists know, Boas came to advocate for a public anthropology that would take a stand against racism, a call many of his students—including Ruth Benedict and Margaret Mead—would take up. Later, several anthropologists became involved in the drafting of the two UNESCO statements on race in 1951 and 1952.[37]

At the same time, research in genetics was also moving away from Mendelian principles. Milislav Demerec—a Croatian-born geneticist whose research with drosophila, and later on the genetics of bacteria and their viruses, led to significant interventions in our understanding of antibiotic resistance—became acting director of the Department of Genetics at the Carnegie Institution in 1942 (and director in 1943). Steggerda must have seen the writing on the wall, because he sent Demerec a letter outlining the twelve years of research he had conducted with Navajo in New Mexico, Maya in the Yucatan, "Negroes" from Alabama, and whites from Michigan under the auspices of the institution, an "inventory of accomplishments," as he stated. "I see," he wrote, "with the change of administrators that my work does not fit in exactly with the present program of the department.

You have not told me so, but others have." He proposed to shift his interests slightly, to devote his attention to growth patterns in fifty sets of twins across "these four races."[38] Steggerda's plea seems to have worked, at least temporarily, but he left the Carnegie Institution in 1944 to teach anthropology at the Hartford Seminary Foundation in Connecticut.

By the mid-twentieth century, other physical anthropologists were being influenced by geneticists and evolutionary biologists such as Theodosius Dobzhansky and J. B. S. Haldane, who were synthesizing Mendelian theories of genetic inheritance with Darwin's view of evolution through natural selection. Their thesis, which quickly became the anthropological baseline, was that human groups must be understood as dynamic populations in which genetic composition changes as a result of many factors, including natural selection, mutation, migration, and isolation. Their understanding that human bodies are porous and unstable made it clear that "the idea that race was something consistently passed down from one generation to the next was oversimplified and inaccurate" (Keel 2018, 118). For biological anthropologists like Jonathan Marks (1996), if genetic diversity in humans is clinal and ephemeral, then "racial classifications represent a form of folk heredity" (131).

THE PERSISTENCE OF POLYGENIST APPROACHES TO EVIDENCE

Despite these shifts, it is also true that anthropologists did not immediately jettison polygenist points of view. My own department, for example, boasts the very first professorship in anthropology in the United States, Daniel Brinton. Although he was trained as a medical doctor, Brinton was hired in 1886 as a professor of archaeology and linguistics, having previously held the position of professor of ethnology and anthropology at the Academy of Natural Sciences. Brinton was also president of the American Association of the Advancement of Science (AAAS) during the last years of the nineteenth century before he died in 1899, and he was an avid segregationist (Baker 2000). In 1896, while president of the AAAS, Brinton argued in *Popular Science Monthly* that "the black, the brown, and the red races differ anatomically so much from the white . . . that even with equal cerebral capacity they never could rival its results by equal efforts" (Brinton, quoted in Baker 1998, 27). Brinton publicly advocated theories of scientific racism across several scientific institutions in Philadelphia. He believed that "traits" developed in particular environments were passed down from generation to generation.

In the mid-twentieth century, this line of thinking would be continued by Carleton Coon. Carleton Coon graduated with a PhD in anthropology from Harvard University in 1928, when he began as a lecturer there. During World War II, his academic career was interrupted and he began work with the Office of Strategic Services (the precursor to the Central Intelligence Agency [CIA]). In 1948, Coon left Harvard and took a post at the University of Pennsylvania (Penn), where he was also a curator in its museum. Coon, whose early publications included *The Races of Europe* (1939), was a racial typologist who believed that human races evolved independently and at different times as the result of different environmental conditions. This would place him squarely within the legacy of scientific racism, carrying on a lineage established by Samuel Morton and Daniel Brinton.[39] Coon advanced his thesis in his 1962 work, *The Origin of Races*, in which he argued that humanity's division into five races preceded our evolution into a single species, and that this is what had caused a hierarchy of civilization, with sub-Saharan Africans existing as the most "primitive" (1962). At the time this text was published, Coon was president of the American Association of Physical Anthropologists, but he resigned following the controversy that emerged from it.

Coon also had a connection to the Pioneer Fund, which, we will remember, was established by Wickliffe Draper, who also funded the Race Crossing study. By the time the fund was incorporated in New York in March 1937, in large part to support "study and research into the problems of heredity and eugenics in the human race... and... into the problems of race betterment" (W. Tucker 2002, 43). Wickliffe Draper had already traveled to Berlin to take part in the 1935 International Congress for the Scientific Investigation of Population Problems, hosted by Nazi Germany and chaired by Wilhelm Frick, the German minister of the interior. Draper selected Harry H. Laughlin, editor of *Eugenical News* and head of the Eugenics Record Office, as the fund's first president. Laughlin was a great admirer of Nazi eugenics programs and an energetic legislative activist for immigration restriction and compulsory sterilization. It was Laughlin who first brought Earnest Sevier Cox's book *White America* (outlining a program of repatriation of African Americans to Africa) to Draper's attention.[40] Laughlin was succeeded by Frederick Henry Osborn, who purported to be more moderate and who attempted to "rescue eugenics from its long association with bigotry and discrimination" (W. Tucker 2002, 48). Osborn nevertheless directed considerable funding to oppose the Civil Rights Movement, and Draper himself secretly sent US$255,000 to the Mississippi State Sovereignty Commission to support anti–civil rights violence and intimidation (Blackmon 1999).[41] In the post–Civil Rights Movement era, the fund continued to support research that undermined integration and political equality, and it focused on purported racial differences in intelligence and capacity through the 1980s and 1990s.[42] Throughout the mid-twentieth century, Delta Airlines CEO and pro-segregationist Carleton Putnam brought many eugenics-oriented scholars into the Pioneer fold, including Wilmot Robertson (a pseudonym), author of *The Dispossessed Majority*, a book that was endorsed by Carleton Coon, Putnam's cousin.

One might argue that Coon's career-long excavations in Iran were oriented to finding fossil evidence of modern human origins earlier than those discovered in Africa in order to solidify his claim that Europeans were older, and thus more advanced, than Africans. Physical anthropologist Wilton Krogman, whose specialties were child development and forensics (and who was an apologist for the racism of Davenport and Steggerda; see Krogman 1976), and paleoanthropologist Alan Mann continued this evolutionary typological focus in physical anthropology at Penn. In all this work, bodies—dead or living—were understood to provide traces of "otherwise invisible processes and events" (Crossland 2009, 71).

TRACES AS EPHEMERA

We should not imagine that the kind of racial accounting Davenport and Steggerda performed in relation to the measurements they collected in Jamaica would have been unfamiliar to West Indian audiences. Indeed, their categorical reckoning might have been seen as very crude in comparison to the highly detailed vocabularies describing racial mixing that planters and other observers had elaborated in Spanish, French, and British imperial theaters. We need only think of the eighteenth-century Latin American casta paintings or the complex naming structures developed on plantations throughout the West Indies.[43] These structures were meant to clarify genealogical inheritances, wherein proximity to whiteness was socially and legally policed, by identifying the various traces Blackness left in and on the body. Indeed, within the contemporary Caribbean, *tracing* also refers to the act of rehearsing an adversary's genealogical history in public in order to shame them, a practice we should understand as an inheritance of this colonial legacy (F. Smith 2023). As Faith Smith (2023) has argued, "imperial power provides the vocabulary through which people in the region imagine power or freedom" (6), and this linguistic heritage means that *we* also speak in language that reads innate racial difference and mixture on the body. Our own racial terminological arsenals are replete with slurs like "coolie," "coolie-royal," "Chinee-royal"—slurs that define various bodily inheritances and that also imply particular kinds of ethnic and racial (and classed) investments and allegiances on the part of the speaker.

We might also think the problem of "race mixing" as a kind of parallel to the problem of so-called plural societies, a concept that anthropologist M. G. Smith would develop a generation after the Davenport study was published. The plural society theory developed by J. S. Furnivall in Dutch colonial contexts had posited that the different communities making up colonial societies maintained their own cultural, linguistic, and religious practices, practices that were unified only through the colonial market and political subordination. Smith applied Furnivall's theory to West Indian societies, understanding them as hierarchical conglomerates of corporate groups (organized in racial-cultural terms) that shared little in the way of family organization, language, or religious practice, and that were united only through imperial (and later, national) domination (Furnivall 1945, 1948; M. Smith 1965). Within this view, Black Jamaicans, because they were not assimilating to European norms, were able to maintain ontologies and epistemologies that differed from (and were often opposed to) colonial modes of being, but the practices that upheld these ontologies and epistemologies—practices that anthropologists and other ethnographers studied extensively throughout the mid-twentieth century—were routinely denigrated as evidence of a negative inheritance, of pathology, and of absence.[44] Measuring the fitness or innate inferiority of the individual body in this light was a way to measure the fitness of the collective body in a world order increasingly reckoned through nation-states.

Another way these older modes of racial measurement recursively enter our consciousness occurs when their visual archives are recirculated, such as in the Dutch exhibition that Geertje Mak (2020) details, in which images from Bernard Hagen's "Atlas of heads and faces of Asian and Melanesian people," published in 1906, were reworked for contemporary audiences in ways that erased the context of their collection. Or, in a more critical context, by artists like Paul Vanouse, who explores the "entanglement of race, science, technology and colonialism" (M'charek, Schramm, and Skinner 2014, 459), or Sasha Huber, who amends the photographs taken by Swiss biologist Louis Agassiz of enslaved people on a South Carolina cotton plantation by clothing them and suturing their wounds.[45] Or, in Tina Campt's (2017) discussion of colonial photographic archives in South Africa, archives that, in some cases, aestheticize Black South Africans "into a temporal elsewhere outside of history" in order to justify policies like the Native Land Act of 1913 (the precursor to formal apartheid), and in other cases, "identify, classify, isolate and distinguish" their physical attributes in order to claim and control their bodies. Campt argues that these images evoke "haptic temporalities" (57) and that reclaiming them through an archival practice that emphasizes touching and feeling, rather than only the visual rubric of comparison, can produce affective encounters in relation to time and in relation to other similar sets of images. These are all attempts at resignifying, and therefore repairing, the traces of one kind of inheritance—the various forms of violence wrought by anthropometric measuring and its allied technologies—after the fact. But we have other inheritances, too.

As I was making my way through the sixteen boxes in the Steggerda collection in the Otis Archives at the National Museum of Health and Medicine, poring over measurements and music tests and form discrimination tests, cringing while looking at photographs, recoiling when encountering hair samples, still preserved as Davenport would have received them from Jamaica in their small wax-paper coin envelopes, I came upon a sheet of paper headed "My Autobiography." It began:

On the 22nd of August 1905, the people in the village of Bluefields, in the parish of Westmoreland, shouted for joy when I was born. Everyone said that I was one of the best babies he or she had seen in our village since the last five years. When I was three and one-half months old, my mother took me to church to be baptized. Little did I know what baptism meant, until I felt water pouring down on my face, and at the same time I heard the minister saying some words, which I do not remember. At the age of six, I was sent to school, and oh what a place it was, when I entered the door on the first Monday morning. The children at first laughed and hit me on my back, but when they found that I was quiet, they made me their friend. I made rapid progress in school. Many of the boys had to ask me to show them how to work problems in mensuration and Simple Interest. On the cricket field, I was also good, and on many occasions my number of runs alone exceeded those of the opposite side. I got many prizes for doing well on the sports field. In 1920, my age was limited, but I took private lessons from teacher [Mr. X], and sat for the yearly Pupil Teacher's Examination. He was a very good man, but often he would get into passion, fling my book from his table, and would tell me that my essay was rubbish. I had to smart under such pains and write the essays over. I took good positions among the number of passes each year. Once had I failed to pass my First Year. The reason was that I was sick for four months, and so could not do any studies. I pass my final examination in the year 1925. In January, Nineteen Hundred and Twenty-Six I took the "Mico College" Entrance Examination and passed it. I was then admitted into the College. The tutors are very intelligent and enthusiastic, and their chief aims are to impart all the knowledge that they can to the students, and to see that no student fails the annual examination for "Training Colleges."

This was the first of forty-two autobiographical accounts of the students at Mico College, collected in November 1926.[46] Needless to say, I was stunned, both because these autobiographies are not mentioned in *Race Crossing* and because they are beautiful reflections of the embodied experiences and aspirations of those who were being positioned to become leaders in Jamaica. Many of the names, which I cannot reproduce here, were familiar to me, which is to say that some of them are names of families who were, or who have become, prominent in Jamaican society. One was familiar because he came from the same village in St. Catherine where my father was born and raised. It is unclear whose idea it was to assign autobiographies: the request might have come from Steggerda himself, or it might have come from one of the teachers or from the principal of the school, capitalizing on Steggerda's interest to introduce the students to a new mode of narrative writing. My sense is that it may have been the latter, since autobiographies were not elicited from any other group subjected to Steggerda's anthropometrical and psychological testing, not even the young women attending Shortwood College. If we judge from the penmanship, some of the autobiographies were written by the students themselves, and some seem to have been told to Steggerda's assistant at the time, Sydney Carby, who recorded them on paper.

Earlier, I defined trace evidence juridically, but these autobiographies provide different kinds of traces, traces that exceed the juridical sphere. I want to think about these kinds of traces in the way José Estéban Muñoz (2001) approached the question of evidence in relation to queerness. "The key to queering evidence," he wrote, "is by suturing it to the concept of ephemera. Think of ephemera as trace, the remains, the things that are left, hanging in the air like rumor" (423). For conventional archivists, ephemera consist of flyers, paraphernalia, and other seemingly transient materials, often mass-produced, that are not seen as the stuff of cultural or historical value. Ephemera are messy and uncontainable. But ephemera also provide important sources for counterhistories because they stand as the "material corollaries of cultural practices and collective memory for their respective communities of origin and use" (Brownson 2023, 310) and they thereby also constitute an affective archive.[47] Something that is understood as ephemeral is also something that escapes permanent capture, and thus something that must live on in memory, in an affective association that includes the context of experience. That some of the narratives were recounted orally, and thus performed, is critically important. Performance, as well, is inherently ephemeral.[48] To think about these narratives as performative and therefore embodied ephemera, as gestures toward sovereign Being, is to rescript the conceptual context that framed their capture.

The autobiographies of the students at Mico are, in essence, narratives of achievement. We often move quite quickly from birth to education, as in the following: "On the 27th of April 1907, I was born in Kingston, Jamaica. Though of humble parentage, I was privileged to go to school at the age of seven." These men are accounting for how they got to Mico Teacher's College and articulating goals for the future. The autobiographies are also narratives of social mobility and respectability; they emphasize the marriage of their parents (whether formal or informal) and their professional histories. We learn of mothers who were teachers and of fathers who were cultivators and shopkeepers, teachers and pastors, tailors and carpenters, produce dealers and overseers, policemen and architects. We learn of connections to Central America, to other islands in the Caribbean, and to Nigeria. In some cases, we learn they were Methodist, or that they were baptized, or that they attended "Sabbath School," which would reflect the denominational diversity in early-twentieth-century Jamaica. We also learn of their birth order and of the death of brothers and sisters. We learn of fathers who "refused to accept the offer for my working with a Fruit Company with a view to sending me to a College," and of brothers who taught them when they were sick at home with measles, influenza, typhoid, whooping cough, chicken pox, or other ailments. We learn that as young people, they took joy in their studies: "It was well known for miles around that I could recite by heart the *Ancient Mariner*." And we learn about how they navigated the difficulties of life while pursuing educational goals, as, for example, in the following: "Being the biggest of the boys, I had to act as the man for the home when my father was away from home, which was often, on account of his work. I had also to do a lot of other rough work about the house, looking after the animals, cultivation etc. My father being a large cultivator, during his absence I had to represent him at times; which, however, did not impede my school work."

Our narrators name each school they attended and each teacher they had, and we see parents making decisions about where to live (or where to send their child) based on the strength of the school in their district. We learn of elementary school teachers who, on determining that our narrators were bright, encouraged them to sit the Pupil Teacher Exams—some passed as early as eleven years old, others when they were fifteen—and then to take the additional exams that would eventually lead them to Mico. We learn of their experiences at Mico, which are generally positive, with one exception. One student cited Thomas Gray's eighteenth-century "Ode on a Distant Prospect of Eton College"—a poem that juxtaposes the joy and innocence of youth and the loss and frustration wrought by knowledge and adulthood—as an apt summary of his experience at Mico. We learn about changes in people's lives wrought by the "outbreak of the Great War of 1914" and by changing immigration restrictions in the United States. And we learn of other kinds of migrations, such as that of the student who was born in Nigeria to Jamaican parents who were both teachers (his father, in fact, was also trained at Mico and his mother trained at the Bethlehem Training College) and missionaries. In his narrative, he tells the story of their return from West Africa to Jamaica: "I was made to understand afterwards that I was among the youngest and smallest of the children on board the ship from Africa to England, but even then, I could do some amount of drill, according to orders, and could eat with my small pair of knife and fork quite well, though just two years old." In a way that resonates with Faith Smith's (2013) analysis of the letters West Indian parents of students at the Tuskegee Institute wrote to Booker T. Washington and other administrators, these autobiographical narratives reflect experiences and dreams "that exceeded territorial boundaries even as they also reflected the hopes of colonial and imperial subjects who sought more mobility and resources *within* the boundaries of their respective territories" (n.p.) Smith argues that the Tuskegee letters reflect a "register of simultaneity—national and transnational, imperial and diasporic, vocational and professional, subservient and assertive, idealistic and expedient." We should read this same simultaneity into the autobiographies of the Mico students.

Toward the end of their narratives, and always toward the end—suggesting that they were given a series of prompts from which to write their stories—we learn of their pastimes and hobbies, likes and dislikes. One student wrote, "Poetry is one of my hobbies but I do not like novel-reading. I prefer to read an essay, the report of a speech or any current event rather than to sit over a tiresome book." Another shared: "My chief recreations, besides cricketing, are walking, riding, and occasionally night drives in motor cars." Another admitted to "a special fondness for the poems of Shelley and Wordsworth" and mentioned that aside from various sports, he enjoyed long walks. "When all these got tiresome," he wrote, "I fell back on sea-bathing." There are others: "As a boy, I was very fond of visiting the woods, oftentimes alone. Not very fond of play, I would often wander through the hills, probably trying to see how well I could climb over the tall sharp stones." "Mathematics, Science and Languages are the subjects I am most keenly interested in, and which I like very much." And, "I am a great lover of music." One student recalled that his father was not only a self-taught blacksmith and tinsmith but had also learned how to extract and distill the oils from plants and fruits. "I was never more pleased than to spend an afternoon at his workplace," he remembered. Another, as a child, "found time to go bird-nesting, and flower-hunting." One student learned to play the piano; another became his church's organist at the age of sixteen. Another who recalled being very "tricky" as a child also said he enjoyed dancing. Several were fond of riding horses: "My parish being famous for good horses, I was like a Cowboy, and as it was with horse-riding, so it was with cycles." The students' senses of themselves also shine through, as in, "Bashfulness hinders me from acquiring some of the qualities of a good society man—dance, music, and athletics"; or, "I find great difficulty in grasping theoretical knowledge except such as may be easily obvious after explanation"; or, "In stature I am small and am of a quiet disposition, genial nature, and prefer a quiet and gentle life to a course [sic] or rough one." These students are gifting us with traces of their humanity. They are demonstrating their multifaceted personhood and thereby countering their designation as innately inferior.

It is not incidental that some also limn their genealogical histories in their own racial terms. "My parents," one student offered, "are of the negro race so I have followed in the line and am a negro and the fourth child of a number of eight. . . . Though I am a negro by colour, yet many of my grandfather's descendants are coloured." Another student wrote, "My mother is the daughter of a Jew, hence I have a tip of Jewish blood." Another noted that his grandfather was born in Central America and that some of his mother's ancestors were "descended from persons belonging to the East Indian peoples." One student who came from a family of "poor cultivators" stated that his father was the "great grandson of a Scotchman who came to Jamaica sometime in the early part of the nineteenth century," and that his mother was "a pure African." Another wrote, "My father's grandfather came from Wales but his grandmother was a negro. My mother's grandfather came from

Scotland to Jamaica where he married a negress." Indeed, as mentioned earlier, many of the family histories that Steggerda culled from his research participants included some Scottish ancestry, and one wonders whether Davenport and Steggerda knew the historical causes of this phenomenon. Did they understand the history of indentured labor, which brought Indians to Jamaica and elsewhere in the Caribbean to "save sugar"? Did they know that Portuguese Jews escaping the Inquisition were some of the earliest settlers in Jamaica, and that after the British conquest in 1655 they were granted British citizenship and given the right to practice Judaism openly? Did they know that by the end of the nineteenth century, a quarter of the working-age male population of Jamaica was overseas, cultivating bananas in Costa Rica, growing cane in Cuba, building the canal in Panama? Would knowing these histories have changed their research protocol?

Another student claimed that his great-grandfather "was the son and heir of Derby of the Mandingans, and on his arrival in Jamaica was made free." It is possible that this student was referencing the Mandingo peoples of the upper Niger valley, who embarked on a series of wars with the French in the late nineteenth century as the latter began to solidify imperial domination over Mali, Guinea, and Côte d'Ivoire. I have not, however, been able to find a reference to "Derby" or "Darby" in this context. What is notable, however, is that the great-great-grandfather of someone who was about twenty years old in 1926 could have been an adult sometime close to the British abolition of slavery in 1834, which might have accounted for the bestowal of his freedom when arriving in Jamaica. Did Steggerda wonder about the significance of someone passing this story on to this student? Did he pause when he read the words of another student who wrote, "With the greatest pride and as a citizen of Jamaica, I boast that I am in no way separated from the Negro Race; and still more do I esteem the family from which I am." Did he ask himself what it would mean to call oneself a "citizen" of Jamaica, to embody this kind of racial and nationalist pride, in the early twentieth century?

Some of our narrators began their autobiographies by reflecting on what it meant to write accounts of themselves. While some of these students merely admitted that while they would never have thought to write their life stories, because they'd been asked they would try their best; others explicitly grappled with the relationships among history, memory, and life writing. Narration, anthropologists have maintained, and in particular self-narration, draws attention to and simultaneously refuses "the power of social scientific generalization" (Abu-Lughod [1993] 2008, 15). Stories are inherently partial, they are situated, and they require particular intimacies between teller and audience. And despite the fact that self-narratives outline individual experiences, they are social rather than individual events in which language co-constructs histories, meanings, and realities.[49] As Judith Butler (2005) has argued, no account of oneself exists outside a "structure of address" (36), which is not merely an interpersonal frame but also a discursive one. For Butler, this frame makes us opaque to ourselves and therefore makes us unreliable narrators (we cannot, for instance, authoritatively tell the story of our own birth); it requires of us a third-person stance, which dispossesses us of ourselves. We are thus unable to escape the conditions of our own recognition as subjects of our own stories.

At the same time, personal accounts are *given*, and as gifts, they emerge from and constitute relations, which is why Hannah Arendt understood narration as political (1998). Butler argues that the very opacity at the heart of the self is what creates the conditions for these relations, and for the elaboration of ethics and responsibility, a point she develops using Italian feminist philosopher Adriana Cavarero's (2000) work on the "narratable self" (34). Cavarero argues that a narratable self *desires* the narration of its coming into being. She insists that as we entrust our narrations to other "narratable selves," we jettison the third-person stance and "recuperate the constitutive worldly and relational identity from which the story itself resulted" (36). This creates a vulnerable embodied relation of exposure that can exist outside the conditions of violence that produce subjectivity.

Consider the following two examples:

I often wish to recall the events of my past life in a more or less chronological order, but as often as I would attempt to gratify my wish, I find my memory sadly ineffective. Early childhood days and incidents in connection with them seem very much blurred. Nothing but what will cause wonderful resuscitation of memory will enable me to produce a well balanced auto-biography.

For a long time it has been growing more and more in my fancy to write an account of myself, but I could never get started. At last the time has come. The reader must go with me even farther back than memory takes me, that is, to the time of my birth; and he must follow me closely, else he might find himself struggling alone in the dark.

It is true that the students typically began their narrations with stories of their birth. If in Bluefields, villagers "shouted for joy" as our first writer came into the world, in Stepney, St. Ann, the parents "were in great perplexity—which was soon followed by great joy . . . [which] was brought when it was announced that I was born." Another student "recalled" what must have been a defining moment in his life, as he narrates his own position in it from the vantage point of an observer (rather than a participant):

> One day, over nineteen years ago, I found myself standing and leaning over the shoulders of my mother. She had a baby in her lap. Suddenly, a violent shaking of the earth, accompanied with a roaring noise was felt. The reason for this I enquired, but do not remember exactly the answer I received. Later on, it was found that my terrible experience was no other than the Great Earthquake of 1904, I being at that time two years and nine months old. This is the earliest of my life I can remember.

After relating this story, our narrator goes back to his birth, in St. Thomas, to "very poor people who get their means of sustenance by cultivating."

With these stories, the students were doing more than creating a relation of narratable selves. Our narrators were *placing* themselves, geographically, historically, and familially. In accounting for their origins, they were laying claim to places, moments, and positions, which means that they were rescripting the context in which their autobiographies were being solicited:

> On the 16th of July 1905, I was born in the little district of Retirement in the parish of St. Ann, in the Island of Jamaica.

> On the 29th of March 1906, I was born of a fairly reputed parentage, and grew up to find that there were seven before me, and three after, making a total of eleven children of whom I was the eighth, and the fifth of six boys, the other children being girls. Never, never shall I forget my home; for I was born on the Pedro River in the "Garden Parish" of the beautiful island of Jamaica, where the skies are ever bright and cheery and the birds sing always.

> In the year 1905, and on the 31st day of the month of March, I first saw daylight at "Airy Castle," a district of the Parish of Saint Thomas, Jamaica B.W.I., where my father and mother are still residing.

> I am the heir-in-law to my parents, and at present have seven younger brothers and sisters alive; two are dead.

I was born in the year 1902, in a little village by the name of Rejoin. The family consisted of four children, and I was the third.

I [name], the beloved son of [names] (both Jamaicans), was born on the 8th of December 1907 in Old Harbour (Jamaica), which was then a prosperous town.

Moreover, the third-person stance taken in some of these accounts does not, in my opinion, reflect the dispossession wrought by subjectivity, but instead speaks to a rhetorical expectation of a certain kind of audience. Indeed, all the autobiographies hum with a keen sense of reader. On one level, they are writing for their teachers; on another, they are writing for Steggerda. But one wonders, based on the performative flair that infuses so many of the narratives, if they aren't writing for one another, as well as for audiences further afield. It is important to remember that some of their accounts were in fact explicitly performed to the scribe Sydney Carby, who would not have been unfamiliar with the performative conventions they were using, forms of rhetorical eloquence that Roger Abrahams (1983) long ago characterized as central to West Indian modes of expression. Abrahams defined the West Indian "man-of-words" as someone who could, on one hand, "stitch together a startling piece of oratorical rhetoric, and, on the other, capture the attention, the allegiance, and the admiration of the audience through his fluency, his strength of voice, and his social maneuverability and psychological resilience" (xxx). Abrahams argued that these kinds of performances "represent a model of interpersonal relations in the surrounding community" (18). Other (earlier) observers such as missionaries and planters also noticed this model. Bryan Edwards's proto-ethnographic account of plantation life in eighteenth-century Jamaica, for example, included the following:

> Among other propensities and qualities of the Negroes must not be omitted their loquaciousness. They are as fond of exhibiting set speeches, as orators by profession; but it requires a considerable share of patience to hear him throughout; for they commonly make a long preface before they come to the point; beginning with a tedious enumeration of their past services and hardships. They dwell with peculiar energy (if the fact admits it) on the number of children they have presented to *Massa* (Master) after which they recapitulate some of the instances of particular kindness shown them by their owner or employer, adducing these also as proofs of their own merit; it being evident they

think no such kindness can be gratuitous. This is their usual exordium, as well when they bring complaints against others, as when they are called upon to defend themselves; and it is vain to interrupt either plaintiff or defendant. . . .

One instance recurs to my memory, of so significant a turn of expression in a common labouring Negro, who could have had no opportunity of improvement from the conversation of White people, as is alone, I think, sufficient to demonstrate that Negroes have minds very capable of observation. It was a servant brought me a letter, and, while I was preparing an answer, had, through weariness and fatigue, fallen asleep on the floor; as soon as the papers were ready, I directed him to be awakened; but this was no easy matter. When the Negro who attempted to wake him exclaimed in the usual jargon, *You no hear Massa call you? Sleep*, replied the poor fellow looking up, and returning composedly to his slumbers, *Sleep has no Massa*. (Edwards [1793], cited in Abrahams 1983, 30)

Abrahams (1983) argues that though the linguistic performances of working-class West Indians might resemble European practices, in fact, we should see them as "more characteristic of African performance patterns" (33)—and here he is invoking the work of Alan Lomax and Robert Farris Thompson—due to extralinguistic patterns like the expectation of some form of call and response. He sees West Indian oratory, in other words, as a different inheritance, as "evidence of the continuity of African attitudes toward eloquence and the adaptation of selected European forms into this value and performance system" (33). In this context, he argues, eloquence and effective speechmaking are evidence of "being a good person and a good community member" (38).

Clearly, Davenport and Steggerda could not hear this other inheritance. Or if they did notice their participants' rhetorical eloquence, in the same way that Steggerda occasionally noticed the beauty or charm of one or another woman he was measuring, they may have understood it as an African continuity that could only reflect their innate inferiority, rather than an emblem of personhood and sociability. As I argued earlier, the people Davenport and Steggerda were testing and measuring as representatives of three racial groups had enormously more complicated ways of representing and understanding their embodied inheritances than could possibly have been evidenced through the protocols they developed to create an equivalence between physical "traits" and mental capacity. The researchers had no way either to appreciate the evidence they were eliciting as forms of ontological and epistemological difference that bespoke a humanity reckoned in terms other than their own, or to understand their participants' insertion of themselves into a Jamaican future in which they would be drivers of worlds within which their efforts would be central. As one student put it: "I look forward to the close of my College career, when I shall go out, with all the discipline and moral virtue obtained in College, to mould the lives of the rising generation. . . . I will ever respond to my country's call."

2

TESTIMONIES

In early 2019, I received a voicemail from Patrick White of Fairfield, Iowa. Patrick said he had seen the film that Junior "Gabu" Wedderburn and I collaborated on with Junior Manning and John Jackson about the Coral Gardens Incident of 1963, *Bad Friday*. He went on to say that he had lived in Jamaica for many years with the Coptics and that he had hundreds of hours of archival footage of the group. The Ethiopian Zion Coptic Church—or the Coptics, as they are known locally—was originally one of several branches of Rastafari that eventually consolidated in the small village of Hall's Delight, in the hills above Papine in St. Andrew. From the late 1960s through the 1970s, several white American hippies caught wind of the group, and they traveled to Jamaica to see for themselves. After several leadership transitions—possibly due to disagreements regarding whether to fully include the foreigners in their community and whether to engage in the commercial trafficking of ganja—the Coptics built an empire. They grew rice and other subsistence crops (in fact, they had the only working rice thresher on the island); they employed thousands of people across Jamaica's countryside; and they cultivated and exported ganja to the United States through an entirely vertically integrated operation until the US Drug Enforcement Agency (DEA) and the Federal Bureau of Investigation (FBI) developed enough evidence to bring nine of the group's (white and American) brethren to trial in the summer of 1981 for having smuggled more than one hundred tons of ganja into the US over the course of several years in the late 1970s. Ultimately they were convicted of operating a massive marijuana smuggling ring under the cloak of religion.

Patrick ended the message by asking whether we thought we could do anything with his footage, if we could make a documentary like *Bad Friday* to show people "all the good the Coptics did for Jamaica." I was apprehensive. To that point, what I "knew" about the Coptics was that they had been used by the US Central Intelligence Agency (CIA) to destabilize Michael Manley's democratic socialist government toward the end of the 1970s. Junior was equally apprehensive, since what he "knew" about the Coptics was that they fractured the Rastafari movement at a time when it was gaining significant traction locally and internationally, bringing Jamaicans as a whole to an anti-imperialist, antiracist consciousness that embraced Blackness and Africa as beautiful and desirable. Our apprehension notwithstanding, and after several conversations, in December of that year, we decided to travel to Iowa to meet with Patrick and his brethren David Nissenbaum.

We had many questions, quite beyond the obvious ones regarding how they became involved with the Coptics and what activities they had engaged in. What happened to the group after the DEA and FBI finally succeeded in bringing them to trial (and, subsequently, jail)? What were we to make of the insulting ways Coptics spoke about dreadlocked Rastafari (as "ropeheads")? Of the demeaning ways they discussed His Imperial Majesty Haile Selassie (as an imposter)? What did it mean for the Coptics to be the largest private landowners in Jamaica at a time when Michael Manley's democratic socialist government was promoting "Jamaica for Jamaicans"? Who supported their incorporation as a church, a status that afforded all the usual tax benefits, and more important, permission to perform their "sacraments" at a time when other Rastafari were being terrorized if caught with even the smallest amounts of ganja? Why were the Coptics allowed to operate for so long without significant government oversight of their businesses? How were they able to obtain farm equipment and (custom-built) jeeps from the US during a time of intense scarcity in Jamaica? What relationships did the Coptics have with the Jamaican government (under both Manley's and Seaga's regimes)? And, critically, what does the current decriminalization of ganja mean to them?

We have since embarked on a journey with respect to the Coptics—with those who were (and are) followers and those who were (and are) detractors—and this is a journey that has required wrestling with the relation between testimonial (and spiritual) forms of evidence on one hand and juridical (and geopolitical) forms of evidence on the other. We might understand the latter, as it is articulated by Rastafari who felt undermined by the Coptics or by scholars who have examined the ways Jamaica during the 1970s became a proxy Cold War site, as "circumstantial." Circumstantial evidence, in this case, is "indirect evidence that does not, on its face, prove a fact in issue, but gives rise to a logical inference that the fact exists." It is probative, but it requires that we put two and two together, that we build "additional reasonable inferences in order to support the claim."[1] The circumstantial evidence surrounding the Coptics is what informed our initial hesitations, and what framed our approach to some brethren's disavowal of their various levels of involvement (knowing or unknowing) with either the Jamaican or the US government. Circumstantial evidence also shaped our attention to the questions regarding both juridical and spiritual inheritances (of land, of an epistemology the white brethren did not originate).

The questions of ownership raised by the Coptics' practices bring us back to an analysis of sovereign notions of imperium and dominium, at the same time that they force us to grapple with articulations of testimonial evidence that undermine these. Here I am not evoking testimony in a juridical sense, in which a witness under oath offers a direct experience of events to a representative of the state. Although this iteration of direct experience is, in fact, what many of the white brethren gifted us, their testimonies were shared not to prove a relation (or lack thereof) to law but instead as tributes, as forms of what are sometimes framed as religious testimonies. If the etymology of "testimony" originates with the Hebrew word uwd, meaning "to repeat" or "to bear witness," then the white brethren were bearing witness to the transformations they experienced because of their journeys with the Coptics and, as a result, to the transformations they saw manifested through their collective action for Black Jamaicans as a whole. They were arguing that God will do it again. And because the Coptics, as is also the case with all Rastafari, believe that God is man and man is God (hence, the "I and I"), that the divine is not outside of us but exists in each one of us, their testimonies also signal the continued circulation and embodiment of spirit that motivated their earthly blessings, even as one or another particular physical manifestation of those blessings fell apart. Whereas Christian testimonies have their roots in the early apostles' witnessing of Jesus's resurrection and spreading of the "good news,"[2] contemporary testimony typically narrates how God has changed the testifier's life through a personal relationship with the Holy Spirit, and allows insight into how new beliefs propel new actions and produce new senses of personhood.[3] This is the case not only for evangelicals (and Pentecostals in particular) but also for faiths like that of the Quakers, who are encouraged to bear witness to their beliefs through action in their everyday lives.[4] Bearing witness is also the root of the Islamic Shahadah, a testimonial required of all Muslims and the first of the Five Pillars of Islam.

The testimonies I limn in this chapter are motivated by similar impulses, but what the testifiers are bearing witness to is their commitment to what they understood as the reconstitution of Black Jamaicans, collectively and on earth, as full persons rather than as merely inheritors of slavery and colonialism. The white brethren offer testimonies that invoke the evidence they needed to forsake a world that had previously lacked meaning for them and to participate in a life of spirit that would lead to the radical decolonization not only of Black people but of humanity as a whole. Sometimes this evidence was bodily. But it was also material in terms of the scale of what they were able to build at a particular time (political jockeying during the Cold War) in a particular place (a land fertile for ganja production and a population committed to its cultivation). Building the "Black man's Kingdom on earth" became the worldly evidence of their spiritual rightness, a mode of being in relation in which generosity and care were mobilized to counter generations of trauma as the result of poverty, disenfranchisement, dispossession, and misrecognition. This, for them, constituted repair. The demise of the kingdom not long after the 1980 elections and the death of the community's most charismatic leader were the result, for some, of becoming preoccupied with law (in this case, Moses's law) and, for others, of the growing inability to sustain the network that generated the resources for the mode of relation they were trying to produce in the day-to-day through testimony, prayer, and good works. But for believers, the church never dies. As one of the American brethren we interviewed put it:

> People say the church crashed. You've gotta remember the church is not a physical building; it wasn't a piece of paper. The doctrine is that man is the

church. The spirit of God is not housed in a physical building, it's housed in every human being in the community. So when people say the church crashed, the physical part kind of dissipated, and the brethren went their ways. But the spirit that we all carry, the spirit that we're talking about right now, it will never die. It can only grow and it will manifest in another way later.

The testimonies of the Coptics' detractors, on the other hand, offer circumstantial and indirect evidence of potential CIA alliances, of the Coptics' presumed insincerity as Rastafari grounded in their rejection of Emperor Haile Selassie as the Messiah, and of their seemingly exclusive preoccupation with the cultivation and circulation of ganja. The emphasis on these forms of evidence also emerged in a particular time and place, shaped by a complex and violent political history in which the white brethren had not been socialized, to which they had no particular allegiances, and for which they had no time. Most of the American brethren would have had no visceral understanding of the material, ideological, or affective realities that structured the imaginative possibilities of the majority of (Black) Jamaicans at that time. However, if we believe as anthropologists that one of our aims is to bear witness to people's theorizations of their own circumstances, histories, and potential futures, then we must also assume that they are giving what they understand to be true accounts of themselves. We must read their testimonies generously and in relation to the analytic modes through which they are offered, knowing also that they are given within discursive and material fields that are constantly changing and within social bodies that are always dynamically debating the parameters of belonging and belief (C. Price 2022). We must also recognize that the Coptics and their detractors were operating within two different and incommensurate evidential realms—the juridical and the spiritual—and that these are realms that require different readings of the evidence that undergirded their truth claims. I argue that it is, perhaps not unexpectedly given the context, the latter, through the genre of testimony, that offers a sense of life outside but in relation to oppressive modes of sovereign being.[5] I should also note here, at the outset of this chapter, that the American Coptics feel that this movement cannot be captured through academic understanding, and that therefore my attempts to write about it—though potentially comprehensive and well meaning—ultimately cannot reflect the spiritual knowledge they gleaned from their experiences in Jamaica.

THE GNOSIS OF RASTAFARI

Rastafari has typically been understood as a refusal of Western white supremacist norms of being and self-determination, a reorientation of sovereignty that grounds it in dignity and full interiority with and as God, the unmediated divine within. It exists within a continuum of practices in Jamaica that emerge from what has been understood as a myal complex, a complex that comprises many variations, including maroon practices, *kumina*, and revival, and that insists on moral and cultural equality for Black people (Chevannes 1998). Sylvia Wynter (1977) has proposed that we understand Rastafari in the same way we might approach the Gnostic heretics who critiqued early Christianity, so that gnostic knowledge is understood as something that propels spiritual and imaginative revolution, as something that has the power to transform not only psychic but also material infrastructures. She draws from German philosopher Hans Jonas to think through the relationships between knowledge, salvation, and Being. For Jonas, "the ultimate 'object' of gnosis is God." The "event" of this knowledge "in the soul transforms the knower himself by making him a partaker in the divine existence. . . . Thus . . . the knowledge is not only an instrument of salvation but itself the very form in which the goal of salvation, i.e., ultimate perfection is possessed." The goal, moreover, is a return to oneness with God, which Jonas articulated as one's "native land": "The goal of Gnostic man's striving is the release of the 'inner man' from the bonds of the world and his return to his native land . . . it is necessary that he knows about the transmundane God and about himself, that is, about his divine origin as well as his present situation, and accordingly also about the nature of the world which determines this situation" (Jonas, cited in Wynter [1977] 2022, 469, 470–71).

Wynter argued that Leonard Howell (considered the founder of Rastafari)— and here we could extrapolate to include other early Rastafari leaders and messianic figures, such as Alexander Bedward—came to *know* the reality of Rastafari and was therefore transformed both politically and symbolically. This was a transformation that required the rejection of the dominant material and semiotic system and the elaboration of a new symbolic order, which, she argued, displaces both imperialist and Marxist paradigms that reduce our creative possibilities by identifying us merely as labor, and instead embraces and values Blackness and Africanness:

> Thus Jah guarantees his identity not as *pieza*—interchangeable productive unit—or as *Lumpen*—structurally unemployable, and therefore expendable,

because of no "economic value"—but as the son of the most High, the son of Jah. This sonship guarantees that man will eat bread not by the sweat of his brow but by his sonship. Thus, the provision of his material needs is no longer the end, but rather only a means, a secondary activity which enables man to realize himself, in his true destiny; to partake in divinity, here and now. *It is therefore this radicality of a desire which refuses all limits* that is the central revolutionary impulse of Rastafarianism. (Wynter [1977] 2022, 478)

For Wynter, then, Rastafari is anarchism in its true sense, "freedom *for* the realization of selfhood, the negation of serving an imposed end, the end of the dominant order of Babylon, the return from *negro* to *Prieto*, from cog to creative agent, therefore to the now autonomously created sense of the self" (488). This is freedom that produces a liberation from material and psychic dispossession.

For this reason, the inclusion of white Americans in a Rastafari commune would have been a subject of intense debate and reasoning. Many versions of Rastafari practice have developed since its emergence in the early twentieth century, but for many, the intervention of the Coptics called into question one of the fundamental tenets of the movement, which can perhaps be encapsulated as "'The Rasta is one who never forgets that he is an African'" (Campbell 1987, 115). This also explains why American Coptics would have felt excluded from other Rastafari camps that were advancing a "back to Africa" argument. As one of the white brethren explained, "I have no inheritance of that message." Indeed, another of the white brethren who ended up settling permanently in Jamaica remembered that Brother Wally, one of the original Black Jamaican elders in Hall's Delight and ultimately the spiritual leader in the St. Thomas compound, had told him that when he first saw the white men, he didn't think they could be saved. It was Brother Ivy, the community's leader for ten months at the end of 1969 and the beginning of 1970, who welcomed the white brethren to participate in the realization of this project of exorbitant sovereignty.

While there were undoubtedly many Americans who arrived and left, who chased after ganja and went home, those white Americans who moved sincerely with the Coptics during the 1970s and early 1980s and who continue to profess the doctrine were, nevertheless, transformed by their experiences in the Ethiopian Zion Coptic Church community in such a way that they came to know their divine purpose—the realization of ultimate perfection. This was to be manifested not only in a new attunement to their own embodiment but also in the building of a kingdom for Black Jamaicans in which they could become the creative agents they were meant to be. At the same time, there can be no question that their white and American bodies afforded them certain privileges, and that those bodies allowed them to maneuver differently from their Black Jamaican counterparts in relation to the global geopolitics that governed the legal boundaries of belonging and accountability, and therefore also of the movements that generated the kingdom's material wealth.

COPTICS AND HIPPIES, HOLLYWOOD AND HATERS

If you were an American hippie in the late 1960s and early 1970s and not entirely destitute, you likely traveled (or wanted to travel) to India, Mexico, or Jamaica. If you went to Jamaica, you were most probably in search of ganja, and you might have heard of the Coptics, possibly through their internationally distributed (free) newspaper, the *Coptic Times*. If you knew someone who had encountered them or who had even gone to live among them, you might have imagined a lifestyle in which you would live communally, praying and singing, gaining enlightenment from both weed and doctrine. And if you were an adventurer, the prospect of being involved in the massive transnational movement of ganja might have excited you. This is the story of the Coptics that is foregrounded in *Square Grouper: The Godfathers of Ganja*, a documentary released in April 2011, directed by Billy Corben, and distributed by Magnolia Pictures.

The film features interviews with Brother Clifton, Brother Louv, Brother Butch, Brother Gary, and Sister Ilene, all white American Coptics, alongside comments by Arthur Tifford (Brother Clifton's attorney), Manny Funes (former special agent with the Florida Department of Law Enforcement), Tony Darwin (a former Coptics pilot), Hank Adorno (former Florida assistant state attorney), and Milton Ferrell Jr. (attorney for the Coptics). It details the various properties purchased by the Coptic Church, incorporated in Florida in 1975, including its "Embassy" on Star Island (in Biscayne Bay within the city of Miami), for which it paid US$270,000 in cash; farmland in South Dade, Marion, and Citrus Counties in Florida; a 149-ton freighter and several other good-sized boats, as well as fleets of cars and buses; and a business called the Coptic Container Corporation. All told, the church's assets in the United States exceeded US$5 million, assets purchased with capital amassed through the trafficking and sale of ganja. In the film, Manny Funes assesses the organization's scope: "They were making so much money from the sale of marijuana, the smuggling itself, that they were basically monopolizing

Jamaica. I read a report one time that they had taken in over a billion dollars and that US$200 million was coming back to the government." The pilot Tony Darwin speaks from his own experience: "I made many, many millions off the Coptic Church. I was moving probably thirty to fifty thousand pounds a week, and it was nothing. It was maybe 2 percent of what was going on. We would load up the airplanes we had in the middle of the night, and there were suitcases and suitcases of money. We took tens of millions, maybe hundreds of millions, to Jamaica from the United States. . . . They couldn't have had the size of operation they had without the government being involved."

The film includes clips from an October 1979 episode of *60 Minutes* titled "Holy Smoke" in which Dan Rather reports from the Coptics headquarters in St. Thomas. In one clip, Rather discussed the economic impact of this trade: "Two years ago this was wilderness. The Coptics brought in electricity, constructed an irrigation system, and built roads. Hundreds, perhaps thousands of people on the east end of the island depend on the Coptics for their livelihood. The church already is reported to have US$3 million dollars invested here." This assessment was corroborated by several of the brethren. In *Square Grouper*, Brother Gary, for example, explains: "We established a trucking line where we trucked the food all over the island. We established supermarkets where we sold our own food. We established Marcus Garvey's Black Star Line, where we had ships bringing containers from island to island as a business. The Coptic Farms was the biggest employer in Jamaica at the time. . . . There was a thousand acres of farmland, houses, and it was all centered around the church."

"The ministers of government would come to us for help," Brother Gary concluded. "We naturally kept the country afloat." This statement would later be corroborated by Edward Seaga, who became prime minister of Jamaica in 1980, after the bloodiest battle for political leadership during Jamaica's postcolonial period, a battle between Michael Manley's democratic socialist People's National Party (PNP) and Seaga's US-backed Jamaica Labour Party (JLP). This battle resulted in more than eight hundred deaths, and many have analyzed it as a proxy for the broader Cold War between the United States and the Soviet Union.

Square Grouper details the various agencies that were investigating the Coptics, including the Miami Beach Zoning Department, the Miami Beach Police Department, the Dade County State Attorney's Office, the Florida Department of Health and Human Services, the Florida Department of Law Enforcement, the US Coast Guard, the DEA, US Customs, the FBI, and the Internal Revenue

Service (IRS), the last of which in 1979 revoked the 1975 recognition of the church as a tax-exempt religious organization and demanded US$2.3 million in back taxes. It also chronicles the history of the Coptics' busts and arrests in Florida, a history also outlined in the *60 Minutes* segment. We learn about the November 1977 bust in Marion County, in which thirteen tons of marijuana were found hidden in a tunnel on a church-owned farm. We also learn about the February 1978 bust in Citrus County, in which twenty tons of marijuana were removed from the vessel *Our Seas*, also owned by the church. In that bust, sixteen persons were arrested, including Brother Keith Gordon, leader of the church in Jamaica. While brethren sat in county jails after these busts, in both cases, the charges were dropped due to lack of evidence; the state found church members in proximity to marijuana, but it was unable to establish a direct link between the Coptics and the ganja. These Florida arrests did not lead to charges that stuck, but in 1981 nine of the US brethren were convicted on federal charges of conspiracy to smuggle marijuana, convictions that resulted in long prison sentences and that marked one beginning of the dissolution of the organization, in the United States and in Jamaica.

Both *Square Grouper* and the *60 Minutes* report featured Jamaican journalist Dawn Ritch as one among the camp of Coptics detractors. Her argument was that the Coptics pretended to be a church but in fact operated "a factory for the export of ganja." This is a point that Ritch elaborated in a series of newspaper columns in the *Jamaica Gleaner*. Hers was a complex position in that she was in favor of legalization but her pro-legalization position was grounded in the nationalist assertions that the trade of ganja should contribute to Jamaica's GDP (gross domestic product) rather than to that of other nations, and that small farmers should be able to capitalize on their own crops within a competitive field, rather than from cultivating and selling illegally for a monopoly. In her columns, she referred only rarely to the Ethiopian Zion Coptic Church, focusing instead on the Ethiopian Zion Coptic Farm Company, and her arguments were that the Americans benefited from ganja-oriented retailing and paraphernalia industries; that Americans in Miami were exporting everything, leaving little for Jamaican dealers in Jamaica; and that while ganja farming and trading were what was supporting a flailing economy in Jamaica, the government itself was "afraid to handle decriminalization, much less the industry as a whole . . . [which left] the nearly half million small farmers in this country who also farm ganja . . . without the protection of law" (Ritch 1979a, 8; see also Ritch 1979b, 16; and Ritch 1979c, 8). She also asserted that the Coptics were buying properties in Colombia and farming ganja there,[6] and she argued that this would ultimately lead to an increased presence of cocaine, heroin, and guns in Jamaica (Ritch 1979b).

These positions made Ritch few fans, in Manley's government or among Coptics. Victor Whitely, a Black Jamaican and general secretary of the Ethiopian Zion Coptic Church, responded to one of her columns—the one that suggested that the only US organization that had the capital to institutionalize the marijuana industry was the Mafia—by arguing that she was part of a broad conspiracy to "bring the Ethiopian Zion Coptic Church and its teachings into disrepute" (Whitely 1979, 8). "Our deity is not one of commerce," Whitely continued, "yet of Unity. Love and charity among the races of the world." He argued that ganja was an offering, not a commodity—an offering designed to unite mankind in redemption. Furthermore, he contended that the government was "the only mafia we know" because after emancipation, "blackman" remained squatters: "It is the politicians who use guns as their defence; the chemists use cocaine and heroin; while the people of Goud [sic] are redeemed by the spirit of the herb they grow, because through the teachings of the Ethiopian Zion Coptic Church, their eyes are now opening to the hidden truth" (Whitely 1979). Ritch's response to Whitely was to call the Coptics ungrateful, noting that the "Jamaican government is largely responsible for what little legitimacy the farm company may have acquired over the past two years, whether by providing lucrative haulage contracts for Coptic Containers (their Orange Street sister company) or most recently when its courts acquitted farm members of ganja charges." She railed against the Coptics' practice of buying crops while they were still in the ground at prices 200 percent higher than those that Kingston-based dealers were able to offer; asserted that no one but the Coptics were able to amass the kind of foreign exchange that would pay for the custom-built American-made jeeps they were driving; and insisted that Jamaican small farmers were being recolonized by "an extremely dubious Miami outfit which proposes to use an indigenous cult—Rastafarianism—as its religious cover so that it can be free to market ganja . . . in the United States" (Ritch 1979c).

Ritch was not, of course, the only one making the last-mentioned argument. Even today, many Jamaican Rastafari do not regard the Coptics as true believers but only traffickers. Brother Bully, for example, told us that while Coptics used the name Rastafari, in fact they didn't believe in the Solomonic line, and because they didn't view Emperor Haile Selassie as the Messiah (a point to which I return below), for them Rastafari was not "a spiritual ting" but instead "a money ting and a herb ting." Another Rastafari, Ribs, remembered the Coptics only as "an organization that was dealing with herb." He knew some of the drivers who ran their trucks, and argued that Coptic "was a business, it wasn't really to teach people about Rasta. . . . All of them was just using Rasta as a stepping-stone to better them financial endeavors." Jerry Small claimed that while the original compound in Hall's Delight, St. Andrew, was not unlike Leonard Howell's compound at Pinnacle, which based its sustenance on the economy of small-scale ganja trading, once the white Americans were involved, the Coptics became a group organized around the "worshipping of ganja." They also developed connections, he maintained, to lawyers in the highest echelons of the People's National Party government, and in 1980 they began to bring high-powered weapons into Jamaica, including M16s and AK-47s.

Other Jamaican journalists, however, were sympathetic to the Coptics. Dennis Forsythe, for example, sought to counter Dawn Ritch's accusations of "Coptic ingratitude" by pointing out their commercial successes (their haulage operations and land purchases, both in Jamaica and in Colombia); the professionalism of the *Coptic Times*, which, he argued, contained "some of the most provocative and mind-expanding articles obtainable by the masses"; and the fact that the Coptics, unlike other multinational companies that have sought to extract Jamaican natural resources for their own profit, have converted "the rocky mountain wastes of Jamaica into American dollars which are then distributed in Jamaica" (Forsythe 1979, 8, 15). Barbara Blake Hannah (1980a), a journalist and author with a long history of public advocacy of Rastafari, visited the Coptic "embassy" on Star Island and reported on her experience. She first sought to outline the church's beliefs: "They say Garvey expresses a truth on behalf of the Black people, to erase the sins of their slave-master ancestors to the Black race, by restoring to the Black race the divinity and greatness that is in them. And of course, they claim that ganja is a holy sacrament to be used in the worship of God, and to obtain the wisdom and knowledge to live a Christ-like life without sin . . . to live, as they describe it, 'a true Rasta life.'" She then described Star Island, the members' prayers, their campaign for the removal of anti-ganja legislation, and their understanding of ganja's medicinal benefits. And then she mentioned, in passing, that Coptics also condemn "'ropeheads,' Selassie-worshippers, reggae music, and Rastafarianism" (Blake Hannah 1980a, 203).[7]

It was these condemnations that led other branches of Rastafari in Jamaica to vilify the Coptics, and that also raised speculations about their connections to the CIA. Arthur Kitchin (1980, 8, 13), for example, himself a Ras and *Gleaner* columnist, noted in May 1980 that the previous months had seen a "significant increase in the anti-Rasta campaign being orchestrated by the Coptics of Star Island, Miami" (8). Kitchin detailed the insults Hannah mentioned, arguing that Coptic beliefs were confusing, and that they ran counter to normative understandings of the Rastafari movement. He also intimated that the Coptics' reverence of Marcus Garvey led them to accept some of Garvey's criticisms of Emperor Haile Selassie after he was refused an interview with the Ethiopian monarch:

> Their use of Marcus Garvey's philosophies and writings, especially those which criticized Emperor Haile Selassie I, could be seen as the voice of Esau spouting the words of Jacob in a vain attempt to convince the people of their authenticity, without giving any consideration to the historical perspective of Garvey's utterances. . . . One wonders if much credence can be placed on Garvey's criticisms of Emperor Haile Selassie I as these were made at a time when the UNIA founder was far past his zenith, a broken and rejected man spending the last years of his life in a foreign country. Naturally it would suit the Coptics to think otherwise. (Kitchin 1980, 8)

Kitchin also positioned Coptic hostility toward dreadlocks as part of a broader "deprogramming" strategy against the movement, and he argued that it bore uncomfortable similarities to "the ill fated designs of Jim Jones and his People's Temple, who were also encouraged to establish a community outside of the United States to practice their religion." He continued by noting that in both of these cases, the countries in which people settled were run by socialist-oriented administrations. "One cannot help but ask," he concluded, "why the Miami hippies have been allowed to operate for so long without official investigation by the government, who seem to be turning a blind eye to their large-scale marijuana deals which are conducted under the guise of religious duties" (13).

Other observers, too, have raised these questions. Political scientist Horace Campbell (1987), for example, argued that "unprecedented levels of violence and a crude anti-communist campaign had been the signs that in the struggle for political power in Jamaica there was intense outside intervention," such as that undertaken by the CIA (114). By the time Henry Kissinger traveled to Jamaica in 1975 to warn Michael Manley not to side with Cuba in its support of Angolans who were fighting against the South African invasion of their country, the Rastafari movement had been at the forefront of this kind of pan-African support. Alliances developed between Rastafari and members of the Jamaican left, and in response, Campbell wrote, "the United States imposed a pseudo-Rasta group to promote confusion in the ranks of the Rastas," meaning the Ethiopian Zion Coptic Church (115). Indeed, he noted that the incorporation of the Ethiopian Zion Coptic Church in Jamaica happened in the same month that the United States announced its support of the South African invasion of Angola.

For Campbell, the Coptics were primarily capitalists who amassed lands and other assets and who used their newspaper, the *Coptic Times*, to promote the use of ganja while also promulgating anti-communism and distorting the lessons of Garvey. "Instead of presenting thoughts on those tobacco and alcohol companies who lobby the UN to ensure that cannabis remains a narcotic," he argued, the *Coptic Times* "carried out a virulent anti-communist campaign among Rastafari and youths in Jamaica" (Campbell 1987, 116). By "fetishizing" ganja, in Campbell's view, they also encouraged young people to embrace capitalism: "Because of the indiscriminate nature of the present smokers of the herb, contrary to the former communal use by the Rastas, the Coptics have used this to promote commodity fetishism among young people, and in the process tied them closer to imperialism" (117). Campbell concluded that "imperialism" worked to "reinforce the regressive elements of Rasta" by inculcating individualism and "alienation from the revolutionary features of Marxism" (118).

Horace Bartilow, an international political economist based at the American University School of International Service in Washington, DC, has argued that the Coptics were, in one way or another, being used by the CIA. Bartilow argues that at first, the Coptics' involvement in marijuana trafficking was not condemned by the majority of Jamaicans because of a belief that white traders might make it more legitimate for Black Jamaicans to be involved in the business. However, once the Coptics started accumulating wealth and properties, and once this wealth wasn't seen to "trickle down" to Black Jamaicans, "there was some degree of distrust and resentment."[8] As Bartilow began doing archival research on CIA propaganda in Jamaica, he learned that the Carter administration had considered whether the US government should clandestinely finance the *Gleaner*.[9] He then began to conduct content analysis of the frequency of various "code words" in *Gleaner* articles about the Manley government—such as "Soviet puppet," "communist pawns," "mismanagement." Because he also realized that one of the ways the CIA infiltrated Jamaican society in general was through front organizations, he started paying attention to what the Coptics were saying about Jamaican Rastafari, and noticed that they were using similar words and framings, as were journalists known to be working with the CIA. "The words were almost the same," he said, "as if they were reading from the same script. . . . So it is highly unlikely that this was simply just coincident."[10] Why would the CIA want to smear Rastafari, he wondered?

Bartilow notes that most historians believe that the United States was trying to destabilize the Manley government because of the Cold War and fears that Manley was aligning himself too fully with Cuba's Fidel Castro and other communist leaders. What he wants people to understand, however, is that these fears were not only about anti-communism but about the ways white supremacy and anti-communism were entwined. The US viewed the Manley government, he explains, and the people around Manley like D. K. Duncan, Arnold Bertram, and Anthony Spaulding (all leaders in the People's National Party) as exemplifying a kind of Black nationalism. "[US officials] saw in Jamaica's socialism not so much communism," he argues, "but that it was empowering Black people." They also saw that Rastafari had a strong influence on this empowerment and on the elaboration of Black radicalism and pan-Africanism, which, Bartilow asserts, they feared would spread to the rest of the Caribbean and beyond:

> As Henry Kissinger also said, . . . Jamaica's influence in the world is bigger than its size, that's the exact words that they used. . . . Jamaica poses a threat to us, especially in Black Africa in ways that Fidel Castro and the Soviets don't pose, because here is a country, a small little country, whose leadership is Black, articulate, English-speaking, and would have far more influence in Black Africa than Castro or the Soviets would ever have. And that was their main fear, what that represents. So smearing the Rastas is part of that process.[11]

Of course, any alliance with the CIA or any other foreign governmental body is something Coptic brethren vehemently refute. As early as April 1976, church members were charging the Manley government with harassment, pointing out that the Narcotics Division of the Constabulary Force had accused the American members of the church of being CIA agents, among other things (*Daily Gleaner* 1976, 19). And toward the end of September 1980, as pre-election fervor was heating up, they complained about government intervention in their activities, as when the Jamaica Defence Force (JDF) seized farming equipment and a light plane valued at more than US$2 million through an air and ground attack on their property at Bogue, St. Elizabeth (*Daily Gleaner* 1980b, 1). A week or so prior, following an announcement by Deputy Prime Minister P. J. Patterson that the government was cracking down on illegal airstrips, one was destroyed by the JDF at Bogue. The Coptics argued afterward that they had no such airstrip, that it was instead an access road to their rice lands, and that because of the military's actions their workers and equipment were no longer able to access those fields. Although people in the community told journalists that they got work from the Coptics, that they saw planes landing at all hours of the day and night, and that because they saw the Coptics as having become involved with the Jamaica Labour Party, they would have to move out of the area (which was part of a PNP constituency),[12] nothing ultimately came of this seizure, and the equipment was returned to them later that year.

Even though the speculations about Coptics' involvement with Jamaican politicians or with American intelligence services remained circumstantial, what these accusations reflected was the curiosity about and suspicion of them that began to develop, especially as they amassed more properties during the run-up to the 1980 elections. This mounting interest was reflected in contemporary press reports, as in the *Gleaner* column "Listening Post":

> I hear that the Coptic Church is buying up property right, left and centre throughout Jamaica. For example, the airstrip photographed and published in the *Gleaner* which is over 4000 ft. long (longer than Tinson Pen) is in the area between Manchester and St. Elizabeth and is on land sold I hear to the Coptics by one of Jamaica's famed land-owners. The Coptics have bought a large house and property in Westmoreland, and yet another in St. Elizabeth. What's up? A Coptic infiltration? Time the Government tells us something. (*Daily Gleaner* 1980b, 1)

> I hear that concern is growing over the expansion of ownership of Jamaica by the foreign body the Coptic Church whose *Coptic Times* signs are seen on more and more properties in Jamaica. As I reported before, St. Thomas and St. Mary have been infiltrated. St. Elizabeth has lost at least one large property, and Manchester and St. Ann are in the queue. It is being said that it is the Coptics who can facilitate some land-owners with foreign exchange, in the same way as their own avowal of the herb and their "no funds" licences have developed Jamaica's parallel economy. Here scarce goods arrive in the island on "no funds licences." But the point is why are foreigners being allowed to buy up our land by a government which preaches self-reliance and land for the people? Yet let it be said the Coptics are employing people and for that the

people in the rural areas are grateful. Time to hear the PNP and JLP speak on this matter! Should this body be allowed unregulated expansion in ownership of Jamaica? (*Daily Gleaner* 1980c, 3)

I hear that the Coptics are buying up everything in sight. Of course there is no bill of sale to the Coptics as such. It is all being done through intermediaries. Hence it appears that some of the vendors are unaware that their property has gone to the Coptics. The most recent to be acquired by intermediaries of the Coptics, I hear, are two in Trelawny—the sales to be effective next year—Brian Castle and Pantry Pan. Both are famous cattle land. (*Daily Gleaner* 1980d, 3)

The JBC-TV [Jamaica Broadcasting Company TV] recently showed a film dealing with the Coptics. In it we were regaled with pictures of members of the cult at their headquarters in St. Thomas smoking the "weed" (ganja) quite openly without let or hindrance, despite the fact that it is illegal to do so. On the other hand, almost daily there are reports in the press of the "small man" living perhaps in a shack at Wait-a-Bit, being heavily fined for possession of a "spliff" or ganja. (*Daily Gleaner* 1981a, 3)

By April 1981, Jamaican journalist Lloyd Williams (1981a, 8) was calling the Coptics "a country within Jamaica." Williams sought to clarify the history and beliefs of the Coptics, noting that they began in Alligator Pond, Manchester, and that they came to more public attention after they began making large land acquisitions. He also noted that the Ethiopian Zion Coptic Church had been formally vested and incorporated in Jamaica on April 2, 1976.

This incorporation was the result of mobilization by Enid Bennett, the JLP member of parliament for Central St. Catherine, who then chaired a select committee to explore the Coptics' petition. Other members of the committee in the House of Representatives were Dr. Adrian Bonner, Dallas Young, Noel Silvera, and Rev. Roy Robinson (later Arthur Williams was appointed to the committee after its leadership passed from Representative Bennett to Representative Bonner) (*Gleaner* Parliamentary Reporter 1976a, 5; 1976b, 17). The Ethiopian Zion Coptic Church (Incorporation and Vesting) Act (No. 11–1976), signed into law by Governor-General F. A. Glasspole, passed in the House with four amendments on March 2, 1976, and in the Senate on March 26, 1976 (Government of Jamaica 1976). The act, which names "Keith Gordon of 20 Sirgany Drive, Kingston 2 in the Parish of Kingston, Chief Elder; Laurenton Dickens of 8 Crieffe Road, Kingston 5 in the

Parish of Saint Andrew, Elder; Walter Wells of Mandeville in the Parish of Manchester, Elder; Isaah Williams of 22 Sirgany Drive, Kingston 2 in the Parish of Kingston, Elder; and Victor Whitely of 22 Sirgany Drive, Kingston 2 in the Parish of Kingston, General Secretary" as executives of the church, seems mainly concerned with the establishment of its property interests. Nowhere does this act of incorporation mention anything about freedom to partake in their "sacrament," the unfettered smoking of ganja.

The act confers on the corporation (the Coptic Church) the power

a) To acquire, hold, purchase, lease, possess and enjoy any lands and hereditaments whatsoever in fee simple for leasehold or for any other estate or interest therein, and all property, real, personal, or mixed;

b) To give, grant, let, charge, improve, manage, develop, exchange, lease, mortgage, sell, convey, assign, dispose of, turn to account or otherwise deal with all or any of the property, both present and future, so held or any part thereof;

c) To borrow, raise or secure the payment of money in such manner as may be thought fit and in particular by the issue of debenture or scrip charged upon all or any of the property (both present and future) held by or vested in the Corporation, and to redeem and pay off any such securities;

d) To appoint a person or persons as the Attorney or Attorneys of the Corporation either generally or for a limited period and for such purposes and with such powers as may be stated in the Power of Attorney and to revoke any such appointment;

e) To make such rules and by-laws as it may think fit in order to carry out the purposes of this Act. (Government of Jamaica 1976)

The act also stipulates that all of the lands specified within the law (which it lists), and all that the corporation would later purchase, would legally and equitably remain property of the church or would be held in trust for the purposes of the church by its officials or members.

Because of this vesting, Williams noted, the church became "big business, with vast land-holdings and farms, productive, well-organized, and efficiently run" (Williams 1981a, 8). Williams listed the properties: five in Western St. Thomas totaling 4,000 acres, where members raised cattle and grew coconuts, bananas, yams, tobacco, timber, sugarcane, ginger, carrots, and cucumbers; another six properties totaling 3,000 acres at Bogue, St. Elizabeth, where they also kept cattle and goats and where they cultivated rice (Williams noted, as well, that next to their rice-threshing and polishing mill, which daily produced five tons of rice, was a warehouse holding 350 tons); 350 acres at Whitehall in St. Mary, where church farms produced coconuts, bananas, vegetables, and cocoa; 25 additional acres in St. Mary; 25 acres in Trelawny; and several properties and businesses in Kingston and Mandeville, with villagers in some parts of Hanover and Clarendon claiming that Coptics owned property there as well. Williams argued that the "rice farm at Bogue, which employs about 120 people, makes the Government's Brumdec rice-growing project nearby appear amateurish by comparison" (Williams 1981a, 8).

The Coptics were, Williams explained, equipped with two-way radios, vehicles, and comfortable, modern properties; they took pride in what they had accomplished in terms of their goal of "feeding the nation"; and, though they eschewed politics, they were nonetheless operating within a politically polarized context in which resentments were developing, as mentioned above. "The fact is that they have good and influential friends in both major political parties," Williams wrote (1981a, 8). His article was mainly descriptive, of the church's beliefs and practices and of the role of ganja in its understanding of doctrine. Both Brother Keith (by that time, the Jamaican leader of the Coptics) and the white American Brother Louv (aka Brother Thomas Reilly, or Brother Tommy) sought to disabuse Williams of the assumptions underlying his questions to them regarding the trafficking of ganja and the connections between ganja and guns. "Coptics don't have any time for guns," Brother Keith told Williams. "Gun is a crime. Guns can't stop crime." Crime, he said, was not caused by ganja. "Crime is found in the human heart. Everything destructive man prepared for himself. . . . Religion, politics and commerce are responsible for destruction." And Brother Louv simply stated that "the last time the American generation smoked ganja, it ended the Vietnam War" (both quoted in Williams 1981a, 8). They both denied that they exported ganja; instead, they said, "we spread religion, not ganja, because if a man is sinful then ganja will be of no use to him." Williams ended his essay by discussing the November 1980 indictments of nineteen members of the Church on drug charges, cases that had not yet been resolved when the essay was published.[13]

Meanwhile, government pressure on the Coptics was mounting in Jamaica. In a November 10, 1980, interview with a *Washington Post* reporter, just after he was elected prime minister, Edward Seaga said, "The ganja trade in the last several months was virtually what was keeping the economy alive. . . . It supplied black market dollars which were then used by industrialists and other persons in the economy who wanted to import raw materials for which they could not get Bank of Jamaica dollars. On that basis they were able to avert a lot of closures and very substantial layoffs" (C. Dickey 1980). Seaga argued that the big question as far as ganja was concerned was not whether to eliminate it but whether to decriminalize it, a question that hinged on the problem of corruption rather than any purported concern regarding its consumption. And in January 1981, during his visit to the White House, the prime minister stated that the ganja trade mostly benefited persons in the United States, with only minor "rub-off" to the Jamaican economy (Williams 1981b, 8).[14] It must have felt like a slap in the face to Coptics and other ganja producers when, not long after the interview was published, Seaga began a series of measures meant to strengthen cooperation between the US and Jamaica in the interdiction and eradication of ganja production and distribution. In March 1981, he sent a telegram to President Ronald Reagan, on the heels of a "lengthy discussion" of the issue of ganja trafficking with Ambassador Loren Lawrence, DEA administrator Peter Bensinger, and Deputy Assistant Secretary Joseph Linnemann during their visit to Jamaica. The telegram was introduced by an operative who wrote that Seaga was requesting assistance with a drug eradication program, but that he wanted this to be "treated with the utmost sensitivity as the whole question of U.S. Jamaican cooperation in this field has the potential for generating a political hurricane in Jamaica."[15]

In the telegram, Seaga also mentioned his concerns about "the corruption that illegal drug smuggling has generated in my country, the attendant illegal traffic in weapons of all kinds, the association of drug smugglers with international and local terrorist and radical groups, domestic violence due to drug activities, threats to the territorial integrity of Jamaica and the sovereignty of my government and threats to the safety of legitimate air transport by undetected violations of air traffic routes." He linked these concerns to "the tie-in between the Coptic Church groups here and in the United States and their growing economic power and land ownership in this country." Seaga went on to acknowledge his inability to attend to these issues without assistance, in part because, he argued, Manley's government had not provided the security forces the necessary equipment to stem trafficking. Of Reagan he was requesting assistance in the form of "trained and trustworthy experts from your Drug Enforcement Agency," of equipment for compliance and monitoring, and of a crop substitution program, which he argued was "absolutely essential to the success of any effort on our part." He further stated that he had initiated a study of Jamaica's laws pertaining to drug trafficking and that he had already increased bail requirements.

By May 1981, legislation was being drafted to strengthen the government's capacity to deal with illegal airstrips throughout the country (*Daily Gleaner* 1981b), and the Jamaican Bar Association was urging the minister of national security to investigate breaches of the Dangerous Drugs Law by the Ethiopian Zion Coptic Church, a plea the police then began to answer (*Daily Gleaner* 1981c, 1981d). And, although Seaga continued to argue as late as 1985 that ganja was not a significant contributor to Jamaica's GDP—an argument that conflicted with DEA figures suggesting that 1,850 metric tons of marijuana, with a wholesale value in the US of about US$2.13 billion, was packed in Jamaica and shipped to the United States (Harden 1985)—the Jamaica government was passing new laws requiring licenses for the operation of airports and allowing for the seizure of trucks, airplanes, and boats. US officials felt that Seaga wasn't taking serious-enough measures to eradicate the trade despite the infusion of more than US$10 million by the US government into what became known as Operation Buccaneer III (Priest 1987).[16] Of course, the prime minister would also have felt pressure from small farmers and their political representatives who opposed the attempts to eradicate their crops. What the Coptics had developed was proving difficult to disband, even as their own organization was crumbling.

HISTORY AND PROPHECY

The story of the Coptics I have just outlined does not reflect how the Coptics themselves would like their history told. And it certainly wasn't the story Patrick White had in mind when he first called me. In fact, he explicitly denounced *Square Grouper* as a sensationalist film that in focusing on the ganja trade misses the true story of the Coptics. But this was, nevertheless, the story that informed our own skepticism and our hesitations about what kind of work might be possible together. I shift here to the way the Coptics write their own history and practice, which also requires that we shift from the juridical realm of geopolitics to the theological realm of testimony. Walter Wells, more commonly known as Brother Wally, was one of the Jamaican elders of the Coptic Church. In his later years, he went blind, but until his death he was the spiritual center of the Coptic community in St. Thomas. Brother Wally authored "Ethiopian Zion Coptic Church, History in this Present Generation,"[17] in which he presented history as something that exists in the body, an inheritance passed down from "generation to generation":

It has been said by modern historians, that the scarcity of written records has enshrouded the history of Africa in mystery and ignorance; this is not so, the first recorded history is man, and so history could not be that written piece of paper, but the experience of an individual or people written on the tablets of Man's heart. The history therefore of any Nation belongs only to its people, and so the history of we Ethiopians has been told from generation to generation even until this day. . . . It is for this reason that, although the forces of evil conspire against us, we of the Coptic Faith know that the leopard cannot change its spots, neither can we alter the commandments and precepts handed down by our fathers; from generation to generation, as a guiding light to lighten all nations, even the gentiles and for the glorification of his people Israel.

The Coptics' history begins not with ancestral kingdoms in Africa but with the "punishments" of slavery across several empires, punishments that emerged "among Israel" because "we failed to respect each other and in time we became covetous and rebellious against each other. There was no brotherly louv [sic] or trust among brethren of the different tribes and so the strong preyed upon the weak, and sold his own brother into slavery; for the sake of money (caesar) which Europeans taught us was the savior from our miseries." From this perspective, it was disunity that caused them to be disobedient to "Goud," and thus cursed, but salvation was immanent because the "Ethiopian Zion Coptic Church is now in the process of igniting this flame [the eternal flame of desire to free oneself from political slavery], and very soon we will see billions of blackman worldwide and the strangers within their gates; uniting and giving acclaim to RASTAFARI, KING, CREATOR; who with blessings has returned to reign, reign over HIS PEOPLE:—ISRAEL."

Brother Wally tracks the histories of persecution from the Roman Empire and through the modern versions of imperialism imposed by the British, Spanish, Portuguese, and French, who "under the disguise of missionary priests were used as the agents of pagan religion to spread propaganda and subvert the Goud given Culture and beliefs of the people who they found living in the lands wherein they traded and settled." In this telling, imperialism and slavery engendered wars for global dominance, which Britain had won by the eighteenth century, at which point the "seventh and last plague" was inaugurated, that of "British/American world power." Notice the conjoined power structure here. It is here that we get a sense of Brother Wally's intended audience for this history.[18] He writes:

> Let me bring you closer however to the present situation, as it affects us today: And so I start with the period 1765. This was the period Brother Editor, when you the suffering people of America; pressured by your colonial masters to the point of extinction, placed your shoulders to the wheel in a united effort, to once and for all remove the shackles of British supremacy and corrupt oppressive administration on your colonies.
>
> You stood up not because you were British subjects on British soil, yet because you had a moral conscience in the equality and rights of every man to live upon the earth as a free man; without enslavement from his brother. We as a people admired your courage for the steps you took in those times. . . . As the years rolled on the British world power by itself became weakened as many of her colonies gained independence. As a result, she had to share her power with her younger sister America. The center of power was removed from Britain and vested in a mixed worldwide international political organization, the League of Nations now called the United Nations, a cage of hateful and unclean, corrupt political birds.

Brother Wally then moves on to discuss Paul Bogle, the Baptist deacon and leader of the 1865 Morant Bay Rebellion, waged by small farmers attempting to address the various injustices of the plantation system. He argues that Bogle, now a national hero, attempted to challenge white supremacy, but "because we were divided among ourselves," this effort failed. Then Brother Wally introduces Marcus Garvey, the Black nationalist and pan-Africanist founder (in 1914) of the Universal Negro Improvement Association (UNIA), whose "message was the same as that of Bogle, only that as a son he was wiser and did not believe in the use of guns and bayonets." Garvey, we are told, "started the preparation for the spiritual resurrection of the world at large," but he first had to "rebuild the moral conscience of black man" which had been scarred by slavery and the divisions this created between "black and white." In Brother Wally's telling, the United Nations fought against Garvey in the same way that the American government in Brother Wally's day persecuted the Coptic Church and the use of "herb," which was made illegal "under the bogus agency called the United Nations . . . in its effort to keep the people divided and thus weak." Garvey, in Brother Wally's view, awakened a new spirit of unity between people in Jamaica and America, and because of this alliance Garvey was persecuted.

At this point, Brother Wally turns to a discussion of the introduction of mass politics in Jamaica, and he indicts Alexander Bustamante, founder and leader of the conservative Jamaica Labour Party, whose "help to the masses," he asserts, "was only an opportunity to seek power and riches for himself and to further divide the race against itself." There is no mention of Norman Manley, founder of the People's National Party, the first nationalist political party in Jamaica; it is Bustamante who "failed to resurrect the moral and ethical principles of the people and guide them to a land of peace." It was Bustamante who organized the people "into divided political forces, thus weakening their strength for liberating themselves." And it was Bustamante who set up trade unions to "control the people's labor." These innovations, Brother Wally argues, caused the Black masses to again lose the "spirit of a moral awakening." Even Garvey's most ardent follower, St. William Grant, is seen in this reckoning to have been "captured by these political forces who with the help of the various pagan religious groups, returned to the pagan religious practices of worshipping an imaginary sky god."

Finally, we arrive at the dawn of a new millennium, when one fervent (and patient) disciple of Garvey took on the "mantle of Faith, Hope and Charity" to bring the masses to enlightenment, and this disciple was Louva Williams, known among Coptics as Brother Louva. Brother Louva, whose mission was "the spiritual awakening of his people from the bonds of moral slavery," first "started his declaration of Rastafari's Holy Trinity (The Man, The Herb and The Word) at Mountain View in southeastern St. Andrew." Brother Wally does not mention Leonard Howell, considered by most to be one of the three Jamaican founders of Rastafari, or his Rastafari camp at Pinnacle, but Junior and I would later learn that there was traffic back and forth between Howell's camp and Louva Williams's camp. He does, however, mention those who, during the 1950s, were adhering to a "false doctrine of Rastafari" that had developed in western Kingston after the 1954 dissolution of Pinnacle, by then the largest commune of Rastafari in Jamaica, following a number of raids by the colonial government. Brother Wally contends that this "false doctrine" was "formulated by the unprincipled ones in Louv Williams Camp who would not live up to the Divine principles of the Holy Bible as taught and were therefore not allowed to partake in the Sacraments as they were disorderly." Because of police persecution, Brother Louva's camp moved to August Town, to the subdivision of Kintyre, on land that had been legally owned by

"Mammy Louv" and that had been captured and occupied for a long time by a Coptic brother named Son Latuce. There, Brother Wally writes, Brother Louva's group was also subjected to political harassment by the member of parliament for rural eastern St. Andrew, Keeble Munn, whom he calls "Feeble Dunn," who argued that they should be removed further from the university, "as they could not take the Cumina that we played."[19]

This was the point at which the camp moved to Hall's Delight in St. Andrew, on land owned by "Massa Bouy Brooks." There, Brother Louv "prophesied the unification of black and white under one Holy Trinity." This prophecy was fulfilled, Brother Wally continues, when, in the late 1960s, "we saw the first white man set foot in camp and being individually convinced of the TRUTH of the doctrine accepted Christ as his Saviour confessing his SINS and partaking in the daily worship, equally with the black brethren." On Brother Louva's passing in 1969, leadership was transferred to Brother Ivy, "who fully opened the doors of Salvation to the white inhabitants of the world within this dispensation; and taught black and white to unite together for one common cause." Brother Ivy, he argues, also prophesied the removal of the Church to western Jamaica, but this was not to happen before his own passing in 1970, at which point Brother Keith Gordon took on the mantle of leadership. It was then that the camp was moved to Trelawny, where it received "both Jews and Gentiles"—by which he meant Black Jamaicans (the Israelites) and white Americans—and where the group "grew from strength to strength increasing in numbers daily."

Brother Wally writes that this was the moment when the Coptics increased their agricultural production through land ownership and began to rear cattle and poultry. But because these lands were mountainous, they began also buying land in St. Elizabeth, Manchester, and Kingston, finally settling at Coptic Heights, St. Thomas, "once more in the East for the final battle with modern Pharaoh." There, they established "a fully accredited farming institution" (the Ethiopian Zion Coptic Church Farms Eternal, Limited), which covered more than one thousand acres of land, fully cultivated with vegetables, ground provisions, fruits, peanuts, scallions, thyme, onions, peas, melons, pumpkins, okra, bananas, and sugar. Notably, he does not mention ganja here. The Coptics also grew to hold more than 1,000 head of cattle, horses, donkeys, goats, and mules, and more than 2,000 head of poultry, and they established a trucking department. In the end, Brother Wally argues, because religion, commerce, and politics have all failed to inspire today's youth and have proven to be riddled with corruption, the Coptics were the "only LIGHT and SOLUTION in these times of troubled waters."

Patrick directed me and Junior to this history after we first met with him and David Nissenbaum in Iowa in December 2019. During our time together there, we deliberated about process. We told them that if we were going to do something together, they would have to trust that the story would unfold as we moved forward, rather than determining from the outset what the story should be. Prior to our meeting I had forwarded Patrick and David a PDF of the relevant pages from the Horace Campbell text I cited earlier, both to give them a sense of the baggage we were bringing to the project and to see how they would respond. Predictably, both rejected the theory that the Coptics were involved in some way with the CIA, and they argued for a distance from politics that other Coptics we would eventually interview also emphasized, as revealed below. Nevertheless, after two days of discussion, they decided we were sincere, and we decided they were sincere, and we resolved to plan a trip to Jamaica together to track down some of the elder brethren to document their testimonies.

In January 2020, while Junior and I were in Jamaica on our own, we decided to go to Coptic Heights to check it out. We called David from the road, and he put us in touch with someone who was working with Denroy Morgan (reggae musician and father of the five members of the band Morgan Heritage), who also lived in St. Thomas and who could accompany us to the compound. Though mostly abandoned, it was still stunning as a testament to what the Coptics had been able to build and create. The stone gates to the property read "Ethiopian Zion Coptic Church, the Church of the Living Man, The Gatherer of the People . . . Enter into his Gates with Thanksgiving and into his Courts with Praises (Psalm 100)," and the graves of Brother Wally and Brother Keith were well kept. While many of the buildings where brethren and sistren had lived were in various stages of being reclaimed by the bush, the main house and the red, gold, and green tabernacle still stood majestically. It was not difficult to imagine how awesome that compound would have seemed in 1980, a beacon for the reclamation of self during a year of extraordinary violence and scarcity. That March we returned to the compound prior to our scheduled meet-up with Patrick and David, but now there was suspicion around our presence. What were we looking for? What did we want? We left the compound.

The day before we were due to meet Patrick and David, I went to the airport in Kingston to pick up Farrah Rahaman and Melissa Skolnick-Noguera, two PhD students at Penn who had agreed to help with the filming. After we left him in Iowa, Patrick had also tracked down Dennis Ivy, Brother Ivy's son, now living in the United Kingdom, to invite him to join us for our trod. Dennis decided that we needed to start at the beginning, going with him to Hall's Delight to meet the elders who were still there, so we embarked on the drive into the hills above Papine. As we approached the community, Dennis had us pull to the side of the road near a big boulder. He explained that for this "first time," one would have to stand on that boulder and call out to the valley below, stating the intention to visit. He told us that if butterflies began to gather (which they did later as he was standing on the boulder), then it was OK to proceed. We pulled off the main road and parked, and while we unloaded our gear and began to attach a lapel mic to Dennis, we were met by Brother Clive, a brother whom Dennis considered to be an original and faithful follower of the doctrine.

We trekked down the hill along a dirt path, which was difficult for Patrick because of an injury he had sustained to his leg when he fell in the Jamaican restaurant he had opened in Fairfield, but his joy at being back in Jamaica was palpable. On the way down the hill, we stopped to greet Sister Lily, who recited a psalm with and for us. By the time we reached closer to the community, we looked for a good location to interview Brother Clive. Born in Kingston on March 29, 1939, Brother Clive Russell originated from lower Hall's Delight. He grew up mostly with his mother, as his father died when he was young. When he was eighteen, he got a vision in which he was "inspired by God to be a Rasta." He went to Brother Louva to interpret the vision, "and so I was caught up to be a part of him." Louva Williams, he said, had come to Hall's Delight from Hope Road where he had been an acolyte in the Catholic Church, but he got "a different spirit" and departed from Catholicism. Brother Louva had, apparently, also spent some time with Leonard Howell at Pinnacle, and Brother Clive described a fluid milieu in which brethren would come and go from Pinnacle to Hall's Delight and back. They were all brethren, he said, united by their persecution for herb, but there were two different "assemblies." And raiding, he said, was constant: "When it come to like Friday, Saturday, Sunday, you can almost look for a raid. . . . So me is a man that know about enough brutalization. Is police kill Brother Louv, you know, them coulda kill me here too. Is the mercy of God."

Brother Clive described the early days of the compound in Hall's Delight, where brethren from all over the island came to live. In the morning, he said, they would have prayers, and then they would reason and "live with the culture as Rasta." He described the music: "We had repeater, that is one of the drums, we had a *funde*, and we had a big drum." He added guitar, shaka, and cowbell, and a rumba box. Brother Clive called their music "Rasta chanting," not *kumina* or revival, but a "hills and valleys, rocks and mountains vibe." Food, he said, was not an issue because people farmed. He himself planted banana, yam, plantain, coco, *gungo* (or pigeon) peas, beans, and pumpkin, "and what we didn't grow we could afford to buy." Others would plant herb, others cassava, others pineapple, others breadfruit, and they all shared.

When we asked Brother Clive about what it was like when the white Americans started arriving, he said that because they accepted the doctrine as truth, "they made themselves a part of us." Because of this, he himself came to understand that "God elect from every nation," and as a result, "you can't tell exactly who will come at your home no time." Salvation, he argued, "is something either you accept or reject," and everyone must make that decision on their own. We also asked about the changes in leadership, and Brother Clive noted that after Brother Louva died and Brother Ivy became the leader, "there was some contrariness among brethren; brethren didn't continue on the same track, so it caused a separation. For you taught to walk in a way, and you know the way you're structured, and once you see brethren going another route you're not going to stick to it because you know the right way. So there was dissimulation. Those times Brother Keith assemble to himself." The following day, as we walked to the original compound, Brother Clive elaborated. He told us that there was a disagreement about the commercial trading of herb, and those who agreed to move forward with this endeavor left with Brother Keith for Trelawny, and those who didn't stayed in Hall's Delight.

As it turned out, this was the story Dennis was really interested in telling. On the second day of our trod, he was intent on giving us the full experience of what the compound was like through his eyes as a little boy during those times. Dennis grew up mostly with his mother, but after she and his father split up, Dennis was charged with collecting a monthly maintenance payment from his father, George Baker Ivy, so he would spend periods of time in Hall's Delight. Describing himself as a "rude little child" back then, he recalled for us what became a defining moment in his life. He had mischievously loosened the boards at the back of Louva Williams's chair, so that when he went to lean back with his ganja pipe, he would fall. Enraged, Brother Louva called for Dennis's father, who then disciplined him harshly, "boxing" him across the face and leaving him to bleed. At that point, Dennis was sent back to his mother, but when next he returned to collect the maintenance funds, he stole some money from the brethren and used it to purchase ice cream and other treats for some of the white children. When his father found this out, Dennis was flogged before the congregation with tamarind and guava branches, which incited a rage in him against his father. Nevertheless, the story Dennis really wanted to tell as we walked through the bush, was that his father's leadership of the community was usurped by Brother Keith.

The previous day, we had been confused by how quickly Brother Ivy's leadership came to an end and about the circumstances of his death. Dennis wanted to set the record straight and to reclaim an aspect of his birthright: "I'm saying that people were looking on him [Brother Ivy] as the Messiah, and from people see you as that, a man will come kill you, because Judas sell out Christ for thirty pieces of silver. A nuh the same thing? Brother Clive give a reasoning up the hill, which is very important. Him show you that when my father dead, a whole heap of people move. . . . Those who go away and make big feast and everything, those are the killers, those are the perpetrators." He continued by arguing that his father (and therefore himself and his mother) had been removed from Brother Wally's account of the history of the Coptics, and that once Brother Keith took over leadership of the community, no one came back from Trelawny to check on him, or on Brother Clive, or on Sister Lily. "Once you get wealthy," he said, "you become blind." On another day, when Patrick and David weren't with us, Dennis said he felt that the white Americans really came only for the ganja and that they united with Brother Keith to kill his father, whom he believed did not support the large-scale commercial trafficking of ganja. These were the contentious dynamics into which walked the white Americans who arrived after Brother Keith took on leadership of the Coptics.

TESTAMENTS AND TESTIMONIALS

Later that week, David invited us to his home outside Ocho Rios, so that we could film both him and Patrick talking about their own experiences with the Coptics. It is a lovely home, near a golf course, with a pool and a number of guest rooms. There was an abundant amount of herb on the table. David goes to the house at least once a year for a month, and while he is not there, a staff maintain it. While we were setting up the cameras, we asked what they had thought about the experience in Hall's Delight, where neither of them had been previously. They were both moved to have had the opportunity to visit with Brother

Clive and to hear him talk about what it was like in the early days. And they were ready to share their own testimonies.

I should reveal here that my rendering of the testimonies offered to us by those involved with the Coptics are not entirely verbatim. I have sometimes changed the order of statements in order to create a flow for you and to allow statements from different interlocutors to exist in dialogue with one another. I have removed verbal tics like "um" and "er," and I have fixed grammatical errors. Sometimes, to preserve the sense of these offerings as testimonies rather than interviews, I have streamlined digressive or repetitive storytelling, and in some cases, I have corrected historical or factual mistakes, fixing a date here or a name there. While I have never altered the meaning of what was shared with us, in a couple of places I have edited out short phrases or throwaway remarks that I believe would have distracted from the overall point I wish one or another narrative to make. These kinds of editorial interventions are not uncommon among anthropologists working through the genre of life history, which often requires the triaging of multiple and long interviews and conversations alongside the "deep hanging out" of ethnography.[20] I have made these interventions to encourage a complex and generous reading of stories of individual experience that might, in more usual circumstances, generate cynicism. My intention is also to model a particular form of relation and intersubjectivity—between us and our interlocutors—a form that reflects a dialogic approach to narrative rather than an approach that understands their statements as transparent and exact reflections of experience, or one designed to prove one or another aspect of the broader Coptics story. Finally, I have made these interventions to call into question the ways inheritances circulate and live in the worlds of our interlocutors, and our own. Let us begin with David.

My name is David Ross Nissenbaum. I'm seventy-two years old, I was born in 1947, and I grew up in an affluent Jewish family. My father was a jeweler, my mother a housewife. I had a couple of siblings, a brother and a sister. I grew up with a silver spoon in my mouth, basically. I was a very straightlaced, typical Jewish boy back then. I went through the motions, but I was a member of a conservative Jewish community, and I didn't even understand Hebrew. To say I was a practicing Jew would be lip service actually. It was something I was required to do as a youth, but it never brought me any spiritual understanding or a desire to seek any further knowledge about it.

I went to high school in a small suburb of Springfield, in Western Massachusetts, at a school called Long Meadow from 1965 through 1969. Golf was my love; I was the state champion, and I spent most of my time playing golf. I had summer jobs—nothing that was toward any type of career, but just to get some pocket change. My father wanted me to work; though we had plenty of money, he really didn't supply me with anything other than opportunity, which was a blessing in itself. I worked on labor crews, and I had a couple of factory jobs, filling in for summertime employees on vacation.

I went on to the University of Iowa. I think 98 percent of my class went on to school, so it wasn't really an option in my mind: When you were done with high school you went to college. I was in no way prepared for college education. I just wasn't ready to immerse myself in what was required, to find a career. I was more into the fraternity life, party life, and after three years of that, the Vietnam War started to become an issue for me. My number was coming up in the lottery, so that was one of the reasons I stayed in school. Once my number finally did come up, I failed my physical, so I realized the war wasn't going to be an issue in my life, and college wasn't providing me with the answers I was looking for. I wanted to learn more about what I was doing on the earth, what life meant. So I started a journey from Iowa. I quit the last semester of my senior year, and I went to San Francisco, where I heard love and peace, and that was the beginning of my spiritual journey. This was disconcerting to my parents. They had a vision of me living what they considered a normal healthy life, and I also began using marijuana in those days, and that was an issue for them. I really lost contact with them for a number of years.

Most of us went out to California, searching for something greater than we'd been given by our parents, something more spiritual, more "meaning of life" than what we'd accumulated. Eventually, my wife of today joined me and we got an apartment. There was always marching and a political thing going on. And it attracted me, but I was testing every water. I attended a lot of meetings of spiritual endeavors—you know, every telephone pole would have ten or twelve postings about this or that meeting and such.

I went to one, and there were a couple of white men saying they'd been to Jamaica and that they had found the answer to life, and that God is a Black Rastaman from Jamaica. Three of my friends went down one after the other, and each came back with a similar testimony, so my wife and I went to Jamaica. We were penniless at the time. In those days, there was a service where you could drive other people's cars across the country, they called them drive-away cars, so we found a drive-away car, and we drove from California to Miami, and we flew from Miami to Jamaica, asked the cab driver to take us to the place we were told to go in Bethel Town, which was in the hills above Montego Bay. This would have been 1969, maybe possibly 1970.

The cab driver brought us to what I'd consider the jungle, and we'd never experienced anything like that before. All of the sudden out of the bush came a white stallion, with a Rastaman on top, with garments flowing and some sort of jeweled crown and a machete, and the horse started rearing up at the cab driver, and I'm hearing curse words, and I thought we were going to die there. Finally, we were ushered into the compound, and that was one of the worst weeks of my life. I considered this Rastaman to be a madman. The camp he'd set up was convoluted; there was no conscious argument. It seemed like there was a lot of LSD floating around. I just couldn't wait to get out of there in the end. So I left Jamaica with the attitude that I didn't want to hear anything more about Rastafari, and I never want to return to that spot or that culture. I went back to California, and I didn't even want to be around my friends who had gone before us. So my wife and I ended up deciding we were going to leave California and return to my roots, and she was pregnant at the time. We hitchhiked from San Francisco to Massachusetts. Everything I searched out appeared to be a lie or a sham, and I found no answers in my search. We found a little one-room cabin with an outhouse, no running water, and that was the place to escape from everybody, you know. We were really disappointed in our journey.

My brother had actually gone to Jamaica before I did. He was three years younger than me, but he made the trip when he met my friends, who had returned from Hall's Delight. He had a spring vacation from the University of Miami coming up and he decided he was going to go. There, he became convinced by what he saw and heard. The elder at the camp at the time was Brother Ivy, and Brother Ivy told him that because he was so young, he would have to return home and let our parents know what he was doing. When my brother went back and told my parents he wanted to stay in Jamaica with the Rastafari brethren, he was immediately institutionalized. They dragged him to McLean's Hospital in Boston, and we had family group therapy. When I would leave the sessions, I was thinking that my brother made much more sense than either the doctors or my parents, so that intrigued me. He was institutionalized for a few months. Actually, with my help he escaped. I picked him up and he got on an airplane and he was back in Jamaica that afternoon.

It wasn't long after we got back to Massachusetts that these same friends of mine from Jamaica came to my door. I had the intention of getting them on their way, but one of the brothers who showed up was a college fraternity brother of mine who I knew quite well, and I saw such a profound change immediately in his person. In college, he was just a drunk, partying, and all of the sudden he carried a divine spirit. Something touched him and changed him completely, and I had to go find out what it was. I was basically in poverty at the time, I had a minimum-wage job, and the trip to Jamaica was a big move, and it took close to about a year before I saved enough money to make that pilgrimage. But many of the white brethren at that point would come visit me and stay with me, so I was learning about the doctrine all the time as well. I didn't get back to Jamaica until about 1971, 1972.

Ultimately, Keith Gordon assumed leadership, and he started a camp in the deep bush of Trelawny, in the Cockpit Country. They went there because the police wouldn't even go there—it was too hard a terrain to penetrate. That's the camp I came to. I remember meeting the elders. It was actually a tremendous pressure on me at the time because to walk with the doctrine, to really take your first step, I was told, I had to confess my sins to the congregation, which is an uncomfortable thing. These are strangers, and it's up to you to stand up and tell them those things that were haunting your conscience. It wasn't really easy for me to take that step, and I was never told in America by the brethren that that was going to be required of me, but I went through with it, and at that point you're welcomed into the community. To be honest with you, that confession didn't make me really feel any different; I felt I had already been filled with the spirit, from the testimony I'd received, taking that step in faith and receiving those words in faith. I already felt the spirit, that this is real and true.

Most people would call us hippies in those days, but we were really people looking for something. We were idealists. So it was a union of the disenchanted, the outcast of American society and the outcast of Jamaican society, that was the union. The union began in abject poverty physically, but the spirit was blessed, and that blessing slowly grew through the blessing of the ganja into a kingdom.

My name is Patrick White. I was born on August 31, 1959, at Emerson Hospital in Concord, Massachusetts, which is a suburb about twenty-six miles west of Boston. I grew up in an Irish Catholic family, and my father was an educator. I lived a pretty comfortable Irish Catholic life: The perfect Christmases, dad worked and mama stayed at home and raised the kids. From about the age of six until I was seven, I was molested for about a year by a twenty-year-old man, which greatly diminished my sense of self-worth as a human being. And then my mother and father split when I was about nine, so I became very introverted, filled with despair, despondency, sadness, depression. I became suicidal. I knew I didn't know why I was here. And then I took a draw of some herb. I was about thirteen, fourteen years old, and that time Bob Marley was coming up. And he was singing songs that were profound. I was hungry to hear some words of hope. I was starving. Because it was either commit suicide or find a reason to live. Is there a God? How were we created? Why is there so much evil on the earth? I couldn't make sense of it at all in my mind. Then I got shipped out to my father's house because I was so troubled. I got separated from my brothers and sisters and went to go live in Albany, and I got back when I was about sixteen.

I finished high school, but during those two years, I'd heard this reggae music, and I heard the psalms, I heard the Bible being spoken by these great chanters like Big Youth and U Roy. My brother had a friend nicknamed Kathy G who would bring me out to these camps that they had in Amherst, Mass, where they brought apple pickers, Jamaicans who had come up to do farmwork. I just wanted to know about their culture. I'd go and get them herb, so they were happy, so they loved "Little Patrick." It was great! I'd hitchhike out there, about two hours from my home, and go spend the weekend with them. Because I just loved to be with them. And I wanted to know about this word. I knew I was searching for truth. I said, "I'm going to Jamaica," that's all I was talking about. I graduated high school in June 1977, and Sunday morning, October 2, 1977, I stuck my thumb up in front of my house and hitchhiked from Maynard to Miami by myself, with one change of clothes, US$300 in my wallet, and a backpack and a sleeping bag. It took me about three days to get to Miami. I had to sleep on a bridge, in people's backyards, but there was only one focus in my mind.

I got off the plane in MoBay [Montego Bay], and I said, I want to know Rastafari. Kathy G had told me about a person up in the hills some-where, and I went up there, but he said, "No room at the inn." So there was a hotel next to the Pelican Grill and I stayed there. There was a little place next to the Holiday Inn called the Reef Club, and on the other side of the wall from there was a squatters' beach. And I ended up living there for some weeks with these Rasta brethren, and they treated me with the greatest love. I said I wanted to know about Rastafari, and they were talking about "back to Africa." But I couldn't identify with the pan-Africanist mindset. "I'm white," I said; "I am not going back to Africa." So they said I couldn't be a Rasta and my heart was broken. I made all this effort and came all this way, and they didn't reveal anything to me that was going to answer my questions. What are we doing here? What's this all about? I went back to the US and I got the one job I've ever had, working at a hospital as a housekeeper. I started growing dreadlocks. And I still had this urge to get back to Jamaica.

The next year, I got fired. And after I got fired, I went to a "free ganja" rally at the White House, a "smoke-in," during the Carter adminis-tration. I had no job, I was homeless, penniless, and there were thousands of hippies there. The police were on horses and they pushed us back onto the National Mall. On the Mall, I found this mountain of newspa-pers, about ten thousand of them, and they were called the *Coptic Times*. And I opened it, and learned about people in Jamaica, in a place called St. Thomas, who said, "We are the true Rasta," Black and white together. And because I was still searching, I said, "Let me try this again." I hitch-hiked back to Boston, and a friend said he had some work in Nova Scotia raking blueberries, so I did farmwork for about two and a half months to get the money I needed to return to Jamaica. That was from July to October, and then I hitchhiked from Nova Scotia to Miami, a five thousand–mile journey, just to answer these questions. Why are we here? Is there a God? I was still struggling with this depression, and I needed to hear something, somebody had to say some words to me that would give me some understanding of myself.

I got to Star Island in Miami and there was a gate man. This was October 1979, and I didn't know what they were going through. The gate man told me, "We can't take anybody in right now, we're going through too much ganja persecution and police raids." And I was like, *What?!* I said, "What are the words that I need to take out of my mouth to convince you that I know that I am standing at the right gate?" Because I wasn't going to budge. A man came out from the compound, and he was huge, he was six foot eight, Brother Tommy, Thomas Reilly. He reasoned with me a little bit, and then he went into his pocket and pulled out US$300. He said, "We're really under a lot of pressure here right now, and we just can't take anybody in. If you want to know about this, go and reason with the elders at our camp in Jamaica." I went to the airport, got a ticket, and got to the camp, and when I got to the camp, I gave them back the change. That's how innocent I was.

I went first to a property which is right along the roadside called Rozelle, and Jungle was the head man for the property. He took me in and fed me, put me to sleep in a room, gave me a fifty-pound bag of ganja as my pillow, and he said that we would go up to the camp in the morning. I felt content, that my journey was over. At two in the morning, Jungle got me up, gave me some cerasee tea, and we started walking up the long road to camp. We got to the gates at about 3:30, the Ethiopian Zion Coptic Church, Church of the Living Man, Gatherer of the People. There was the moon over the sea. It was majestic. And everybody was gathering for prayer, which was every morning at 4:00. I was speechless. There was a congregation of about 100, 125 people that morning, in this circular temple. And we reasoned amongst ourselves, and we read the scripture. The temple was just so beautiful, red, gold, and green, all of the artwork was God's word. Prayer was thunderous. They had a recitation of about twenty psalms, and nobody was reading a book. Not man, woman, or child. It was very intense. And everybody was burning herb, furiously. This was right after what we call the dedication of the temple, on August 6, 1979. There were a number of white people who had come for that, but most of them had legal obligations in America so they had to go back. It was really unbelievable.

The sun was rising and they took me to the chief elder, Brother Wally. He said, "What do you want from us?" People I'd never met before, they said, "You want to know about the things of God, don't you?" And I said, "Yes." It just broke me down. They said because I had sinned against God, a veil stood between me and the God that created me. They were giving me fundamental Christian doctrine. There was no difference, except that they opened the books of the law, and when they did that, they showed me that I was actually a condemned person because I had sinned. In my Catholic church, we never talked about any of that stuff. But these elders showed me, in the Bible, laws of immorality. I was guilty of breaking Moses's laws, so I had to confess my sins. About two weeks later, after kicking and fighting and biting every step of the way, I stood up in the big congregation and told them some of the most shameful things that I have ever done. And that is how I became a member of the faith.

After I confessed my sins, Brother Wally, he called me and said, "You can't stay here. You have to go home, and you have to tell your parents." So they sent me home. But when I got there, it was just drunkenness and drugs, immorality, nothing Christian. People were out of control, a whole heap of drugs and confusion. So I told my mother I was going to live in Jamaica, and I got out of there as quick as I could and got back to the camp. I flew back; I didn't have to hitchhike this time. The brethren owned Jamaica—money was no problem. They knew I was coming back. They knew I was all in. This was November 1979, and that's when everything started to dwindle down because they had the bust in Maine. And I didn't know anything about ganja or the ganja smuggling, that for ten years they had been moving herb. I just came into this heaven. They said I couldn't work on the farm, I didn't know the language or the custom, so my job was to go to prayer and get grounded in the scripture. And then I worked in the kitchen.

Both David and Patrick, as well as others we interviewed, narrate an odyssey, a search for the meaning of life and something bigger than themselves. Where David was fleeing the boredom of convention, Patrick, like some others, was seeking a path out of self-destruction. Public confession freed them of their pasts and opened them to salvation. Both found their answer in the communal partaking of ganja, which they saw as the mystical blood of Jesus, the communal sacrament, an embodied enlightenment into the divine consciousness. Patrick understood this as having been outlined in Revelations, where it is written that God would reveal himself by a new name and a hidden manna, which he took to be ganja. Whereas many Rastafari have understood the "new name" to be His Imperial Majesty (HIM) Haile Selassie in Ethiopia, the Lion of Judah, the last in the Solomonic line of kings from David, the Coptics believe that although Selassie was a king, he was not himself the Messiah. How could he have been when he himself let it be known that he prayed to God three times a day? One of the white brethren put it this way: "Haile Selassie didn't have ropes, he didn't have dreadlocks, he didn't smoke ganja either, and I know he didn't talk to any Jamaicans other than the prime minister. He had some good speeches, but he was a political king." Or, as Brother Tony, one of the Black Jamaican Coptics we met the first time we went to Coptic Heights, told us, "Our king, Rasta, is a Black man who laid down his life for the sins of the earth and then took it back up. Our king, Rasta, doesn't have a palace," he continued, "he doesn't have an army. We are sheeps of his flock." He elaborated:

> The greatest problem that the Black man suffer in life was when he was deprived of the knowledge of his God. When the Black man was deprived of knowing that the Christ that laid down his life for the sins of the earth was a Black man, the moral equilibrium became deteriorated. When you speak about African history in my generation, the most African history you read about is slavery onward. It took some effort to dig deep and realize what was my ancient glory. It was the utterances of Marcus Mosiah Garvey and his revelation that made me realize I am a character of supreme being, and all I have to do is be perfect in all conception. Out of Marcus Garvey came forth the Coptics . . . we are the offsprings of that faith.

And within that faith, ganja became a Christian sacrament, that which was blessed by Christ at the last supper.

Indeed, David understood the Coptics' doctrine as Christianity in its purest form. "That's what I received from these brethren," he said. "It's the understanding of revelation, and dispensation of Christianity. I know I received the gift of the Holy Spirit; it made me a new creature, and it changed my life fifty years ago. We received ganja as the blood of Christ," he continued, "and that was the true Christian communion, not the wine":

St. Thomas became a kingdom literally, and it afforded us to help many poor people in the community. We helped get a lot of children educated. I can speak for myself and those I was intimately affiliated with: None of us were into this for personal gain at all. We were in this because we had received what we feel was the gift of the Holy Spirit, and we had a message to offer the whole world, and we were preparing a place to receive multitudes of people: We were building an airstrip on the top of the mountains that could take large commercial aircraft. We were really expecting the leaders of the world to come here to hear this message. And I still think this message is appropriate for them. Nothing's changed.

Building the kingdom, however, required funds, and while Patrick claimed to have not known about the extent of the movement of ganja prior to his arrival in Jamaica—"I was just clueless; I was thinking about God"—David was open about being given that duty as his primary contribution to the community:

The part I was to play in helping to build the community was fiduciary, to supply financial funds by selling ganja in America. Prior to my coming that year, some of the brethren who were bringing ganja to America would visit me, and I would help them distribute it up there, so I was involved in that business prior to my ever coming to Jamaica. There were certain men chosen to do work to provide for the physical needs of the community, so that other people didn't have to work. We felt that God provided us with a "plant of renown" as the scripture says, that would take that burden off of us.[21] We could live a totally spiritual life, we wouldn't have to be dependent on Babylon at all, we didn't have to go work for wages, God gave us the gift of the ganja. And this gift provided income and the ability to build an unbelievable community in St. Thomas where we were able to provide for the needs of pilgrims rather than ask them for donations.

David himself, like many of the American brethren, never lived in Jamaica full-time. At the time, the longest stay allowable in Jamaica on a tourist visa was three weeks, and he would go and come, helping to facilitate the movement of ganja. "Sometimes it was off-loading the cargo, sometimes it was transporting it, and sometimes it was staying in my house and selling it." He described a separation of duties in which Brother Wally ran the gospel camp, the prayer services, and the administration of the divine, while Brother Keith administered the "physical necessities" that were required to keep the compound running. This was a division of labor that seems to have been first established after the "scattering" from Hall's Delight. The white brethren, David said, gravitated to Brother Keith, who "controlled what was going on with government officials to make it easier on the brothers." This is one of the reasons other Rastafari view the Coptics as a ganja organization rather than a true Rastafari way of life. But here is how David responded to such claims:

> There were some who wanted to move the ganja and be a big ganja man, but that's not what I came looking for. I was happy to do the ganja moves, but that wasn't the reason why I was amongst us. That wasn't the thing that attracted me. They always want to say the church was the front, but the ganja moving was the front. . . . It's really a shame that this reproach is brought down on the Coptic Church, concerning ganja and importation, because otherwise, the ganja was just incidental to something that was already happening, and the ganja wasn't what was happening.

As mentioned earlier, the commercial trading of ganja was one of the points of conflict among those who gathered in Hall's Delight, the other being whether white Americans should be allowed to participate as members in the community. But these conflicts were not known to David and Patrick, who entered the fold when there was already a union between the Black and white Coptics. As David explained:

> The gift is a free gift, the gift of this spirit, that I received at the beginning. The blood of Christ has freed us from sin and made us new creatures. I became a new creature, not because I did something. All I had to offer was the sin. Sin brought me separate from my understanding and brought me to the darkest in my life, and I knew that I didn't know why I was here on the earth. And now I know why I'm here on the earth. It's a universal message: It's not for the Blacks or for the whites, it's Christ's message, to all nations.

This focus on prayer and on spiritual development also seems to have kept them mostly unaware of what was going on more generally in Jamaica's political culture at the time. "When I was coming to Jamaica back in the 1970s, early 1980s," David recalled, "I never even heard of Bob Marley—that's how isolated I was from any cultural and political events in Jamaica. . . . The gospel camp was total immersion, this was twenty-four seven." Patrick felt he was a bit more aware than David, and he acknowledged that "there was like a civil war going on, between Manley and Seaga. There was a lot of pull and tug," he said. When we asked whether anyone at the camp ever discussed what was going on politically, David said they were apolitical. "There may have been that kind of conversation," he allowed, "but it didn't appeal to my ear, so I didn't pay it much attention. . . . Politics was one of the evils on earth. We didn't want to participate in any way."

Brother Tony, however, narrated the relationship between the Coptics and Jamaican politics somewhat differently. Here is his testimony.

The basic factor of the 1970s and 1980s was that Jamaica became a victim of circumstance and the IMF [International Monetary Fund]. We were indebted to the IMF and we were under a financial strain. The prime minister of Jamaica at the time, the Honourable Michael Manley, was offered a choice. He was offered US$500 million if he would discourage Fidel Castro from sending troops to Africa to defend Mugabe,[22] and this would ease the tension of the CIA off the back of Jamaica. Instead of that, Michael Manley sent Jamaican troops with Castro's troops down to Africa. The next thing we know, it was the poison.[23] And the next thing we know, it was the gas crisis. And the next thing we know, it was a strain on all infrastructural resources of the country. Policeman strike. Fireman strike. Water man strike. Telephone company too. Everything gone bad. Because they had to get rid of Michael Manley. Based upon that, Michael Manley government fell.

But before Michael Manley government fell, in 1976, my king, Nyah Keith, called Michael one morning, and said, "Mikey, what the foreign debt of Jamaica?"[24] And Michael Manley told him. And Nyah Keith in turn said to Michael Manley, "Monday morning I clear it off for you." This is not hearsay—I was very much there. They had a short conversation and Michael Manley call him back the next day, about three, four o'clock in the morning.

And Michael tell him that, from him talk to him the night before, Michael had not slept, because all heads of state were gathered to discuss the matter of that meeting. They all gathered, and they refused to entertain Nyah and his offer. Some proclaimed that Nyah was going to take over the country and ray ray ray, and they spoke evil of the Coptics. And a few weeks after that we suffer the fate of a robbery. Political gunmen came in. I was very much there also. That was where we saw the destruction of the PNP in that time.

Then came the JLP, and when Eddie come,[25] he finds a government in bankruptcy. The whole country broke. So Eddie himself come stretch out his hand to Nyah Keith also. I was very much there when he send to collect. That's the time when he said it, "Only little ganja money that keeping Jamaica alive." Even Grace Kennedy had to send to Nyah for get a little dollars. Right? Yeah. Because there was such a tight shackle placed on us by the CIA, that the entire Caribbean was under sufferation from that type of commercial venture that was instigated against us. These are not things that I have been told by people outside. Michael Manley told me about the Kissinger story personally, me and him sit down and talk. During that time, all those days, Nyah was the one who keep feeding the nation.

This kind of political involvement wouldn't be unique. I have heard similar stories about Reverend Henry, head of the Peacemakers compound in Clarendon, who is also said to have offered to clear the national debt for Manley. And while there are some who would vilify Brother Keith for this kind of political engagement, both brethren and those he worked with outside the church sang his praises.

I bring another voice into this conversation now, that of Alan Meyerson, whom Junior and I interviewed in his home in Cape Town, South Africa, in February 2024. Alan was born in Detroit, Michigan, in 1943, and he arrived at the compound in Hall's Delight before Brother Ivy died. Alan was one of the brethren to accompany Brother Keith to Trelawny and then to St. Thomas, ultimately becoming Brother Keith's right-hand man, living with him in Kingston, and, like Paul the Apostle, bearing witness to the day-to-day life of the kingdom they had built, to the material manifestations of the teachings of the Bible and of Garvey. Alan, like David and Patrick, has a testimony that emphasizes transformation— his own but, perhaps more critically, also that of a generation of Jamaicans touched in one way or another by the Coptics. Because he was the American who was closest to Nyah Keith, his testimony offers a perspective that in some ways brings together a geopolitical and theological exegesis of the 1970s and that sheds a different kind of light on what it means to be "political." Let us begin with his arrival narrative.

I was living in Berkeley, California, in the early 1970s, and I was kind of a hippie, you know, psychedelics. And I was doing some research for a sociology project called Violence in America. I'd lived in Berkeley about a year, two years, and it was a time of very revolutionary and political thinking, and it was a time of psychodelia, and it was a very hippie time. And all those things that had been interesting to me, and life-changing, were losing their luster; the politics had become quite divisive. The psychedelics certainly had a limit as far as I could think and move. One day, in the mail, I got a letter from a friend, and in it he said, "I was just in Jamaica, and I brought some Jamaican ganja back in my sleeping bag." He sent me a spliff, and he said, "Smoke this—this is the best weed you'll ever smoke. And if you smoke it and like it," he said, "go to Jamaica and visit the Rasta camp in Kingston, above Hall's Delight. Ask for Brother Louv's Rasta camp." I didn't think much of it, except "Well, that's really nice I got a joint in the mail." At that time in the early seventies, there was no Rasta, there was no Bob Marley. We weren't really familiar with the Caribbean, and most of the ganja we were smoking had come from Mexico or Thailand.

I was living in a communal house—there were five or six of us—so one night I waited until everyone went to bed and I smoked the spliff. And, wow, it was really good. My mind had been perforated by psychedelics, but when I smoked the ganja, all the sudden my mind started thinking very spiritual things, things I had never thought about: Who am I? Where do we come from? Typical spiritual questions of the 1970s. And then, at the end of the evening, I said, "I've got to meet the people who grew this because they have a message for me. They know something I should know." I woke up in the morning, and I told everyone in the house, "I smoked this weed and I had a revelation, and I'm going to Jamaica." And they all said, "That weed must have really been strong, because it made you crazy." And I said, "No, I'm going." And that time, you know, it was a time of exploration, not like the time we're living in now. People were picking up and going to India, people were going to Mexico. It was not unusual for people to pick up and go. No one was really going to Jamaica, but people were much freer in the spirit, and transportation was quite possible. You didn't have any roots. So I sold all my worldly possessions, and I said I was going to Jamaica.

In those days you would hitchhike, because there were a lot of hippies, and counterculture-type people, and a lot of them had vans— these were their homes—so it was easy to get a ride. Everyone had a sign, some said "Reno," "Sacramento," maybe "Denver." My sign said "Jamaica." People would pick me up, they'd share food, they'd share weed. Sometimes I'd go fifty miles, sometimes I'd go two hundred miles. When I got to Florida, I went to see my aunt, the one relative I had there, and she didn't want anything to do with me. She asked, "What do you want to do?" And I said I wanted to go to Jamaica. She said, "I'll send you," because she didn't want me to come in the house or ask to stay there, you know? I'd been on the road, I didn't look good, I didn't smell good. She let me take a shower, and she took me to the airport, and I got on the 10 p.m. flight to Kingston. I arrived in Kingston at midnight, and someone had told me about a guesthouse at Sandhurst, which was in a suburb of Kingston, so I stayed there.

The next day I went to the market in Papine, and I was the only white person there. I asked a woman who was selling if she knew where Brother Louv's Rasta camp was, and she said, "Oh, don't go there—they're going to kill you, they hate white people." I went to another guy and asked, "Do you know Brother Louv's Rasta camp?" And he said, "They're going to put you in the pot; they cook white people." I thought "Wow, this is not great." But I was still determined to go. Two little Jamaican kids walked up, two Jamaican boys—must have been ten or eleven, barefoot, real country boys. And they said, "White man, what are you doing here? You lost?" And I said, "No, I want to go to Brother Louv's Rasta camp." They said they knew it and that they would take me there for twenty bucks Jamaican. These two little boys put my suitcase on their heads and started running up the hill. Where the camp was from Papine was a good distance, and it was hot. And I'd been on the road and I'm a hippie, so it's not like I was training for long distance running or anything, and I was really out of shape, and these two little boys, they're flying up the hill. And finally we got to the camp.

They took me into the temple, and there was a brother there and he was painting the sign, very strong brother, and he said, "Welcome. We were expecting you." He was smoking a spliff, and he handed it to me and said, "Here, smoke my spliff, feel how I vibrate." The vibration was so calm, this man was so welcoming, that I just felt comfortable. I never felt any fear, I never felt any doubt. His name was Brother Ivy, George Ivy, and he was the head of the church. He said, "We're the Zion Ethiopian Coptic Church, and we studied under a man called Brother Louva Williams. He was our teacher, our elder, and he told us way back twenty years ago, or fifteen years ago, that there would be a time when white people would come to look for our knowledge. He said, 'They're going to come looking for you, for what you know, for who you are, for your ganja, for the spiritual understandings you have.' So when I see you, this is the fulfillment of that prophecy. So I say, we've been expecting you for many years."

That first night, Alan recalled, they had a prayer session, they sang the psalms, they brought out drums, and they danced. During that celebration, one of the other brothers sat down and smoked with him, explaining what was happening. This was Nyah Keith Gordon. The next morning, they were up early for more prayer and more ganja, and at daybreak, they danced and served tea. Alan thought he would stay for two weeks. "I could only understand part of it, the patois was difficult, and the weed was really strong," he said. "But the vibe was very reassuring. I had no long-range plans." But after several weeks of life in the temple, of prayer and fellowship, of being taught by Brother Keith and others about history, about slavery, about the teachings of Marcus Garvey, Alan was more compelled by the life he was living with the brethren. "When you're in Berkeley, you read all about Siddhartha, you read about Christ, you read about all the different spiritual things in the world, but it's always very unreal because you're reading it in a book and you go outside to American life," he remembered. "Here I was seeing the real enactment of these spiritual things in the day-to-day life: It was quite a revelation to me." He ended up staying for a long time, overstaying his visa: "I had US$100 in my pocket, and I felt burdened by that, so I went to Brother Ivy and I said, 'Brother Ivy, I've got some money and the church has taken care of me, and I want to share it with you. It feels like a burden to me.' And he said, 'That's not necessary.' But I gave him the US$100. And then I was broke. It was my first act of faith in the church."

Alan noted that although he was not the first white man to arrive at the Coptics compound, he was one of the first:

During the time I was there, other brethren, white brethren, were coming. This was the 1970s, so ganja had become very popular amongst the counterculture, kind of the elixir of the hippies. People from the eastern part of the country realized there was this group of people in Jamaica that had ganja as their sacrament, and they took it as something holy. So the braver people came down, and some of them were finding their way to the camp. But a lot of them got very frightened—white people surrounded by Black people, and everyone was very fit and strong, as Jamaicans are. White people would come, and they'd freak out. They'd stay for two hours, and it was too much for them. Out of every ten that came, maybe one would stay like I did.

Eventually, a core of white brethren had arrived and stayed, including Thomas Reilly, whom Alan said was "favored because he had quite a bit of understanding." A while after Thomas's arrival, both he and Alan became "afflicted," as Alan put it. I should say that Patrick, too, in his testimony, spoke of the same affliction, something from which he suffered for weeks. Alan explained that after a while in the temple, learning the teachings of the church, the brethren decided he was developing enough understanding to start working off-site, planting food, building up his body. In doing so, he was besieged by mosquitos, and when he scratched his bites, they became infected. Badly. "It was a messy and painful affliction," Alan said. Pus oozed from his legs. Both he and Thomas Reilly were isolated in the back of the church; they couldn't walk, and they had to watch the prayers and activities from a distance.

We were told by Brother Ivy that this was a spiritual ailment, that we were purging out all the bad things that we did in life, that we were cleansing ourselves, and that this was natural. We were told this was a type of spiritual leprosy. But it was horrifying, and one day the army came and they said, "What's with you?" And Brother Tommy said, "We've got leprosy." And they ran away. They got in their helicopters and left. And they said we chased away Babylon. Everyone started singing and dancing, "Babylon's gone; look at the power of Rasta. Jah bless." This was a lot to take in. The affliction was enough to deal with, and I was dealing with it on faith. Two days later, another raid comes, and all these health workers came in, in hazmat suits, the protective suits—they all thought we had leprosy. They wouldn't touch us, and they took us to the Mercy Hospital, and the doctor said it was a simple fungal infection. He put some purple ointment on it, and then they kicked us off the island, they put us on a plane to Miami. I came back again when it healed up. There were headlines in the paper, "White hippies living in the hills with sores." We were on the front page of the *Star*.

Whereas, for the Jamaican state, Alan's sores were evidence of a public health threat, biblically, leprosy is a symbol of sinfulness; sin corrupts spiritually the way leprosy corrupts physically.[26] For Alan, Tommy, and the other Coptic brethren, therefore, their sores were embodied evidence of coming to spiritual consciousness, of purification; they were the material manifestation of profound internal transformations. Their sequestration at the back of the church reflects the importance of ritual purity to the brethren, as this purity is essential to approaching God and remaining in the kingdom. And, while Alan and Brother Tommy were sequestered at the back of the church, they were also able to better grasp its organization.

Brother Ivy, they came to ascertain, was the clear leader of the church, "the nexus." He was supported by Brother Keith and another brother, Brother Dougie, and while there were many younger brothers who came and went, Alan understood them as "hangers on," many of whom began to disappear once the spiritual core of the church, Brother Ivy, died in 1970. Alan described his reaction to Brother Ivy's death.

Here I was, afflicted, I couldn't walk, and in the middle of the jungle, and you could tell Brother Ivy was the foundation of this, so what's going to happen? A lot of the brothers who were not as invested spiritually began to wonder what they were going to do with these white brothers. A lot of the Black Jamaicans said, "Brother Ivy brought all these white people here, and that infected us with a bad spirit, so let's get rid of the white people." There was a lot of argument back and forth. And they started arguing about the land. A lot of them were there because they could get a meal or they could get work. A lot of them were just learning the doctrine as I was learning it. It really left me in a state of confusion.

And then Brother Keith came to us, and he said, "Look, we all had the same teacher. That teacher was Brother Louva Williams, and he was one of the great Rasta elders, and he taught us this doctrine that we're teaching you. Brother Ivy was the resurrection of his spirit, and he's continuing Brother Louv's work, and Brother Louv prophesied that white people would come and everything that had happened. And now Brother Ivy's passed out." He said, "It's my duty, my responsibility, as the disciple of Brother Louv and Brother Ivy, that I take charge of the church. I have five acres of land in a remote parish in western Jamaica, Trelawny—we're moving the church to Trelawny. I'm going to take the white people there, and who wants to come with us will come with us." And what could I say? I was at the mercy of this. At that time, I became very spiritually and mentally invested in the church. And then Brother Keith took us from Kingston; he drove us to this rural place, way up in the mountains, what they called the Cockpit Country, steep hills, very difficult. We began constructing a church building, a large wooden structure, and that was the movement of the church to Trelawny.

In the Cockpit Country between Warsop and Troy in Trelawny, the Coptics had no buildings, no running water, no electricity. Once they moved, therefore, they had to determine how they were going to fulfill Brother Louva's prophecy. They had to develop a way to build "Black man's kingdom." This, after all, was the reason they were there. As they had come to understand from the Jamaican brethren through their study of slavery, imperialism, the teachings of the Bible, and the speeches of Marcus Garvey, Black people had to realize their own consciousness and work together to build a kingdom for themselves, a kingdom where there were no colonial masters and no white masters. "Our main point," said Alan,

was to bring the Black population in Jamaica, who were all descendants of slaves, to a consciousness of themselves as descendants of the royalty and the greatness of Africa. Marcus Garvey understood it, Louva Williams understood it, Brother Ivy understood it, Brother Keith understood it. And through their teaching we started to understand that we were dealing with people who were really African royalty. And the main project of this church was to rekindle this African civilization and save the world. We used to say, white man had his kingdom for Western civilization, and China man will have the kingdom now for some time, but the world will not be safe until we return to African kingdoms and African living.

They had also come to understand that ganja, like all plants, was given by God, a sacrament equal to the wine of the Catholic Church in that partaking in it would bring them closer to God, not, as some say, "a God in the sky, or a God who was dead, or a God who was a picture on the wall," but the divinity within each of us. "Ganja is an instrument to expand your spiritual consciousness," Alan explained:

> If you smoke it in a spiritual way, not a recreational way, you explore who you are, you open your consciousness, and your consciousness is your spirit. And your spirit is not something that is supernatural; your spirit is just your thoughts. God moves thoughtworthy. . . . Ganja is something that rekindles and awakens that spirit of consciousness. And that consciousness is a spirit of love. If you love that spirit of God inside yourself, you're going to realize that that spirit of God is in every other human being. You're going to have a love for that humanity. So we would say that when you smoke ganja, smoke goes in, smoke goes out, something stays inside yourself, and that's the spirit of Jah, the spirit of God, the spirit of love that you awaken inside yourself. This was the communion of the Ethiopian Zion Coptic Church. This was the communion of a generation, the generation that's here now, hopefully the generation to come.

Ganja, in other words, was both an instrument of embodied consciousness and consciousness itself. Of course, ganja would also become the key to building the kingdom. Alan remembered that before Brother Ivy died, a couple of white Americans had come to the camp in Hall's Delight interested in moving ganja. "At the time, I was afflicted, my consciousness was at a 25 percent level, so I didn't understand what they were saying, but as I look back," he said, "I can see that that was the start of the talking, that moving ganja's going to be our thing." By the time they got to Trelawny, Brother Keith said it was time. The ten or twelve Americans at the camp were, in Alan's words, "the most worthless group of white people that had ever walked on the earth." They were hippies with no material wealth, "strung out" people who "had come to the end of the road." But, Alan recalled, "Brother

Keith looked at it and said, "This is what God sent me, so we're going to make this happen.'" He told them they were a blessing, that they would help them to build a kingdom, to show people a physical manifestation of their greatness and potential, by capitalizing on "the wealth of the Black Jamaican," ganja: "He said, 'The Arabs have oil, the Americans have timber, the English have coal, South Americans have coffee. We have ganja, and ganja here is basically free. In America it's worth a lot of money. In America, they think we have the best ganja in the world. How do we get ganja from Jamaica to America so we can turn it into wealth and build our kingdom?'" Of all the brethren with whom we spoke, Alan offered the most comprehensive discussion of the logistics of building the kingdom, a discussion that perhaps most clearly demonstrates both the imbrication and incommensurability of theological and juridical modes of testimony and evidence. I provide excerpts below, but Alan has also detailed this aspect of the Coptics' activities in a ten-episode podcast available on Spotify titled *I Will Always Be Your Brother*.[27]

Brother Keith said, "You have visas, you're American, you can take ganja to America." He said, "Let's start off small." At that time, cigarette smoking was popular, and there were duty-free shops where you could buy a carton of cigarettes for half the price. Brother Keith said, "OK, buy two cartons of cigarettes at the duty-free shop, and come to the camp." So they came to the camp at Trelawny, and then he said, "What we're going to do is fill these cartons with ganja, and then you're going to carry them back to the airport, and then you're going to sell them. And then you'll come back again, and we'll start to raise money." By that time, we were true believers, and at that time there was no sonar, no dogs, no radar. You would go to customs, and it was just you and the customs man. Brother Keith said, "Everything in this world is a spiritual battle," and by "spirit," he wasn't talking about something superstitious. He said, "The spirit is your thought, your mentality. And if your spirit is stronger than the customs man, you will overpower the customs man. You have to think in a pure way so that you'll pass through without any trouble. If you're nervous, if you're doubting, if you think you're doing something wrong, you'll go to jail." It was a challenge.

So we would take these cigarette packs, and we had a large press which was four steel sides and a car jack and a plate up top, and we'd take all the buds out of the ganja, which is the valuable part, put them in the press, and we would press it until it was compressed. And we would cut it. And we'd take out the cigarette package, we'd carefully take the cellophane off, and take all the cigarettes out, and then we would cut the block of ganja to go into each pack. There were ten packs in each carton. And then we would put the cellophane back, and take a hot knife, and put a towel over it, and seal it back, without showing any burn marks. And we would do that to each pack and put the ten packs in the carton and seal the carton. So, if you would look at it, going through customs, it's a carton of cigarettes, which everyone is carrying. If they find it, you get busted, and you go to jail for two years. Two or three brethren who were much more conscious than myself, who really believed in what we were doing, they did a few trips and they made it. And they would come back with US$1,000 or US$800, which was a lot of money.

I was watching them go, but I was kind of still not 100 percent conscious, and Brother Keith said I wasn't yet ready. Finally, he told me I could do it. So the next time I came, I bought two cartons of cigarettes, and we fixed it all up. We stayed up all night and drank coffee and sealed the ganja, and the next day, I'm full of the holy spirit. And then you get in the car and start driving on the road, and you've got this ganja, and you're like, "Wow, this is a bit dodgy." And you go to the airport, and you have to pass through Jamaican passport control, not too difficult—they didn't really want to bother tourists. But then you got on the airplane, and the first time I got on the airplane, I thought, "Wow, I'm flying to Miami, and I've got these two cartons, what am I gonna do?" If I'd had a parachute, I would have jumped out of the plane. I thought maybe I could take the ganja to the toilet and flush it. You know, fear and doubt. "I'm going to jail," I thought. "I'm never going back to Jamaica. What's my mother going to think?" I was really scared. We were taught if the fear and doubt comes, just meditate on the psalms of David, so I kept on meditating. By the time we landed in Miami, this tremendous calm came upon me. The prayers had worked. I went to the customs man, I gave him my suitcase, I gave him the two cartons of cigarettes, he stamped me, the doors opened, and wow. Euphoria is too mild a term. I had done it. And over time, I ended up doing it a number of times, and eventually we started bringing in money.

This money was, according to the teachings of Brother Louva, through Brother Keith, a tool. "Don't hold on to the money," Alan remembered Brother Keith saying. "Immediately put it into something that's valuable, either real estate or food, something that's real. Money is an image." After that first trip, Alan and the eight or nine white brethren decided they could do more to help the church.

We figured out they had these cigar boxes, rolled Jamaican cigars, so we started buying the cigars, and we could put half a kilo in two boxes of cigars, so we did that. One time, we took a big block of ganja, must have been a kilo and a half, wrapped it in plastic, and we had a friend who was a baker cover it in chocolate frosting, and write "Happy Birthday Sweetie" on it. Someone carried that through customs, saying it was a birthday cake from their mother. People were getting busted round and about. Don't forget, we all had beards, we all wore sport coats like we were respectable businesspeople. Eventually in Miami they realized, "Hey these bearded guys are carrying ganja." So we shifted to New York. Then a couple guys got busted in New York, and we shifted to Chicago. We did charter flights with retirees, and eventually we burned out every airport in America.

There were direct flights from Montego Bay to Montreal and Toronto, so we started going to Canada. And we stepped up then: We realized that if we're taking a chance, we might as well go full on. We started making these ganja shields. We would take four kilos, wrap it in cellophane, sleep with it at night to shape it to our bodies, then we'd put on these orthopedic girdles, and we would carry it on the plane. We were carrying fourteen, fifteen pounds at a time. Eventually we got busted and the only airport left was Toronto. We read in the newspaper that there was going to be an airline strike in Toronto, and that the last flight out would be on a Sunday night. So we figured hey, the airport would be crazy, which meant this would be our chance. Eleven or twelve of us, we carried probably 180 pounds of ganja between us, and we all went on the same flight to Toronto. And the airport was chaotic. In Toronto, when you went to customs and passport control, the man had three cards, a red card, a yellow card, and a blue card. If you got the red card, that meant you were searched. If you got blue, a light search. If they gave you the yellow card, no searches. It was like roulette; you always wanted to get the yellow card. There were twelve of us on the same flight, eleven bearded guys and one woman. And she had a suitcase that just had a block of ten pounds of ganja with a dress over it. It was bold. And we all made it.

Then we decided since we couldn't do the airports anymore, we would buy a boat. We had one brother who was an experienced sailor, and we sold the ganja and we took maybe 30,000 Canadian dollars and bought a boat. With the money we were bringing back, we built our little kingdom in Trelawny. We had houses, we put in a dam, we put in a generator. We built a little kingdom and we planted food. And this is one of the poorest districts in Jamaica, so because of the wealth we brought in, we were hiring people, and everyone saw we could do it.

The Trelawny group expanded. They bought a ten-meter-long boat that could carry seven hundred pounds of ganja, which they would access via a remote bay outside Kingston with a dinghy. They rented a safe house in central Florida near the barge canal where they would land. They distributed to the locations where the brethren had connections—Detroit, Chicago, Boston, and other cities. And they brought the revenue back to Jamaica. Eventually, they were moving two thousand, three thousand, four thousand pounds of ganja by boat, and a good amount of cash was coming in. "We were becoming well known amongst the population," Alan said.

You don't mind me telling a little story? One of the boat moves, I think we had eight hundred pounds, and there were six or seven of us, and we went to Cow Bay. We used to bring a couple of the sisters with us. So we were sitting there with a pile of ganja, waiting for the boat. Two police vehicles pull up, and the women became emotional. I thought, "Well, we're going to jail." And Nyah was there, and two of the cops came over. Nyah said to them, "Look, you're a Black man, I'm a Black man, we're both coming from the same place. You're working for Babylon, they're not giving you what you're worth. We're trying to build this Black man kingdom—here's the teaching of Marcus Garvey—we're trying to build, we're doing this for you, we're doing this for your children, we're doing this for the next generation." Nyah was a very persuasive, spiritual speaker. He knew what he was talking about, and these were policemen, but again, they're Black Jamaicans, they're descendants of slaves. They could be touched by a spiritual understanding of who they were. He talked, and then the cops said, "Nyah, you're right." They took off their coats and they started loading the ganja with us. I said, this is a miracle. My faith of course was building. I had no doubt anymore after seeing something like this. The cops loaded, we shook hands, and said "Jah bless."

We see from this part of Alan's narrative that the interaction with the police initially tested his faith and the faith of those women who had accompanied them to the loading site. We also see the "miraculous" resolution of this trial, in which the state bows to the spiritual vision of the charismatic leader.[28] The evidence Nyah presented was so compelling to the police—representatives of the juridical realm—that they abandoned their duties, at least for that moment. Or perhaps it would also be precise to say that the policemen's subjectivities (and histories) as Black Jamaicans superseded their identification with law, which is presumably why movements like Rastafari (in all its various versions) constantly appear as legitimate threats to the state and its notions of juridical sovereignty. But let us return to the story at hand.

Ultimately, Brother Keith decided that Trelawny was too remote, and that having built a kingdom there—ten houses, twenty acres under cultivation, a water system and electricity, a prosperous and growing district—they were ready to move again. Someone knew about a property that had become available in St. Thomas, six hundred acres of undeveloped land closer to Kingston. By that time, Brother Keith was moving back and forth to Kingston, "integrating into society," as Alan put it, and finding new ways to support their project. They had also announced that if people were growing ganja, the Coptics would buy it at a fair price. "Everybody and their mother started bringing us ganja," Alan remembered—"Catholic priests, politicians, everyone brought us ganja." Even the army. "And this was giving employment and wealth to the people." The Coptics bought the property in St. Thomas and they moved to White Horses.

At that time we got bigger and bigger boats, moving five thousand, ten thousand pounds. We were starting to amass some serious capital, and so we built this large kingdom in St. Thomas. We ended up buying all the properties around it until we had about six thousand acres in eastern Jamaica, which we turned into quite a prosperous place. First, we fenced off thirty acres in the center of the property and we built a large assembly hall. Around the assembly hall, we built these structures, beautiful large houses, each with ten bedrooms, each bedroom with its own bathroom, marble floors. These were first-class mansions, raising out of nowhere, and this became Coptic Heights. We employed thousands of people. Some of the foremen were former members of the church, and we tried to bring in as many people from the district as possible. We tried to spread the employment around so that the money could get into the different communities. And, of course, Jamaicans are some of the most skillful artisans in the world. And we put them all to work, and we paid a fair wage.

This project was, amazingly, completed in nine months. If you remember, I mentioned earlier that if you're going to tell people about a kingdom, you have to show the physical reality. We showed them the physical reality times ten. We showed them the reality in the most beautiful, magnificent way. The greatest thing about it? It was a Black man who was directing it, it was built by Black people, it was for Black people, there was no colonial master, there was no European leading it, there was no politician leading it. It was totally self-sufficient, as Marcus Garvey had prophesied. Marcus Garvey spoke about changing the mentality of the people, that if you work for yourself, or you work for the community, or you work for the collective, it benefits yourself. You had to convince the people that in working for yourself and the community, you're working for your culture.

When the project was completed, it was quite a monumental achievement, not only physically but spiritually, because we were able to keep all these diverse people together. So we decided to have a large celebration to celebrate the stabilization and the building of the Coptic Kingdom at Coptic Heights.[29] We had a three-day celebration, and people came not only from all over Jamaica; people came from all over America, people came from England. We had connections with some nefarious Colombian people, and they honored us by coming. At the same time, there was a film crew there from America from a very dubious news magazine called *60 Minutes*, and they were doing what you could politely call a hit piece on us. And we gathered about five hundred pounds of ganja, and everybody who came got a spliff. We killed a number of cows, we killed a number of goats, we fed everybody who came. It was three days, and I would say maybe a couple thousand people came. Policemen came, politicians came, upper-class people came: This was the celebration that transcended the Jamaican communities. It was monumental, it was a liberation celebration, it was the end of colonialism, it was the first start of where Rasta had really accomplished something physical.

We had daylong music and dancing in the temple area, all day and all through the night people were dancing and singing. And we smoked hundreds of pounds of ganja. Hundreds. There was a permanent cloud over the entire area of Coptic Heights. And the amazing thing is, to us it was nothing, but ganja was highly illegal at this time. If you got caught on the road with a half a spliff, you could go to jail for two years. And there we were, thousands of people smoking hundreds of pounds of ganja, publicly, being filmed—this was the first liberation movement of ganja. Ganja became free for this moment, and nobody felt out of place. This was further proof of everything we had done, something that we had done for the community and for the church. It was a really powerful moment, probably the height of the kingdom. And it's something I'm still very proud of, and I'm sure every brother or sister who was there is proud of it. Everybody who was there was touched by it. The legacy of Coptics, amongst Jamaican people that knew it, is a very warm legacy. It's a legacy of the people that knew what we were doing, the people who will always understand the beauty and the warmth of what we were doing.

What they were doing, on the scale at which they were doing it, was no doubt facilitated by the political moment. As mentioned earlier, many of the American brethren did not seem to know much about Jamaican political history or about the ways the Cold War was playing out in the region. Alan himself arrived not knowing much:

We were up in the hills, we were separated, we were doing Rasta thing. And then as part of the learning sessions we had at night, we would read books about slavery, about the oppression of the white people on the Black people. We had these long learning sessions, sometimes they'd be four or five hours; sometimes we wouldn't sleep, we'd go right into prayer. We only slept two or three hours a night at the most. The ganja was very strong. So we went through all that history. But we were in a spiritual atmosphere, so the real world, the political world, was not sinking into me at that time. When we moved to Trelawny, I got more understanding moving back and forth, but we were kind of in a spiritual bubble. It wasn't until I lived in Kingston for a long time that I understood the political dynamics, what happened in 1972 and the socialist revolution.

Following is Alan's narration of that moment in Jamaica.

In 1972, Michael Manley was elected as the PNP prime minister, and he was socialist. And very anti-American. At that time, there was a fight between capitalism and socialism. Fidel Castro had liberated Cuba with his brand of communism or socialism, and he was very anti-American, anti-capitalist, and America was fighting against him. So Cuba became socialist, and Jamaica became socialist, and then in Grenada, there was also a socialist movement run by Maurice Bishop, so the danger to America at that point was that the shipping lanes between Latin America and the Panama Canal could be shut off if all these islands were in sync. So it became very important to America to stymie this revolution of socialism in Jamaica. And so they went on a program of destabilization. They brought in guns and instituted types of political gangs and warfare. They put embargoes on goods. Tourism went from a million people, which was the lifeblood of the Jamaican economy, to under a hundred thousand in a year.

So Jamaica was being destabilized. The people suffered a lot; the economy crashed. America had given guns to the gangs that supported the JLP, and they started robbing and killing. The police who were part of the JLP gave up, they walked away, because Michael Manley wouldn't give them guns or vehicles. The gangs were more well armed than them. Michael Manley started his own police force, which he called the Home Guard, which was basically his gang of criminals. It was a very chaotic time. Eventually the Cubans armed the PNP gangs, so it became a small civil war between the socialists who were fighting for the PNP that were armed by the Cuban intelligence, and the JLP, which was being armed and supported by the CIA in America. And thousands of people died. It was quite brutal.

Jamaica's social structure, in Alan's understanding, was still very colonial at that time, "run by a colonial upper class, mixed race or white or Chinese" that became wary of Manley's "democratic socialism" and worried that their properties might be nationalized, as had happened in Cuba. They "panicked," in Alan's words.

They wanted to leave the island. Michael knew they were going to leave. He instituted a law preventing them from taking money out of Jamaica, and he established a new part of the police force, called the FIU, the Financial Intelligence Unit. They checked everybody at the airport, and if you had over US$50 you went to jail, and if you tried to transfer your money out of Jamaica, you couldn't do it. He wanted to freeze all these assets. Many of these people were going to Miami, or to Toronto, or to New York, and now they had to figure out how they were going to get their money out. At the same time, we were moving large amounts of ganja, so we had a large amount of American cash. We used to bring it down to Jamaica, which was a hassle. Sometimes, I had to carry it in plastic bags and put these orthopedic girdles on, and I'd have US$150,000 on me. But we wanted Jamaican money. We were the only people in the world who wanted Jamaican money at the time because it was depreciating by the hour, but we had to pay our people.

We worked out a plan. We had a large house in Miami, in a very posh neighborhood called Star Island, that was our embassy. We would tell these rich upper-class Jamaicans: You bring us your Jamaican money, we'll exchange it at a fair rate, and then you trust us and go to Miami; and the brothers there have American money, they'll give you the corresponding amount of money in American money. People were thrilled, absolutely thrilled. They could go through the airport with US$10, but on the other side there would be US$50,000. So, they started bringing us their money. At that time a Jamaican $50 bill was the largest currency, and they would bring us 400,000, 500,000 Jamaican dollars. One time a guy showed up with a pickup truck with twenty crocus sacks full of money. And I had to count it. Finally, after a while, I just did it by size. I don't know whether they ripped us off. We bought a large safe and we stuffed it with money.

These people also had properties and they had equipment, worth a lot of money, but they thought they were going to lose it all. So they were offering us houses in posh suburbs, at very reduced rates. I mean, they panicked. Sometimes we would get a house in a very posh suburb, and a large ganja grower would come and say, "I've got 4,000 pounds for you." And we would trade them the house for it. And he would be thrilled. I mean, living in the bush, and all the sudden he's living in a posh suburb of Kingston; he would show up with the goats and the chickens and his whole family. So we started to integrate all these neighborhoods. They would leave us their cars; a lot of them had equipment they needed to leave. So we had like eight bulldozers, we had front-end loaders, so we started building roads, we started a construction company. And people would always come to us saying they wanted to start a business, and we would support that if we could. So we started a furniture business, we had an ice cream parlor, we had restaurants, we had a large supermarket in Kingston, all run by Black people, all people who had been previously disadvantaged because of who they were.

This was our part of liberating Jamaica; we took advantage of this political and monetary situation to liberate Jamaica, to revitalize the economy, to put Black people in the places that they belonged. We broke the colonial yoke. People will say Michael Manley did, and he helped us. Because of this policy of financial pressure that Michael Manley was putting on these rich people, we expanded tremendously. It was the greatest gift to the church physically that we ever had. We were actually socializing the country, we were the main source. If you talk to people who were there, who really saw what was going on, you would say this is a very warm, important historical point. Because we kind of broke the yoke of colonialism, we broke the yoke of where the wealth was. Some would say we were laundering money. But we weren't laundering money, we were redistributing the wealth. I don't feel bad about it, because I thought that being able to redistribute the wealth to the people who were really responsible for the wealth was a wonderful thing.

What they were doing also required connections with representatives of the state, and their proxies in the so-called garrison communities of downtown Kingston.[30] Some might have understood these relationships to be evidence of corruption, but the Coptics understood them as part of a redistribution of wealth that also shook up the juridical foundations of the colonial, and national, order. "Laws are made by politicians," Alan said, reciting what he had learned from Brother Keith. "They're not made by God." Because they were moving large amounts of ganja and because there were a number of organizations, principally the CIA and DEA, that were trying to stop them, they built a community of people around them who could help if problems arose. In return, the Coptics also gave back to that community. "Some people say, 'Oh, you bribed them,'" Alan acknowledged. "But we were part of a Black community, part of an African community, a community that had been destroyed by slavery, and we were bringing people out of it. So we were not against giving people things, and they would be loyal to us. By being loyal to us, we could help build a kingdom and we could help build more people." Alan told of one example of how the Coptics' support of this community ended up working in their favor.

The DEA and the CIA, the Americans, they knew we were moving a lot of stuff, and they thought we were dangerous, so they sent a squad down to Jamaica. And they checked in at the Pegasus Hotel in New Kingston—it was the fanciest hotel. And they didn't tell the local police, which they should have done. And, in the room, they set up a task force. They put up all our pictures, and they started talking about how they were going to get us. And there was a Jamaican woman there cleaning the room, and they said something to her and she shrugged and acted like she couldn't understand them. So they started talking all the stuff they were going to do to us in front of her. She called Nyah, and we called the Central Police Station, and we told them the CIA was at the Pegasus, that they had come to bust us, and they said, "OK, leave it up to us." So they sent a squad to their room at the hotel; they knocked on the door, carrying a small bag of cocaine with them, and they planted it. They told them it was wrong that they didn't check in with the local police, and that they were moving drugs. And they said, "OK, we won't put you in jail, but you've got six hours to leave the island." And so they left. They got chased away, all because of this lady who was cleaning the room. If you have the people working for you, it's a force of humanity that really controls the island. If you're controlling the people, you're controlling the conversation, you're controlling the vibration, so giving these gifts to higher-up people, the police, coast guard—it wasn't for our benefit, it was to build the kingdom. And I'm sure people misunderstand this, but democracy and all these other things are much more corrupt.

By "control," here, Alan was invoking the teachings of Thomas Sankara, the Pan-Africanist, Marxist revolutionary who served as the president of Burkina Faso after the successful coup he led in 1983 until his assassination in 1987. Alan remembered Nyah Keith quoting Sankara as teaching that the person who feeds you is the person that rules you. That vision of political leadership is grounded, for Alan, in the post–World War II emergence of anticolonialism, of people through-out Africa and the Caribbean "who had the same spirit of Marcus Garvey," people who became leaders "dedicated to educating the uplifting their people." Control here is rooted in sacrifice, in love of their people, rather than in dominion. "There's a difference between a leader and a politician," Alan offered. "A politician asks the people to work for him, and a leader will fight and work for the people." Nyah, for Alan, also inherited this spirit, and it was a spirit that transcended the political divisions that became hypermilitarized in Jamaica during the 1970s.

Like I said, there was basically a civil war being fought out in many places in Latin America and the Caribbean between the capitalist oppressive governments run by the CIA in America and the then-socialist governments, which were supported by Fidel Castro and basically by the Soviet Union. We of course had a doctrine of nonviolence. And Nyah had a deal with everyone. The worst of the gangsters would come to us. Policemen came to us. Politicians came to us. We made a point of never being political. We made it known we had friends who were JLP, we had friends who were PNP. In order to survive in Jamaica in the 1970s, you really had to be nonpolitical. Nyah, of course, was not judgmental. He would tell them what they were doing was wrong and try to show them the right way. We would read from the Bible, we would feed them, we would help them out, give them money. We judged them by their mind, their spirit, the attention of their heart, and that they were a Black person.

Nyah, because of his compassion and his understanding, was the man with the golden heart, and he would help everyone. If you read Marcus Garvey, his point was to bring people back to a consciousness of who they were as Africans, that they should unite, that they were one common tribe, one nationality. Nyah, Brother Louva Williams, Brother Ivy—this was the doctrine, to bring Black people back to a consciousness of the greatness, the royalty, the brilliance that they were supposed to be part of. Nyah had the ability to touch their heart; he could take the most vicious policeman, the most vicious criminal, and he'd have a way to touch their heart, so that maybe for one minute, maybe ten seconds, maybe two minutes, they could understand the divinity that rests inside themselves.

This "divinity," for Alan, was Black Jamaicans' inheritance, and it was something Nyah Keith attempted to bring into being in his day-to-day interactions. After the move to St. Thomas, Nyah asked Alan to stay with him in Kingston, where he lived most of the time, rather than continuing to make the ganja moves back and forth to America. "I was blessed enough to become Nyah's aide-de-camp, Nyah's assistant, Nyah's second in command."

I felt blessed to be able to bear witness to this every day. It was not easy. Nyah was a man who was difficult, who wanted things done his way. But the foundation of any spirituality, I learned from Nyah, was forgiveness and mercy. From Nyah I learned many things, but I learned that forgiveness and mercy and understanding are the three keys if you're going to deal with humanity on a large scale. Everyone would petition him—we had the good, the bad, and the ugly that came every day. They started coming at five in the morning. People knew if they had a problem, they could talk to Nyah, and Nyah would try to solve it. Some mornings I would wake up at five and there were already five people there. When I asked if they would ever stop coming, Nyah said, "If someone's coming to visit you, you have to take that as a great honor. They're taking time out of their life to come visit you. You should accept that these people are honoring you by coming to visit you." People would come without end—in an average day, we'd have a hundred to two hundred people that would come and go. . . . I think it's important for all of us, especially those of us that were in the church, to understand that we were part of something that was great, something that is still moving, as the global south, people of color, now manifesting and overtaking the people of the north, which is basically NATO, all the countries that were colonial oppressors. We were part of this movement. And Nyah was part of this movement. He understood humanity, and he tried to impart that to all of us. He was a leader beyond how the people saw him, to understand the wave of Black consciousness and Black leadership, and I think it's important we understand that. I wondered often why he chose me to be his assistant. I was not the smartest of the brothers, I was not the quickest, I was not the brightest. Now that I look back on it, I think maybe it was so I can give this testimony.

The qualities of the Coptic movement that Alan bears witness to here, and that Brother Tony and Brother Patrick describe in earlier passages, were immensely powerful, and other brethren speculated on what this power must have looked like to the American government. As one said, "America looked at that and said, 'Wait a minute—they're letting this Black man take over Jamaica, and he's a ganja man too? And he actually has white people helping him?' They didn't like that." He recalled that when Reagan was inaugurated president of the United States, the first head of state he invited to Washington was Prime Minister Seaga, "and he promised Seaga more money than Seaga was making off the ganja, so that's where he went and he started fighting against us hard." This is what led to the beginning of the end. As one of the brethren put it, "The closer you get to God the harder Satan fights. When they saw St. Thomas, they thought, Whoa, this is too much." As with most material manifestations of community that are developed in opposition to state logics, there are many versions of how and why they end. Here is Alan's.

When we were just in Jamaica starting to manifest wealth and power, we were quite anonymous, nobody knew us. And then, beyond our power, there was a bust in America and we became a media sensation. And Thomas Reilly, known as Brother Louv, a brilliant and wonderful man, he became the spokesman in America, and America was the media capital of the world, full of propaganda, full of lies. So they publicized the church, but they publicized only the white part, even though Brother Louv would tell everyone, "No, Nyah is the leader of this church." And the propaganda started saying we [were] a CIA organization that was there to destabilize Jamaica. America at the time had killed every Black prophet, Black revolutionary, every Black person who stood up for freedom. We were totally against America; we were moving ganja to America to help ourselves, and also to enlighten a generation in the hope that they would help destroy America. We were very anti-American.

The problem is, especially in Jamaica, through the mentality the people had: A Black man could not be the head of this organization. Nyah was not a man who was educated, he could not read or write, but he was educated in wisdom. But it was easy for the media to say the leader must be this tall, white man, very eloquent and educated. Even the Black people in Jamaica were kind of trained to never think that their own could accomplish anything. It was part of the slave mentality. So it was very easy to spread the propaganda that we were part of the CIA, but we were highly anti American, and everything that we did emanated from this very poor group of people. The white Americans who came were strung out, were not thoughtful, were discombobulated—it was the worst group of white people. If the CIA was going to put a group together, we would have been the last people they would choose. I know the CIA is quite incompetent, but they always recruit the best of the best, and we were the worst of the worst.

Cuban intelligence was also there. At first, Cuban intelligence thought we were CIA because they saw the white people. But they investigated us quite closely, and they came to the conclusion that we were an independent organization, that we weren't affiliated with anybody. Later, the CIA had a study done on us, and the report said, the Coptic Church is 70 percent of the social services in Jamaica, the Coptic Church has a 90 percent favorability rate. The brethren in Miami, they were doing their own thing, and because of different busts, they got caught with large amounts of ganja, and we decided to go public. They were fighting for their lives, and they did that by fighting propaganda with the reality of the truth that we had. But that was quite separate from what Nyah was doing. He trusted Brother Louv and the brethren in Miami, but it was different. That was just an offshoot. We always wanted to be underground; it's only because we got busted. . . . We were there to bring down America, we were not there to build up America.

And following is David's version of how the Coptic Kingdom ended.

By 1980, pretty much everybody was involved with some sort of court problems, so it was difficult to gather. And, shortly after that, many of us were convicted of felonies in America and there were appeals, and it became more of a legal battle at that point. And there weren't people coming to the camp, because there were restrictions on us in America. So the whole focus of things changed.

Our first major problem with the authorities that led to a dissolution of the spiritual efforts of many of us was in a place in central Florida called Dunnellon. We established a spot there, like a safe house. We would bring the herb in and warehouse it there, and distribute it from there when needed. We purchased property, specifically for that purpose. There was a young man from Jamaica who had had some problems with the authorities there, and the brethren smuggled him on a ship into America with some ganja. We were trying to help the young man, show him a life of spiritual life, give him an opportunity to improve his life. He was with us for a number of months, and we became a little too trusting of him. He would drive to town [to] buy supplies for himself, and he ended up starting a relationship with a local woman, and they would come back to the place in the middle of the night, get into the stash that we had, and sell it for themselves. Of course they were arrested, and they became informants. That's when the authorities first found us in America, I believe. I wasn't involved there, and while that case was pending, we were still doing ganja moves.

We brought some into central Florida, through what was at the time called the Cross Florida Barge Canal. It was a project the government had started with the aim of digging a channel that was to go from the Gulf of Mexico, following rivers across Florida to the Atlantic Ocean. They had dug a canal for the deep water, so we could bring vessels, one in near the shore and we would unload there. The marine patrol saw something funny going on, and they called in reinforcements, and they busted us. My wife was there with me, and the two of us escaped. We were out in the middle of bush—it's not the Everglades but it's just as desolate, miles from anything—and we spent the night in the bush. That morning we started walking through the bush because we were trying to work our way towards a safe house we knew was about two miles away. While we were walking through the bush, I heard a vehicle approaching, and I told my wife to go and hide. I was arrested on the spot, and while I was sitting in the back of the pickup truck, they spent a good half hour looking for my wife. There was very little foliage, but somehow she avoided them. She had overheard them talking about a culvert that went under the main highway to the other side of the road on the gulf side, which was totally desolate from civilization. They knew we would all have to cross this highway. It was very flat, and you could see for miles down the highway, so they positioned two people, one at one end and one at the other of the highway, and as everybody was crossing they would just pick them off. Probably twenty or more of us were arrested then. Brother Keith was one of them. But my wife was able to use the culvert to cross the road without being seen.

This was in Citrus County, Florida, what we would call a very redneck community. We spent close to a week in jail before we were able to be bonded out. There were a number of us there, and we would have our prayer services every day, and the chant would resound out into the community.

Everybody in the community wanted to know what was going on in their jail, and the sheriff didn't feel comfortable having to answer questions like that, so he asked us what would be required in order for us to stop chanting. We told him we would be more than happy to remain silent if he could supply us with ganja. Which he did. So while we were in jail that week, we had ganja. There was one other request that we had, and that was for a large carrot, so we could carve a pipe out of the carrot and smoke it as a chillum pipe. While we were in jail that time, in the middle of the night, they came to Brother Keith and told him they wanted to talk to him down at the sheriff's office. Brother Keith just started yelling and screaming to wake up the whole jail and let everyone know what was going on. He felt they were going to bring him out in the street, it would look like he'd escaped, and then they would kill him. So he woke up the entire jail, told everybody what he felt their intentions were, and they backed down. After about a week, we were all bailed out.

At that point, the federal government decided to intervene. They had a superseding indictment, a Florida case that included this particular bust, which they combined with the first case in Dunnellon into a broader conspiracy case. To this day I don't know what happened: I only can assume it was a clerical error, but somehow everybody that had an arrest in Citrus County was included in the federal indictment except me. Maybe my shoulders weren't broad enough to bear that burden, but for whatever reason, I was not included in that case, which saw many of the brethren get double-digit sentences. Brother Keith was out on bond and returned to Jamaica, and I don't think he ever again returned to America, because he would have been a fugitive at that point.

There were many delays in that trial, and so we did another move, this time up into Maine, where I had purchased a home under an alias. Some of the brothers who were out on bail from those original indictments in Florida, or maybe they were out on appeal—it's hard for me to remember how that all went. But we got popped in Maine and they got arrested again. After that bust, the ship was also busted, and I think there were twenty tons on that one. A few of us were able to escape, and it took me about two or three days before I was able to actually surface again from the bush. Later I was involved in the indictment because a real estate agent identified me as one of the purchasers. That would have been around 1980. When they came to my house to arrest me on the conspiracy charge, they found me in my greenhouse tending to some ganja plants. It's a convoluted story, but I was arrested there on the Maine indictment, and also had charges filed with the State of Massachusetts because I was charged with cultivation, and when they did a search of my house, they found more marijuana, so I had significant state charges pending at that point. Both me and my wife were facing a minimum mandatory three-year sentence, and she was a mother of four children at the time. So there was some pressure put on us, to say the least.

Eventually I was convicted and did serve that time. I was given a five-year sentence and served three. It then was extended a bit because during the trial in Maine, there was a recess, and we all went outside to have a smoke and the press mobbed around us. I lit up my ganja spliff and did an interview with the press, and that happened to be on the front page of the newspaper the next morning, and so the judge opened his paper and saw that his courthouse steps were the pulpit for ganja legalization. He didn't react well. I had been convicted on the state charge as well, and during my sentencing for the Maine conspiracy arrest, the judge gave me consecutive time rather than concurrent time, so I paid a little price for that. My wife wasn't arrested for the federal case in Maine. She happened to be with our son at our safe house about thirty miles away, but unbeknownst to us, they had been watching us for quite a while. We had gotten one load in successfully right under their noses, but when we attempted a second load, they busted us. A number of women were there, but mercifully, they dropped the charges against all the women. But my wife was charged for the Massachusetts bust, and she went to trial with me. We presented our religious defense, and we were both convicted. Both of us were facing a three-year minimum mandatory sentence. They offered her a plea deal: They would drop her conviction if I would drop my appeal, and she wouldn't do it. But through another merciful act of God, the law changed while we were awaiting our appeal, and her conviction was overturned. My mandatory conviction was also dropped, and I only got a couple of years, in a county jail.

My arrest was one of the more liberating experiences of my life. It really was. I didn't really come to this doctrine to move marijuana or to make money. I came seeking truth. But because of the necessity to supply the needs of the community without everybody having to sell their souls over to Babylon, it manifested that I did that work. But I lived a clandestine life. I didn't want anybody to know what I was doing. I made no friends. I lived in a remote area; I still live in that little one-room cabin. I wasn't building a kingdom for myself with all the ganja moving. We lived in a one-room house with an outhouse. And sometimes I'd have a million dollars, but every penny would go to Jamaica. The liberation of my arrest was the opportunity now to share the word. No longer did I have to be silent and quiet. It freed me up. Being in prison was wonderful because I was with hundreds and hundreds of people, many with open ears. So I felt as though that was my pulpit, prison. Actually, for the first time in literally decades, I was able to share this message. The arrest was in 1980, but by the time all the appeals worked out, I think I finally went to prison in 1985 and my release date was supposed to be 1988. As I was leaving the courtroom headed to the jailhouse, I remember telling my wife I'd see her at the Olympics.

Brother Tony, one of the Black Jamaican Coptics, argued that it was not just the arrests from the movement of ganja that brought the kingdom down. "It was not the aggravation of the government that destroyed Coptics," he said; "it was the defilation of our own status within, our own environment, that caused the destruction." He explained that by defying the laws that were set before the community, by seeking material prosperity, people defamed what had been created. Patrick, too, who remained at the St. Thomas camp, remembered that while the church had enough to sustain itself for a couple of years after the arrests of the white brethren in America, there was, indeed, a juridical coming to terms (what he called, using biblical language, "a judgment"), one that was incompatible with the spiritual values they had attempted (unsuccessfully, in his estimation) to uphold. Patrick explains.

It was a terrible judgment. Brother Wally and Brother Keith were different. Brother Keith was administering all of these properties, so he was in town, and he didn't really come to the gospel camp anymore. It was intense there. You had to love it. It was very strict, it was not an easy place to be, whether you were Black or white. Anyway, the last time that Brother Keith came to the camp, a lot of people were starting to take set. They were stealing our co-

conut, our cattle. People realized Coptics didn't have the money they used to have, so we were going through a lot of that. The judgment, now, however was that everyone on the farm was brought before Brother Wally and Brother Keith to answer for what they were doing. A lot of elders were questioned. Some of them had been selling everything in the house, furniture, fridge. After that judgment, that's when everything really dwindled down. This is two or three years after I got there, shortly after 1983. The white brethren were gone from Jamaica and they never returned, and then all the elders got judged, and most people never came back to the camp after that. And it came down to just a few little people. During morning oblations, it would be me and Sister Mummy alone in this big old gospel camp that had housed thousands of people, now dwindled down to me and Sister Mummy.

It never restored because the curse was already set in motion. We were living a Judeo-Christian life. We lived very conservatively, or we professed that we did. We kept the dietary laws, we kept the laws of separation for women, we kept the laws of cleanliness and uncleanliness, but we didn't keep all of Moses's laws. And while we performed a number of the Jewish laws, it became a big problem because in our imagination, we became holier than you. So instead of showing you love, we would have this list, this imaginary list, of things that you would have to do. Love could never live under those constraints. We were instructing others to keep Moses's law, and we ourselves did not keep the entire law. The Bible says, "Cursed are those who are under the law and not do all of them."[31] And that's exactly what happened to the Coptics. So that's how it came to be to the camp that you see today, this crumbled desolation, this place that was filled with joy and work and people and activity. Don't play with God's word man.

Following is how David describes the "curse."

We became the largest private landowner in the island of Jamaica, we had huge holdings and enterprises, and we were so blessed, we didn't have room enough to receive the blessing we received. It's really a biblical story, when you see the group and where it started from, from that it became this blessing that none of us couldn't really grasp. The conflict was what happened, the blessing turned to a curse, because the curse was everyone being scattered, everything was taken away. I returned to the church many years later and I found basically a skeleton of the building with cow dung in it—that's a biblical curse, you know? That spirit that I received, that spirit that just encompassed love, it wasn't there, in my mind. My prayer became, if something is wrong with this church, crash it. If something's wrong with me, crash me. That's where my spirit was, because I didn't want to live a lie: I was seeking truth above all else.

One day, I opened the Bible, the book of Galatians, and it talks about a blessing and a curse. And it talks about the apostles and the disciples in the early Christian church, not a bunch of neophytes but the leaders in the church, and how the early church fell into a judgment because Moses's law crept in unawares and bewitched everyone in the church. We talk about sin being the enemy. We know thievery, fornication, these sins are easy to discern. But the law creeping in perverted the message of the gospel, and we started to become judgers of one another through the law.

In these testimonies, it is the problem of law that led to the Coptics' downfall; as Patrick argued, "Love could never live under those constraints." The evidence that they had become too juridically minded was the breakup of the church, the arrests of the white brethren, the bickering attendant to the diminishment of their resources, the eagerness to judge one another. They are speaking not only of Moses's law but also of American law. And of course, their analysis appertains to law generally because what they are pointing out is the difference between law and relation. I remind us here that prior to the dissolution of the church, building the "Black Man's Kingdom on Earth" was the worldly evidence of their spiritual rightness. It validated a mode of being in relation in which generosity and care reigned as principles of interaction, principles that aimed to destabilize the long-term political-economic and psychic effects of capitalist modernity and to create fertile ground for repair. What these testimonies show us, as well, is how precarious it is to build a "Black Man's Kingdom on Earth" outside of, but in relation to, normative infrastructures of sovereignty.

After Brother Wally had a stroke in 1984, Brother Keith brought Patrick from the camp to town to help with the administration of the properties and businesses there, which included the Coptics Containers business, the trucking company on Orange Street, the supermarket in Barbican, the houses owned by the brethren in Cherry Gardens, Beverly Hills, and Barbican, and the gas station, now the Texaco that sits at the fork where Mannings Hill Road diverges from Constant Spring Road. In 1984, Brother Keith was shot at that gas station while he was standing right next to Alan (who was not hurt). Although a bullet blew out one of his lungs, he survived the attack. Alan remembered how stressful it was for Nyah after the busts because people were still looking to him to solve their problems, and the Coptics were no longer the fountain of prosperity they had once been. And the gunshot wound, he said, "took a lot out of him." His condition deteriorated, and the brethren moved him from the house in Beverly Hills to a place in Stony Hill, where he could be more isolated. "You could see he was going to pass on," Alan said. About sixteen months later, Nyah was diagnosed with a fast-moving cancer, and in July 1986, he died in the arms of Patrick and other Kingston-based brethren and sistren. "When Brother Wally and Brother Keith died within a couple months of one another," Patrick reflected, "it was like the hierarchy of the main decision-makers was done."

After Brother Keith's death, many of the Coptics' properties were liquidated after the Jamaican government demanded they pay back taxes. Some of the brethren expected Alan to take up the mantle of leadership, since he had been Nyah's second in command, and he did stay in Kingston for a year or two after Nyah's death. Eventually, he felt he had to leave because he couldn't, as a white man and an American, fill Nyah's shoes. "I didn't think Black Jamaicans needed a white man to be the ruler of the Coptic Church; I didn't think that was the point of our existence," he said. He moved to a piece of property he had in the parish of Portland and took some time to reflect on what they had built and what they had lost. Brother Gary and some of the other American brethren tried to keep St. Thomas running, but they moved away after Hurricane Gilbert in 1988. Some of the younger brethren tried to do a few ganja moves. Patrick, too, stayed for a while at one of the properties in Portland, near San San, but he was eventually busted for herb, so he was unable to return to Jamaica for some time, which was why it had been so moving for Patrick to be with us, to see Hall's Delight, and to meet Brother Clive.

Patrick said that Brother Keith had signed his will the afternoon before he died, leaving the church to three white men: Brother Louv (Thomas Reilly), Brother Gary, and Brother Alan. Patrick thought it was interesting that Brother Keith couldn't find "one of his own that he could trust enough, that could administer the church with honor and respect," and he noted that people have been fighting over the will and the land ever since. Alan, however, disputes Patrick's claims:

> I was there when he made up his will, and I was there when he was on his deathbed. There's a lot of complexity. We had a lot of properties, we had a lot of things that were in the Ethiopian Zion Coptic Church's name, and some things were in Nyah's name. He gave people certain properties; he made sure his children were taken care of, and they got some of the properties in St. Elizabeth and St. Mary. There were a couple pieces of land that he gave me, but I didn't really want to get into it. There's an old saying in Jamaica: The worst thing you can do is get involved with a dead man's things, because people are going to fight over it. And it's going to be messy. The Church property, it was very complex. We had a lawyer, Sylvester Morris, who ran all the church things. I think there had been a change to the church papers. I was not part of that. I think he made Brother Dougie one of the elders; Brother Tommy, he was in America, he really wasn't part of it. Brother Gary was left in charge there, but he wasn't put on the papers. The paperwork was very confusing, like all paperwork. I think some of Nyah's children are still fighting over some of the things.

Another brethren put it this way: "They say when you kill a shepherd the sheep scatter. . . . Everybody wanted to know where the big bag of money was."

After a while, Alan decided to travel. He was back and forth to Europe for some time, and then after 1994, he began going to South Africa. "The minute I got to Africa," he said, "I just felt inspired, and this inspiration has never left me. I think it's a part of the continuation. The Rasta story, the Coptic story; it's not a Jamaican story, it's not a ganja story, it's an African story." He saw his residence in Africa as a fulfillment of the Coptic prophecy:

> I remember that one time Brother Tommy and I were sitting outside with Brother Keith and Brother Ivy, and there were a couple sisters there. It was midafternoon; most people were out working. And Brother Keith and Brother Ivy started talking, and they said, "One day we're gonna have boats and cars, we're gonna run the island, we're gonna have big houses, we're going to have a big boat and we're going to fill it with ganja, and we're going to go to Africa and they're going to welcome us." And I'm sitting there afflicted. We didn't have a dime. It was totally insane, to the outside person. But they were very sure, and

they really believed. And I thought, "Wow, I can't wait." I think because we were the white men, we filled a certain prophecy by being there, and that built their faith. Eventually many of those things came true. And here I am in Africa, so . . .

THE END IS A BEGINNING

I mention in the introduction to this chapter that an analysis of the Ethiopian Zion Coptic Church can give us insights into the imbrication and incommensurability of theological and juridical modes of testimony and evidence. Here, the same evidence is being mobilized to support truth claims in both registers. For the Coptics, the massive movement of ganja—itself a vehicle toward an embodied consciousness and power—was what enabled the manifestation of Black Jamaicans' reconstitution and, therefore, of the elaboration of a universal humanity that centered Africa and Africans. It was what allowed them, under Nyah Keith's leadership, to find their true purpose, which became, as they saw it, to radically decolonize, to meaningfully integrate, and to monumentally redistribute the wealth in Jamaica from the inheritors of colonial privilege to the descendants of those who enabled that privilege. For Coptics detractors, ganja trafficking was a reflection of the opposite: It instantiated the white, capitalist penetration of an economy that was already under siege by the US government, which protected them as citizens and as inheritors of a superpower at the height of the Cold War, whether they disavowed it or not. Although both perspectives would likely position a figure like Nyah as someone in the right place at the right time who was able to play both ends against the middle on multiple levels and toward different ends, the truth claims each camp espouses are irreconcilable. This is because, where the geopolitical-juridical frame directs our attention to the political economy supporting or hindering Black liberation both nationally and globally, the spiritual-theological frame pushes us to consider how profound internal transformations redound to the material world, without being fully consumed by it— that paradox itself being a tenet of Christianity (to be in the world but not of it).

We could think about this as a problem of *gnosis*, to return to Sylvia Wynter's (1977) engagement with Jonas's work, which I limned earlier. If knowledge, for the early Christian heretics, was seen to transform both psychic and material infrastructures, if it is to deliver us from the flawed material existence of the physical world to a spiritual oneness with God our "native land," if it strives toward transcendence through personal religious experience catalyzed by a redeemer (in this case, Nyah Keith, in the metaphysical lineage of Marcus Garvey and Louva

Williams, rather than HIM Haile Selassie, in the physiological lineage of King Solomon), if it is meant to answer the existential questions Who am I? What is the meaning of life? Why am I here?, then what is at issue is the body and its relationality at multiple scales. Patrick, David, and Alan, among others, understood their individual bodily changes (the sores, their intensifying consciousness) as evidence of the strength and righteousness of the body of the church (because the church is not an infrastructure that is external to "man"), and therefore of their oneness with God (because "man is God and God is man"). This oneness then connected them to a worldwide body of Africans and their descendants, now ascendant—through the perfection of salvation. While they worked with and through the infrastructures of the body of the nation-state, their attention to the inherently imperfect world was instrumental insofar as it was oriented toward the building of the kingdom on earth. This is not unlike the ways Florida Seminoles have exploited casino revenues to "generate new forms of inalienability and distinctiveness" for their tribe (Cattelino 2008, 99), creating the conditions for enhanced autonomy and the redistribution of wealth. In this regard, the Coptics would not have been unlike other groups of Rastafari, such as the International Peacemakers, who sought to create "Africa" in Jamaica, or others who continue to envision repatriation to the continent.[32] They would have seen the nation-state and its political infrastructures—those fiercely defended by detractors who understood the Coptics to be undermining a worldly project of sovereignty through a transnational traffic they understood as extractive and opportunistic—as an idol, as image, as myth.

Recounting the story of the Coptics, one that remains unresolved and somewhat secretive in Jamaica, is also a way to think through the relationships between testimonial and ethnographic gnosis. If we look again at their narratives of arrival (to Jamaica, to the worldview of the Coptics), do we not see parallels to the older anthropological arrival stories that often introduced ethnographic texts? Don't their stories of coming gradually into consciousness mirror earlier anthropological narratives of slowly learning the languages and sociocultural processes of one or another community? Aren't they enacting a sort of canonical articulation of moving from a position of radical difference to one of understanding and relation, an articulation that also animates many anthropological texts? As they give accounts of their acts of faith, does this inspire accountability to our own?

CODA

I sent this chapter to both David and Alan for feedback, and I reproduce the feedback from Alan here,[33] to be accountable to him and to his story, and therefore to the spiritual understanding of the Coptics he feels should be paramount. What follows is text from several WhatsApp exchanges in mid-September and October 2024.

Sunday, September 15, 2024

[ALAN]

Hello Deborah . . . Trust you are well and enjoying the last days of summer. Wow, that one chapter is very massive, and well written, kudos to you. I have just skimmed it and since it's an academic study, I am sure you need to cover all aspects. I found it had a very large reliance on all the skeptics and critics. Dawn Ritch, Lloyd Williams, the other academics. Since none of these people really knew nothing of the church, except their own theories, they viewed the church through a highly prejudiced lens. Their testimonies are just conjecture, none of them have any facts. Since the opening salvos are all so negative, and from supposedly authorized sources, I think the reader will get a highly tainted and untruthful idea of what occurred. Of course, I do not think you can explain the story in an academic or literal way, and I understand that the audience that will be reading this are academic and I think they will prefer these explanations. Appreciate that you gave my testimony so much care and featured it.

Very interesting to me to hear David and Patrick talk about the curse. I would never say something like that. These kind of movements cannot be judged in the moment or short periods of time. I know Niah [sic] was not about material gain or gathering riches. This movement was above simplistic biblical interpretation, or self-interpretation of something, that had roots, far from those that had these unusual and unfounded thoughts. David and Patrick never spent significant time in Kingston or with Niah, so their testimonies should be taken in that light. So many of the people you interviewed had limited understanding of the mission or the work that was being done. And because there was a lot of physical wealth involved, a lot of people, to this day, concentrate on that aspect.

Congratulate you on a well thought out and comprehensive writing, as I previously said. I think it is impossible to explain this story in an academic or intellectual way. Hoping the movie takes a different direction. Hope you do not take offense at my remarks, trying to tell you what I really thought. Sending you a lot of love from Cape Town, hope you return soon.

[DEBORAH]
Hey there, wow! Sorry, was in yoga and then had a couple meetings. Now I have to run to a screening but just wanted to thank you for getting to this so quickly and for offering the feedback. I'll write more tomorrow, but I hear what you're saying about the skeptics. My hope was by putting them first and following with the heartfelt testimonies (whether or not some of the others had the full knowledge you had), it would give the sense of dispensing with that skeptical mode of approaching the Coptics as we end with the importance of the spiritual understanding. And of course, you must know that that is still a strong line of thinking in Jamaica, which is why I wanted to lay out what the spiritual mission was. My hope is that in the context of the book, which in all three chapters really seeks to highlight spiritual and embodied ways of knowing, coming to know and living in relation with others, people end up there instead of with the juridical modes we are asked to privilege. But more soon . . . thank you, so much, for reading it! BTW, we will be in Johannesburg next March, doing a talk and some *Kumina* drumming, bringing people from Jamaica. Any chance you think you'd be able to meet us there?;)

[ALAN]

Hi Deborah . . . Very happy you had such a full and nice Sunday, keep up the good work. Forgive me if I am overstepping and giving you too much feedback. I just wonder, when Marcus Garvey was kicked out of America, and the physical manifestation of the UNIA started to crumble, did people say the curse came down on Marcus, because he was using too much symbolism and material things, to make his people[?] Parades, uniforms, corporations, were part of his strategy to make his people understand who they were. They were not the purpose of his teachings, but a tool that opened a certain line of thought within his followers. He understood it was a physical manifestation, yet it had a spiritual understanding. Time has proven that is the spirit of his work that lives on and enlightens millions today. People are aware of the physical things that he did and promoted. But his legacy is in the mind of his spirit and the intention of his heart.

Hope it is not a bother, but there are certain thoughts in the chapter that need serious rebuttal. When I came across the church, the brethren were living in obscurity, as they had been for many decades. Through Niah's work and mastering of the material words and goods, the church became known and discussed worldwide. Affecting many many people and cultures. If we did not use this material wealth to make our message and presence known, would fifty years after people remember us? It is testament to the power of what was done that decades later, books are being written, films produced, we are still a topic of conversation and thought. The work of the church was very complex, and Niah understood the legacy, and tried to pass it on to future generations. Do not forget when things were going good and prosperity was flowing to one and all, everyone said we were partaking of God's blessing. Only when tribulation came and the flow of money and goods, etc., stopped, then these things that everyone said were blessings became the reason for a curse.

The main problem I have with the chapter is that you start out with a large dose of the critics and skeptics, and it seems to lend credence that this was all about money and the material. I am sure you understand the real nature of the movement. I think you have to understand the nature of Jamaican thinking, and the intensity of the times we operated, especially in Kingston, and surrounding Niah. To really get through the superficial and limited thinking that so many promote. BTW, the program in Jo-burg sounds fantastic. Will try my best to attend. Any chance you could bring it to Cape Town?

[DEB]

Hi Alan, sorry I didn't get back to this discussion yesterday—I was on leave last year and have come back as chair of our department, and I haven't quite stepped out of the overwhelm yet! Anyway, I appreciate your comments very much, and also want to reiterate that we are with you on what you are sharing. I agree that it is impossible to explain the story of the Coptics through the discourses of law and politics, which are the discourses being mobilized by journalists and others, and this is part of the point I am trying to make with the chapter. By laying out what the "skeptics" are saying, which reflects their own attachments to the nation-state, or developmentalism, or to socialism, to differ-ent visions of Black self-realization or whatever else, I am hoping to show how their frames for understanding and assessing the Coptics are primarily juridical, and that these frames are incom-patible with the spiritual frames you (and others) are mobilizing to understand the movement toward Black repair. You, clearly, are in the best position to understand and reflect what Niah was envisioning, and what you all were part of, and I'm hoping this is represented by ending the chapter with your words of experienc-ing the prophecy they articulated not long after you first arrived, and how even your presence in South Africa is part of the fulfill-ment of that prophecy.

It is also true that David and Patrick, whose understanding is based on a different position in relation to the movement, also had transformative experiences, even if you don't think what they're saying reflects the deep understanding you would have because of your closeness with Niah. Even the brethren we spoke with in Florida, who were perhaps even more removed from the Jamaican moment to moment, were so profoundly affected by their experiences in that time, and this is, in itself, compelling, not in terms of their narration of the history and possibilities of the movement, but in terms of what it offered them, and how it traveled through them, however incompletely.

I hope it is clear in the chapter that Niah envisioned the material as means to an end (the liberation of Black people)! Of course, others would have had a different relationship to the material—some of the Americans would have been interested in the excitement of the trade; some of the Jamaicans who, as things began to diminish materially, would have moved on. Yet it is my belief (and of course I'm not alone) that movements never "die"; they continue to circulate unpredictably in ways that people later take up and move forward (this is something I wrote about in my last book regarding the International Peace-makers Association—maybe you know about them?). It's also true that there is still interest in the Coptics, as you point out, not only because of the way spirit moves but also because of the material dimensions of what was happening at the time in Jamaica, and how people are still struggling to understand that moment, which was so incredibly formative for my generation, and those before me. A short film recently emerged on the internet (will send it to you but maybe you've already seen it), which is about the Coptics but which misses the history, the expansiveness, and the genius and generosity of Niah. Our hope is that by foregrounding testimonies—like your own, which would feature prominently for all the reasons you list—our own film will create a different understanding of the movement than the one that sees it only through the lens of the Cold War, etc.

A small thought on David and Patrick's testimonies: . . . I don't read in them that they were "all about money and the material." David explicitly says that this was not about the money, that the money was a tool for liberation, and that his duty was to generate it (but that he was interested in the spiritual message). Patrick has another story, but it was also he who brought us to this project, and we want to honor that. We are grateful for having been directed to you. I guess when we were there we didn't talk very much about Sis Lorna, right? Was wondering about it, because when we were there with her, she talked a lot about her own testimony, but didn't want to be on camera (which of course is fine). . . . At any rate, one thing that is possible in the book—if you're interested—is to represent your feedback . . . what do you think? I would like you to feel like your concerns are acknowledged and present, but of course you'd have to be comfortable with this. . . . Re Joburg—really hope you can come!! It might be difficult to also bring it to Cape Town (though this is something we'd really like) just because of the timing of classes, etc., but we'll look into it, maybe at Chimurenga. . . . Have to hear back from my friend in Amsterdam, where we are going after South Africa, about his dates for us.

[ALAN]
Hello Deborah . . . Thank you for such a thoughtful and excellent response. Just starting the semester, as department head, must be daunting. Of course, I am sure you will navigate in the best way. I really appreciate what you are doing and the understanding you have. Since you and Junior are both Jamaican, it gives you certain understandings that those outside of the culture might not get. Do not mean to disparage any of the brothers and sisters. Everyone will take something different away from the journey. Happy most still perceive it as a blessing and uplifting their thoughts. Have nothing but love for David and Patrick. Was upset in the interpretation of a curse on the church. I think that comes from trying to self-interpret the scripture, a trap for many throughout history and it seemed to verify what the many skeptics were wrongly saying. David is definitely understanding of the spiritual nature of the doctrine and is a spiritual brother. Many take spiri-

tuality in a simplistic way, trying [to] separate a reality that exists to something more supernatural.

Let me reread the chapter, in more th[o]rough and relaxed manner. So impressed with the thoroughness of your work, it is amazing to me. Appreciate you are trying to tell the story as it should be told. Thanking you for spending time in considering what I said, it is very meaningful to me. Sending you and Junior much love ♡, from Africa

I guarantee you a full house if you bring your project to Cape Town, sounds so special and exciting

[DEB]
Hmm, yes on their sense of "curse." Could work to clarify this in the chapter . . . will look forward to your thoughts after "relaxed" reading, and we can talk more about it! ☺

We talked again on October 7, and Alan reiterated his complaint that the journalists and academics who were skeptical were getting so much air in the beginning of the chapter:

Dawn Ritch had it in for us, and Lloyd Williams got all his information from a very dubious character, so I don't count them. A lot of people rode us to fame. You know who Steve Croft is? One of the main hosts on *60 Minutes* for a number of years. He did a five-part series on us for local Miami news and that catapulted him from channel 10 Miami to *60 Minutes*.

I think a lot of the intellectual and the academic people, a lot of it has racial overtones, whether they're Black or white. I think there's classist overtones to it. They don't want to accept that this could be a Black man with basically a lot of uneducated people that made all this happen. I find it so absurd that they go into this long thing about the CIA to co-opt Rasta because it was getting too popular and it was revolutionary, we were just following the doctrine. We never had long political discussions. We just wanted to promote this doctrine. Everyone wanted to interpret it like we were part of something, a niche of the 1970s, which was socialism v. capitalism, but we had nothing to do with that. We never talked about that kind of stuff, we just promoted the doctrine as it was given to us. People still hold on to this day to the CIA thing, but everyone went to jail. If you work for the CIA they find a way to get you out!

This was a doctrine that Brother Louva Williams formulated in the 1950s and we were just following his teachings when it came to Haile Selassie, and the schism in Rasta was something we kind of inherited. Reading the statements, it comes off like we invented the schism, but we were inheriting teachings that came down to us. To say we brought this to destroy democratic socialism, like the CIA gave us a template to undermine a higher cause, makes no sense because we were following a doctrine that had been developed 25 years prior to us coming. We fought against communism, we fought against socialism, we fought against capitalism, we were against isms, we wanted a more spiritual understanding.

What Alan is arguing is that Nyah and the Coptics were about the liberation of Black Jamaicans, and they didn't discriminate. When they gave money to help people, whether it was a policeman, a gangster, or whoever, it was always in the spirit of redemption, to help them understand who they were and to hope they would also pass this on to someone else. "We hoped that the charity would redeem their thinking," he said. This was charity that was not partisan, not part of the "schisms" of the 1970s, but instead had come down from Louva Williams's teachings from the 1950s. The dissolution of their manifestation in the early 1980s couldn't, therefore, have been a curse. The death of Nyah meant the movement had to take on a different manifestation, in the hearts of all whom the Coptics touched.

3
EMBODIMENTS

During the Salem witch trials in seventeenth-century Massachusetts a new form of evidence became legally admissible. "Spectral evidence" consisted of witness accounts of their torment by the spectral images of those they accused of witchcraft, images that could appear during a dream or a "fit." In 1692, when Betty Parris and Abigail Williams accused Sarah Good, Sarah Osborne, and "Tituba" of witchcraft, they testified "that they or Specters in their Shapes did grievously torment them" (Hale [1702] 1914, 414). As in other cases, spectral evidence referred to the appearance of ghosts or the spirits of the dead who were threatening the accusers. Spectral evidence, difficult as it would have been to refute, was generally positioned as corroborating other forms of evidence, such as a confession or eyewitness testimony. At issue with spectral evidence is the agency and autonomy of the body; indeed, this has been an issue for some scholars of ritual possession, as it has also been for those attempting to disentangle questions of sovereignty from questions of agency.[1]

In her analysis of the role of the body as a medium in early American spiritualism, and therefore in mediating these trials, artist and anthropologist Erin Yerby (2016) argues that "what is on trial, what stands accused under spectral evidences, is this uncontainable potency of the body" (93). For Yerby, the spectral body is excessive, both materially and temporally; it is a medium "where past and future, before and after, crack open a flattened present" (103). In this cracking open, the spectral body is also a portal to and through the historical processes that frame and generate accusations of witchcraft. Tituba, for example, was identified by Betty Parris and Abigail Williams as their "Indian" maid, but court records describe her as "'a slave originating from the West Indies and probably practicing "hoodoo"'" (V. Tucker 2000, 624), a woman who arrived in Massachusetts from Barbados and who subsequently married an "Indian" man.[2] While the girls may have directly understood themselves to have seen the specter of Tituba, what was really haunting them were the twin processes of their community's dispossession and genocide of Pequot natives (Yerby 2016) and the trafficking of enslaved Africans to the West Indies and North American colonies. Similarly, the "witch hunts" in Cuba near the beginning of the twentieth century reflected elite anxieties about respectability at a time of intensifying American dominance, political and economic (Palmié 2002). And in Paul Stoller's (1994) study of Hauka spirit possession, possessed bodies actually enact colonial memories, which Stoller analyzes as a form of mimesis. For those practitioners among whom he lived, "spirit possession is a set of embodied practices that constitutes power-in-the-world" (636). In other words, it effaces the tenuous border between ritual practice and (geo)political practice.

We are indeed inclined to read witchcraft and other forms of ritual possession through the specter of the sociopolitical, to understand these as responses to the exigencies or uncertainties of any given contemporary moment.[3] James Siegel (2005) has argued that anthropological attention to witchcraft has tended to sanitize the violence associated with phantasms—either the violence generated by those assumed to be witches or that deriving from community attempts to neutralize the witch. This sanitization reflects, Siegel argues, one of the legacies of structural-functionalist and structuralist approaches in anthropology, which is to understand the eradication of the witch as a way to repair whatever social breach the witch has introduced into a community (in contradistinction to an approach that would interpret witchcraft through the language of social deviance and unproductive violence). If a witch—a human being who is able "to cause harm to their fellows by the exercise of powers not possessed by ordinary folk, powers which operate in a manner that cannot be detected, so that the cause can only be recognized when the damage comes to light" (Mair, cited in Siegel 2005, 11)—if such a person can be put to death, the threat to community cohesion has been destroyed and the social can be reconstituted.

However, if we understand the past (and not just one past) to live in the present, and if we do not observe a strict division between life and death, then these matters become more complex. We cannot eliminate the broader histories that cohere in the figure of the witch; their earthly embodiment may be eradicated, but we are still haunted. If, as Siegel (2005) argues with respect to witchcraft in early modern Euro-America, "witchcraft brings people to the limit of their understanding of others in regard to themselves" (10), then it also gives bodily form to what has been disavowed, namely, the global historical processes that created the conditions for Europeans to be in the presence of, inhabiting the land of, and exploiting the labor of others. And if the power of witchcraft lies outside and is unassimilable to the secular state, then it exists as a threat to the state, though in complex and indeterminate ways. In this sense, the ways that people "catch power," which is how the Trinidadian obeah practitioners with whom Brent Crosson (2019b) worked activate dynamic relationships of agency, also allow us to "question unitary conceptions of sovereignty in Western political theory" (609), seeing it instead as performative and as distributed among "powers that exceed and inhabit human frames" (Crosson 2019b, 610; see also Crosson 2020).

The body, here, becomes a medium not only for historical and ancestral meaning but also for the transcendence of Western juridical conceptualizations of personhood. Roberto Strongman (2019) has argued that a kind of transcorporeality is distinctive to African diasporic communities but is reflective of broader African conceptualizations of personhood, in which the human soul is "multiple, removable, and external to the body that functions as its receptacle" (2). The real tragedy of imperialism and slavery, Strongman argues, was not that it positioned Africans as primitive, backward, and soulless but that its discourse of interiority closed off their "philosophical corporeal openness while at the same time legislatively prohibiting precisely those religious rituals of trance possession that render black bodies inhabited or soulful" (4). What Strongman is contending is that bodily experiences predate the transatlantic slave trade, and that we still have a haptic (if not strictly genealogical) inheritance of these. In Jamaica, obeah is part of a broader "myal complex," an African-based religious ethos oriented toward healing and deliverance from the ontological degradations of slavery. This complex generated what Sylvia Wynter (1970) called the "indigenization" of African descendants in the so-called New World, by which she meant the processes through which Black people humanized the landscape of plantation-based slave production by peopling it with their gods and spirits.

Myal was identified by planters as early as the 1760s (Long 1774) as a worldview that, in separating the body from the mind-soul, conceptualized individuals as possessing multiple souls and understood the dead as part of the living world. Having been thus identified, it was simultaneously seen as evidence of enslaved people's inherent backwardness and the source of their resistance to the regimes of the plantation. As such, it was outlawed by the colonial state, which nevertheless meant it was constantly produced by the very legal apparatus that was attempting to eradicate it, though in different ways at different historical moments (Paton 2015). But witchcraft, or forms of spiritual practice that include possession, is now not everywhere juridically prohibited. In Cameroon, Siegel (2005) reminds us, witchcraft is recognized by the state and adjudicated through the justice system, and this kind of recognition produces the irony of a sovereign state recognizing an extrajudicial and, ultimately, irrational power (and by "irrational" here I mean to point to witchcraft and possession as inherently unstable, "sensed or suspected" [Siegel 2005, 2], rather than transparently knowable through reason). Recognition also arrives through the elaboration of postcolonial cultural policy, as in Jamaica, where African Jamaican folk practices have become recognized by the state as expressions of cultural heritage that should be preserved through documentation, instruction, and performance. This kind of recognition is ultimately a form of containment, but in ritual practices that involve possession, we see an openness to different embodiments, temporalities, and modes of being in community. In myal, it is not witches but ancestors who appear to communicate with those inhabiting contemporary temporal terrain, and to "catch myal" is to serve as a medium for these ancestors. It is, by another name, possession; and this spiritual meaning of possession is the B side to the juridical sense of possession I outlined in the introduction. Myal thus marks the nonlinear and unexpected ways something that feels like power circulates and is transmitted from one to another, today, yesterday, and maybe tomorrow.

This *myal complex* encompasses the practice of *kumina*, which emerged in Jamaica when indentured laborers were brought from the Kongo region of Central Africa after the abolition of slavery in 1838. Many of these laborers would have been among those who were enslaved by Spanish or Portuguese traffickers but were subsequently recaptured by British ships patrolling the Atlantic after the abolition of the (British) slave trade in 1807; relocated to either Sierra Leone or

St. Helena, where they would have met the many maroons who had also been settled there decades before (Chopra 2018); and sent from there to the New World as part of postemancipation indentured labor schemes that would bring Africans, and subsequently Indians from the subcontinent, to the Caribbean to work on sugar plantations (Warner-Lewis 1977; Schuler 1980). Scholars and artists alike have probed *kumina* as one of many "folk forms" in Jamaica, evidence both of civilization (or the lack thereof, depending on the interlocutor) and of continuities with Africa (in other words, a cultural inheritance beyond slavery). Artists, other cultural workers, and nationalist states have mobilized *kumina*, like other aspects of Jamaica's "folk cultures," as part of an anticolonial turn away from Eurocentric markers of cultural competence and an attempt to inculcate people into an understanding of their cultural value in the context of new political arrangements. I will have more to say about these processes later in this chapter, but my own interest here lies in what we can glean about the bodily enactment and transmission of the forms of knowledge and relation forged through practices like *kumina*, and what this gleaning can tell us about the practice of anthropology.

For the past five years, I have co-organized (with Junior "Gabu" Wedderburn, Nicholas "Rocky" Allen, and the St. Thomas Kumina Collective) a *kumina* festival called Tambufest. Our intention with Tambufest is to create space for dignity, healing, and collectivity. The festival is part community fun day, part discussion (or "reasoning," as it is called in the Jamaican context), and part performed ritual practice, and it is designed to bring people together in community to reflect on issues that affect their lives. In past years, we've facilitated moderated discussions about political violence, about prostate cancer and healing, and about the various forms of land dispossession that are afoot across Jamaica. Our intention with these reasonings is to chart new futures, explicitly and unconsciously, through the portal of *kumina* and the relations it brings into being. If myal is a *science* of attunement that produces the potentiality of giving-on-and-with others toward a relational, iterative practice of unbounded being, an inheritance in which present, past, and future are repeated and joined, it is this potentiality that we are trying to produce with Tambufest.

Because we have recorded the festival every year, and because others have also recorded it, we have amassed a fairly large visual archive of the practices and discussions we have featured. Drawing from this archive, from interviews with elder practitioners, and from our own reflections on the process of organizing the festival from year to year, this chapter positions bodily surrender (to myal, to one another) as a mechanism of knowledge transfer and community building in which the body—individually, collectively, and ancestrally—is limitless. It is this limitlessness, this unboundedness, that dismantles Western juridical conceptualizations of sovereignty. Myal thus brings into existence an embodied archive of being through which we might experience autonomy without authority, sovereignty without solidity, and surrender without subordination. At the same time, bodily unboundedness generates a range of vulnerabilities that demand a perceptual attunement, also embodied, in the service of ongoing cooperative praxis. Relation, simply put, is hard work and requires the ongoing commitment of interpretive communities that are more broadly defined than has been conventional within anthropology.

THE SCIENCE OF FOLKLORE

During the same period that Morris Steggerda and Charles Davenport were doing their eugenics study, folklorists like Martha Beckwith were also conducting research in Jamaica. Like the eugenicists, Beckwith was interested in processes of acculturation and in the ways the beliefs, customs, and superstitions of "the folk" offered windows on both an African past and a hybrid present. Her *Black Roadways: A Study of Folk Life in Jamaica*, published in 1929 (the same year that Davenport and Steggerda's *Race Crossing* appeared), offered an elaboration of folk ingenuity and an indictment of Jamaica's upper classes: "In every case where a sophisticated and a backward race meet, the problem lies not with the folk who absorb and re-create but with the upper classes who absorb and imitate" (Beckwith 1929, xi). Notwithstanding this critique, Beckwith, like other early folklorists, believed that the study of folklore helped educators and reformers involved in uplift-oriented projects identify "how much African heritage remained to be rooted out" in the context of their efforts to Christianize formerly enslaved people (Baker 2010, 34).

Historian of anthropology Lee D. Baker (2010) points out that this orientation to folklore emerged in the context of US empire with missionaries like Rev. Richard Armstrong, whose work in the Sandwich and Hawai'ian islands during the 1840s measured the success of his tethering of industrial education to Christian civilization by the extent to which folklore and folk practices were disappearing. Armstrong's son Samuel Chapman Armstrong went on to found the Hampton Institute, where Alice Bacon established a folklore society with the seemingly contradictory aims of collecting folklore in order to root out superstitions and civilize rural Black southerners, and preserving the songs and stories that constituted what W. W. Newell, founder of the American Folklore Society,[4] understood as "the learning or knowledge peculiar to the Negro race" and "that mass of information which they brought with them from Africa" (Newell, quoted in Baker 2010, 56). This view of folklore also aligned with the more general post-Darwinian view, adapted by Victorian cultural evolutionists such as Edward B. Tylor, which understood comparative anthropology to be a "'science which undertakes to investigate the development of the human mind, through its various stages of animal, savage, and civilized life'" (W. W. Newell, quoted in Stocking 1968, 121). The study of folklore, which entailed the same processes of collection, classification, and comparison followed in anthropometric research, was therefore initially intended to elaborate an evolutionary hierarchy of mental development.

Martha Beckwith collected stories over six weeks during the summer of 1919, five weeks in the winter of 1921, and then again in 1924. Her first research report, *Jamaica Anansi Stories* (1924), was essentially a list of folktales, "set down without polish or adornment, as nearly as possible as they were told to me" (xi). She divided the tales into "Animal Stories," "Old Stories," "[stories] Chiefly of Sorcery," "Modern European Stories," and "Dance and Song." Her focus was on numbers—how many stories people knew, and how many they were willing to tell on any given day. It is in the endnotes where Beckwith presented commentary and context, "Notes to the Tales," as she put it. Here, we find comparisons with other stories that had been collected by other researchers, as well as discussions of how particular elements also appeared in stories from other African diasporic contexts. For example, in her notes to "Tiger as Riding Horse," she wrote:

> The story is very common in Jamaica and presents no local variations from the form familiar in America. In Parkes's version, the "two misses" become two "post-mistresses." In a version by Knight, a school-master in the Santa Cruz mountains, Tacoomah is the horse and the story ends, "From that day the saddle fasten on Brer Tacoomah's back." Knight explained that "Brer Tacoomah is a large spider with yellow spots and a broad back shaped like a saddle," and that the story was told to explain this characteristic.
>
> Other Jamaica versions are found in Milne-Home, 51–63; Pamela Smith, 17; and Wona, 19–23. In Wona's version, the story is made to explain "why gungo-peas are always covered with Tacoomahs," a species of spider.
>
> Compare Parsons, Andros Island, 30 and note; Sea Islands, 53; for comparative references.

Tremearne, FL 21:205, and Tailed-Head-Hunters, 322, tells a Hausa story of a Hyena who has stolen a holy man's horse. Spider offers to bring the Hyena to him in its place, and persuades Hyena, under pretence of taking him to a dead animal, to be saddled and bridled and ridden by Spider to the holy man, who then mounts Hyena and completes his journey.

In Ellis, Yoruba 265, Tortoise rides Elephant into town to sustain an idle boast.

In Smith's Brazil version, the little animal is tied on for safety, and takes care to slip into a hold when he finally dismounts.

In Ernst, VBGAEU 20:277 (Venezuela), Rabbit rides Tiger across a river. The story is coupled here with the murder in midstream. (235)

Beckwith provides this comparative analysis for each of the 149 stories in the book, an analytic process that recalls Davenport and Steggerda's comparisons of their results to other anthropometric studies. In both cases, the emphasis was on building a global database of sorts in order to further enable this comparative approach.

Black Roadways (1929) is a more narratively presented text in which Beckwith does not merely reproduce particular songs and stories but also provides ethnographic context surrounding Jamaicans' beliefs and customs, with chapters detailing Jamaica's history and geography; fishing, trapping, and stock raising; family practices; health practices; attitudes toward death and the spirit world; and various ritual practices (with special consideration of the effects of the great revival of 1860). Throughout, she argues that while folklore represents the worldview of peasants, its "rhythmic melancholy or rollic, its shrewd wisdom, as even its superstition, penetrate the life and thought of white and colored alike of the literate classes, and leave an impress upon their speech, attitude, emotion" (Beckwith 1929, x). Beckwith ends up indicting the church for what she sees as a narrow focus on spiritual enlightenment in the face of material impoverishment. She also criticizes the British for declining to offer opportunities for work and entertainment that could counter "the problems of folk shiftlessness" (225). And while she acknowledges the richness of Jamaican language, song, and story, she nevertheless positions it within the evolutionary narrative of the colonial civilization project:

> The knowledge of the belief of the folk and especially of its outer expression in life and art, while it leaves much to deplore, also gives encouragement for the future. We find a lively, imitative race with a strong practical philosophy and native wit. Especially we observe that genius for outer form which goes

to the making of a harmonious social life and to its dramatic rendering in song and art as a means for stabilizing the inner passions. Much has been done to encourage that sense of order through the imposition of British law and British social and religious patterns. More must, however, be done to bring the great mass of the folk out of their present social isolation into a more robust and wholesome way of thinking and living. (222–23)

This orientation toward folklore would change beginning a bit later in the 1920s (Baker 2010). The Harlem Renaissance, the US military occupation of Haiti, the renewal of Ethiopianism (as a result of Italy's second attempt to invade and colonize), and the elaboration of pan-Africanism (due to Marcus Garvey's establishment of the United Negro Improvement Association) would catalyze a view of folklore as constituting an African heritage and, therefore, as something to be protected, preserved, and embraced. In "folk" or "popular" cultural practices, scholars and activists began to see modes of cultural memory and tools of resistance to white supremacy throughout the Americas; the stories presented a theory of colonial life in a plantation zone, a theory peppered with tricksters, herbalists, and magicians, persons who could make a way out of no way. Melville Herskovits famously framed these resonances of African cultural practices in the New World "survivals," and his call for the programmatic study of the "Negro in the New World" (1930)—a call that emerged in part from his own prior anthropometric work on racial hybridity and the question of variability (Herskovits 1927)—encouraged anthropologists and other observers to attend to the dynamics of acculturation in conditions of extreme inequality. His own "scale of Africanisms" (Herskovits [1941] 1990) prompted a search for continuities between African and African diasporic ontologies and epistemologies among scholars in the United States, but also throughout the Caribbean and Latin America, and Herskovits himself conducted research in Haiti, Trinidad, and Dutch Guiana, elaborating his continuity thesis with evidence from each location.

While Herskovits popularized the Africanisms paradigm, he was, as Kevin Yelvington (2006) has pointed out, only one scholar within a broader network concerned about thinking through the political uses of elaborating an African cultural heritage. This network included Jean Price-Mars, and Herskovits's unacknowledged theoretical debt to Price-Mars is evident throughout *Life in a Haitian Valley*, in which he discussed the *combite* system of cooperative economic production and marketing, extended-family systems, the institution of *plaçage*, deference toward elders, and especially Vodun as elements of a West African (specifically Dahomean) cultural heritage.[5] In *Ainsi parla l'oncle* (1928), Price-Mars had reevaluated and affirmed African-derived folklore in Haiti as the necessary foundation for nationalist development and cultural self-esteem within the context of the US occupation.[6] For him, the politics of acknowledging Vodun and other peasant practices as central to Haitian culture writ large had to do with the rejection of not only US occupation but also what he called middle-class Haitians' *"bovarysme collectif,"* their rejection of local cultural practices and embrace of all things French.[7]

That the discovery of "Africanisms" in New World Black societies became an important political project in emergent anticolonial movements is also reflected in Sir Philip Sherlock's prefatory remarks to the 1966 edition of Walter Jekyll's 1907 book, *Jamaican Song and Story* ([1907] 1966). Sherlock, a Jamaican historian, champion of the popular arts, and the first vice chancellor of the University of the West Indies, credited Jekyll's efforts, and those of other scholars like him, as having bestowed value on Anancy stories and folk songs in a "semi-feudal Jamaica of the old plantation . . . at a time when they were despised as 'Negro talk' and 'old-time sayings'" (Jekyll [1907] 1966, viii). By 1966, four years after independence, these songs and stories would be repositioned as part of a legacy that provided Jamaicans with a new identificatory certainty.

While the continuity argument shaped much of the intellectual and political attention to popular cultural practices among Africans throughout the diaspora after the 1930s, it also spurred some scholars to elaborate a theory of cultural transmission that positioned popular practices not just as emblematic of heritage or instantiations of resistance but also as evolutions from a cultural baseline within new structural contexts. These scholars critiqued the central role given to slavery as deterministic of the persistence (or loss) of African cultural patterns that grounds both the Herskovitsian and Frazierian paradigms. Trinidadian sociolinguist Mervyn Alleyne (1988) articulated this position:

> It is important to go beyond the folkloristic tabulation of "quaint" artifacts and the matching of them with counterparts in Africa. We must deal rather with evolutionary processes and seek explanatory models that can cover most data and answer most questions about the development of . . . Afro-American culture in general. These questions include not only what things "survived," but why they survived; why are there more, and different, surviv-

als in some areas of Afro-America and in some segments of each individual Afro-American society than in others; and is "survival" the most appropriate term for conceptualizing Africa-based culture in the New World. (4)

Alleyne's (1988) argument is that "culture" cannot be inventoried as a set of traits that can be mapped across the African diaspora (or that have been lost), but that instead it must be conceptualized as both "'becoming' and as 'being'" in dynamic ways (5). Further, he wanted us to see these processes of becoming and being as complex and specific to the particularities of one or another location rather than universal across space and time. In this way, Alleyne argued that the focus on slavery as universally deterministic precluded a more dynamic understanding of the processes by which people who were forcefully displaced from a homeland drew from "memories of, or habits or predispositions acquired from," ancestral cultures as they built new institutions to accommodate their needs and desires in particular new places (23). In his understanding, "culture" did not merely produce "resistance"; instead, the "will to resist required the preservation of some functional distinctiveness in culture" (69). This more processual accounting of the linguistic and religious variation among Africans and people of African descent in the New World marks an understanding of cultural process that is actor driven rather than typological (as it was for the physical anthropologists and geneticists discussed in chapter 1), and it allows us to gain insights into moments of stability and instability, continuity and discontinuity. If we agree with Alleyne, then we must see our inheritances and our embodied archives as iterative and relational.

ARCHIVES OF THE BOUNDLESS BODY

What began with the realm of folktales and language extended to studies of ritual, and in Jamaica, *kumina* was central to these studies. Zora Neale Hurston was one of the earliest ethnographic observers of myal and other spiritual phenomena involving possession. In *Tell My Horse* ([1938] 1990), the ethnography that emerged from her field trips to Jamaica and Haiti in 1936, she wrote, "There *is no death*. Activities are merely changed from one condition to the other" (43; italics in original). Historian Vincent Brown (2008) has argued that this conceptual frame, common to spiritual practices across the Afro-Atlantic world, reflects the Akan *adinkra* "'Nyame nwu na mawu' (loosely translated, 'God does not die, so I cannot die')." This is a conceptual frame that refuses the grip of Western temporal reckoning and it continues to be a feature of many of the diverse religious practices in Jamaica, including *kumina*.

For practitioners, *kumina* is born in you; it is itself an inheritance and it defines a lineage. *Kumina* communities are often small family-based groups, sometimes called "nations" *or* "Bongo nations," led by a queen or king. In a *kumina* ceremony, the counterclockwise dancing, driven by the drums and marked by the singing, is meant to invite myal, that complex of being and knowing that heralds the return of ancestors and a surrender to spirit. In myal, the feet become heavy, the head "grows," consciousness wanes, the community of dancers rallies to care for the possessed individual—ushering in an old-new gnosis in which souls are not contained by bodies, the dead are not dead, the past is not past, the here and now is also the there and then and the possibility of something else to come.[8] It is myal that creates the conditions for healing and well-being, individually and collectively, today and in this world. It thus instantiates what Wynter (1977) identified as "radical difference," a difference grounded in the gods, beliefs, and modes of storytelling that accompanied Black people on slave ships, to build new worlds. In the world of *kumina*, progressive developmentalist teleologies are eschewed, binaries of body and soul are destabilized, and a conception of Africanness as "exponential" (Stewart 2005)—as encompassing both the particularities of ethnicity and a pan-Africanist sensibility—is advanced.

Where early American (or American-trained) observers of *kumina* reflected the acculturation and functionalist frameworks of many mid-twentieth-century anthropologists—for example, Joseph G. Moore (1953) (and Maureen Warner-Lewis [2016], who critiqued his research design and questions), George Simpson (1970), and Edward Seaga (1969)—later (and local) scholars came to understand *kumina* as evidence of the ontological and epistemological continuity of central African notions and practices of being within Jamaica (and here, I am thinking of Wynter [1977], Maureen Warner-Lewis [1977], Edward Brathwaite [1978], Kenneth Bilby and Fu-Kiau Kia Bunseki [1983], Cheryl Ryman [1984], and Dianne Stewart [2005]). These texts offer lists of ki-Kongo words as they are used among *kumina* practitioners; sketch out Bakongo and Bantu cosmologies; draw parallels between central African prohibitions against the eating of salt and the washing of clothes in the river, and those that have perdured among Jamaicans; and outline conceptual continuities in terms of "communotheism,"[9] possession, ancestral veneration, and herbalism. These interventions emerged from a more general effort during the 1960s and 1970s among West Indian scholars to reject the notion that a process of acculturation is what characterized Caribbean societies. They argued instead that the dominant European sector, often absent, did not provide a cultural and social scaffolding to which dominated Africans had to acclimatize, but that Afro–West Indians, in maintaining, reconstructing, and transforming their own cultural practices (especially those having to do with land use and religious expression), underwent a cultural process of indigenization that rooted them in the New World and that rejected colonial logics of personhood and production. For these scholars, and for those who followed them, it was the African heritage embedded in the cultures developed during the period of slavery that should be seen as the basis for Caribbean cultural creativity, and understanding the ontologies of *kumina*, therefore, became part of a decolonial intellectual and political praxis (Wynter 1970; Brathwaite 1971).

At once descriptive and analytic, these texts coalesce around the overarching principle that the body is unbounded. This principle is rooted in relationships between the living and the ancestors, relationships brought into view through drumming, dance, and myal.[10] Consider the following statements found in a selection of these canonical texts:

The relation of Man to his ancestral spirits is a historical and an actual living relation.... The dead are not the negation of life, but part of the life force. (Wynter 1970, 37)

The concept of the "living dead" provides African society with the major basis of its people's sense of continuity—as a family, a clan and a nation. (Warner-Lewis 1977, 77)

The god:spirit:ancestor: remains very close to the living:is in fact *part of the living*, and "worship" (the word is not even appropriate/accurate here) involves the possession of the living by the dead: by ancestors; by the god; or rather, it involves the frequent and accepted incarnation of the spirit: god into the community of the living; and the necessary and equilibrium-maintaining "opposite": the retained intimacy between these interpenetrating worlds. (Brathwaite 1978, 46)

If Kumina possesses a single most important organizing principle, it is the continuity between the ancestral dead and their living progeny.... The express purpose of any serious Kumina ceremony ... is to establish contact with the ancestral dead through the possession of living dancers by their spirits. . . . An essential aspect of Kumina, then, is the link it forges between generations, its maintenance of communication between the living and the dead. (Bilby and Bunseki 1983, 475)

In Kumina, the ancestors, suitably enticed, return to this corporal world through the possession of the living. They are fed and entertained and in return they provide the living with solutions to their problems, offering advice and vital knowledge not otherwise available to them. (Ryman 1984, 81–82)

African identity is restored and epitomized in the transcendent yet accessible ancestral community. Through ritual possession and other acts of devotion, Kumina Africans constantly strengthen the metaphysical continuity between the living and the dead, the visible and the invisible, the Bongo nation and the Bongo ancestors. With the assistance of the Ancestors, Kumina devotees configure a space for accessing and applying African ideas and values to the concrete tasks and challenges they confront in the visible dimension of life. (Stewart 2005, 145)

For these scholars, what is critical is that the ritual practice of *kumina* provides evidence for and access to modes of thinking and being in community that are not tethered to liberal, Western bodies. Instead, it instantiates a different "bodily technology of history making" (Johnson 2014b, 6–7). This history making is not universal, however, even among its community of practitioners. Because ancestral possessions in *kumina* are grounded in particular lineages, as in other Afro-Atlantic religious practices (Richman 2014), the archives to which they provide access are personal and family based, though also intelligible to the broader community of practitioners.

Earlier scholars who attempted to make *kumina* legible from a functionalist perspective, as well as those who sought evidence of an African heritage, saw it as critical to describe ritual process and to write about what it feels like when ancestors inhabit practitioners' bodies and of how community members care for them. George Simpson's (1970) early research on "religious cults" in West Kingston provided an extensive description of dancing myal as it appeared among *kumina* practitioners in 1953, and it is worth quoting at length:

After the gods have been invoked by the drums, the spirits are attracted to the ceremonial and come down close to the dancing booth, but it is believed that they do not enter it immediately.

When the spirits are willing, they are described as coming into the booth to the center pole, then down the pole into the ground; from the ground they go into the open end of the drum, to the head of the drum, and are there hailed by the drummer, the master of ceremonies, and the singer. Then they travel out the other end of the drum, into the ground, and into the feet of the person selected to be possessed. At this point, informants report that the feet become heavy, feel as if they are stuck to the earth; some say it feels like an electric shock. From the feet, the spirit creeps up the legs to the hips while the spirit's own drum beats and songs are executed by the drummer and the singer. The selected individual trembles as the spirit rises and the feeling is described as that of a snake crawling up the legs. Next, the spirit lodges in the spine, and then climbs up to the shoulder where he may ride for some time, feeling heavy to the individual about to be possessed; with varying individuals this is accompanied by a feeling of lightness in the head, or a small pain, or faintness.

When the spirit "feels like it" he mounts into the head of the individual. At this point, the individual loses consciousness; sometimes, he falls to the ground; sometimes he goes into a spin, or leaps into the air. It should be noted that *myal* possession, at its inception, is one of complete mastery of the individual which is not always accepted willingly. When this first phase is completed, the individual has given his body to the spirit and he becomes the physical personification of that particular god or ancestral zombie.[11] In this early phase, great care is given to the individual by the master of ceremonies and his assistants, for, with some spirits, the man or woman must be subdued until the dance can be controlled. In this phase, all individuals claim they have no knowledge of what is happening.

A second phase of *myal* is the dance of the god or spirit which becomes a controlled dance and is identifiable by the master of ceremonies, the drummers, and all assistants. The possessed individual is spoken of now as a zombie, is identified as a named god or ancestral spirit, and is danced with in the manner of that spirit. Sometimes, in the progress of this *myal* dance, there comes a partial consciousness when the individual begins to know himself again, and the spirit possessing him becomes less and less pronounced.

There is evidence that after the period of complete dominance, the spirit comes outside the individual, dancing outside his body. This, also, can be established as the second period of *myal*, for many of the dances of these spirits force the possessed individual to appear to be dancing with someone. Moreover, the assistants handle the possessed individual by dancing as the possessing spirit would dance if he were outside the body. Toward the end of the second phase, the possessed individual dances without assistance, continuing to appear as if he were dancing with someone. It is this type of dance which is responsible for the feeling of many persons that, after the gods have control, they dance outside the body. (G. Simpson 1970, 167–68)

Cheryl Ryman (1984), who conducted research in St. Thomas, Portland, and St. Catherine between 1975 and 1983, also offers a description of what myal feels like and of what the dance does:

The combined and kinetic force of the dance as a dance-music unit, entices the *nkuyu* to possess a living Kumina dancer, thereby making their presence and identity known, and thereby facilitating their entertainment and enjoyment. After the *nkuyu* have been fed and thus satiated in the dance, it is felt the *nkuyu* are more amenable to granting favours, providing information and bestowing knowledge or Power on and through the person being possessed, . . . Generally, sensations of a "cramp" in the leg, the "blood running cold" or "like yu head grow" are also commonly reported with reference to the early stages of possession. In physical terms, an obviously altered style of movement, transformed and intensely fixed or glazed-eyed stares and loss of control of balance are all marks of possession.

Myal possession is often signaled by a somewhat violent control of the dancers' bodies, attributed to the possessing spirit, causing them to lose their balance, spin and totter and eventually fall to the ground . . . the able hands of the Mothers strive to lift or help the possessed to rise and "dance out" the possession phase. To ensure the safety of the possessed and that they maintain their decorum this is advisable; for the *nkuyu* to be identified this is imperative. (90–91, 116)

Contemporary practitioners describe it similarly. "You can feel it," one person told us. "You can feel it move in you, feel your body a rock, a more powerful energy. Most like it come in your feet first, you get weak, yeah. Foot get weak, so you know you're about to drop." Another said, "Your whole skin a raise . . . sometimes I can feel it coming on and I can resist it, like stop dancing, do certain things, cut if off. But when I go deep," she laughed, "I know nothing. When I come back, I dirty. Mud up." She continued: "When persons get into myal you know that the drumming is right, you're doing the right thing, and the ancestors them coming. And it takes a good drummer, proper singing, everything has to be on the right chord, for that to happen. So you can't take a eight o'clock drummer to play eleven, twelve at night." Indeed, one drummer told us that "playing the drum, you can build a new rhythm, and that rhythm can call specific ancestors."

If myal requires particular skills and attunements, ancestral possession becomes a mode of redress and reclamation, what Nadia Ellis (2015) has called a structure of diasporic belonging, but a mode that is really also an embodied model for interaction, one that simultaneously instantiates identification and alterity:

> One belongs, under a spirit's possession, neither to oneself strictly, nor to any one particular moment or place in time. Rather, for an eternal moment, a moment during which nothing but paradox reigns, a subject may be both *here* and *there*; may be, or rather will of necessity be, at once in the current moment, wherein she can be perceived by others, and in another time altogether, perceived only minimally. She will be in place—perhaps spinning—but she will float above that place in a way that enables a perception of expansiveness and travel. She will give herself over to another power; and yet that other power will work with her, alongside her, so that she may feel differently empowered— possessed of knowledge and understanding that she does not usually own. (147)

What is critical in this passage is Ellis's attention to the "knowledge and understanding" gleaned through possession, and the way this gleaning leads to a different kind of possession, a sense of ownership not grounded in the property relations of liberal political philosophy. We might think of the empowerment Ellis indexes as a kind of attunement. In surrendering to the spirit, perception shifts, not only for the person in myal but for the community attending to that person, which requires attention to the temporal and spatial shifts created in and through myal, and to the needs and desires of specific ancestral presences.

There is another sense in which the body in myal is not bounded. Throughout these earlier accounts, as well as in contemporary practitioners' reflections, we hear stories about how bodies in myal are unaffected by the realities of materiality. Cheryl Ryman (1984) noted that "stories of healing, clairvoyance, drums being played by the spirits or 'invisible musicians,' walking medicine pots, rising calabashes of sacrificial blood, the 'sprouting of wings' and 'flying' back to Africa while still alive, and even the revival of the dead, abound both from oral and written sources" (118). For her, these stories were important because they were passed down. In this way, they constituted an inheritance, they contributed to the mythologies of particular elder practitioners, and they provided evidence of the efficacy of *kumina* practice. Today, we hear stories of elders climbing up banana trees as if they are teenagers; of men in myal on their knees in the grass, making sounds like horses as they graze; of a woman swallowing a wooden stick that had been set afire without scorching her lips or burning the inside of her mouth; of someone's auntie climbing up the center pole of the *kumina* circle, sliding back down headfirst, picking up the glass of sugar water in front of the drum, crushing the glass in her mouth and swallowing it without even the tiniest cut. These stories defy the material logics of cause and effect, and they ask us to think differently about how the body—and therefore personhood—is constituted. These are also stories about the "power" of *kumina*, a power that is grounded not in the logics of containment and control but in the capacity to channel and use energy in both individual and collective ways.

TAMBUFEST

Aside from being important to scholars, *kumina* was also one of the cultural practices elaborated by artists and intellectuals in Jamaica as part of anticolonial agitation oriented to the development of an awareness of Afro-Jamaican cultural traditions (Thomas 2004). In this way, though it emerged in Jamaica as an instantiation of the elaboration of life outside the plantation system, *kumina* became a cornerstone of a nationalist sovereignty that imagined the state as the container for liberatory aspirations.[12] Tambufest, on the other hand, emerges from our intention to create space for world-building outside of (but in relation to) the juridical structures of modern collectivity that were founded in settler colonialism, imperialism, and slavery.

The idea for Tambufest emerged when Junior and I were looking for ways to generate grassroots discussions about political and drug-related violence in Jamaica. We, alongside Deanne Bell, now associate professor in Race, Education and Social Justice at the University of Birmingham's School of Education, had been working on a project with residents of West Kingston after the "Tivoli Incursion" in 2010, when Jamaican security forces, supported by the United States, entered the Tivoli Gardens community in search of Christopher "Dudus" Coke, who had been ordered for extradition to the US to stand trial for gun- and drug-running charges. The search for and arrest of Coke resulted in the deaths of at least seventy-four civilians. During our work with Tivoli Gardens residents, we sought to provide a platform for them to memorialize loved ones they had lost and to narrate what had happened during the four days the security forces occupied their neighborhood. While we were doing interviews and beginning to amass archival footage regarding the long histories of political violence in Jamaica, Junior suggested we hold a drum circle to commemorate the anniversary of the incursion at the downtown arts space, Roktowa. We provided refreshments as *kumina* and Nyabinghi drummers played and attendees danced the circle. The following year, we organized a similar event at Liberty Hall, a downtown cultural center that was formerly the site of Marcus Garvey's UNIA, an event that members of the Hannah Town Cultural Group (who had worked with us on the Tivoli project) attended. Similarly, when our exhibit *Bearing Witness: Four Days in West Kingston* opened at the Penn Museum in November 2017, we brought *kumina* drummers, revival singers, and Nyabinghi drummers to bless the space, and once we finished our film *Four Days in May: Kingston 2010*, we held community-based screenings in Kingston, St. Thomas, and Portland, as well as at the University of the West Indies, Mona Campus, following them with moderated discussions and opening and closing them with drumming.

Our aim with the "Tivoli Stories" project was to disturb the normative frames through which crime and violence have been represented in Jamaica by juxtaposing assemblages of archives—visual, oral historical, colonial, and postcolonial—in order to think through the relations they bring into being among the psychic, material, prophetic, and political dimensions of sovereignty, the broader historical and geopolitical entanglements these relations make visible, and the possibilities they generate for a redefinition of human recognition. Given the intense political polarizations in Jamaican society, we held screenings in spaces where people were already accustomed to coming together across partisan political boundaries. During the discussions that followed the screenings, people talked about their own experiences of state violence, about the broader history of violence in Jamaica and the legacies of the Cold War and US intervention, about the effects of the transnational trades in drugs and arms, about the psychological trauma influencing their contemporary decision-making, about the impossibility of measuring the long-term impact of states of emergency, and about the extent to which they feel transformation is possible.

What was notable about these discussions is that when confronted with the narratives of people who directly experienced the violence of the state— narratives that detailed both the quotidian and extraordinary ways violence shaped their lives—audiences reevaluated what they thought they understood about the events of May 2010. They rethought their assumptions both about how political violence operates and about the humanity of people who live in areas where it is rampant. Following these kinds of responses, we became interested in the extent to which this kind of format—an artistic engagement followed by *kumina* drumming—could generate greater dialogue and collaborative solutions to the ongoing problem of political and drug-related violence in Jamaica, solutions that would move beyond the security-oriented strategies of the Jamaican state. We began doing screenings in different areas of Jamaica, and when we went to St. Thomas, Rocky suggested that, rather than just using one group of drummers, we convene people from a range of *kumina* groups to form a kind of collective that could play at these screenings in order to release potentially difficult discussions by coming together in music, dance, and song, which would also serve the purpose of rehumanizing ourselves and rebuilding our collectivity. Junior saw this project as an extension of the work he had been doing most of his adult life to preserve and reinvigorate the traditional musical practices associated with Afro-Jamaican rituals. As a result, we felt that building a festival that centered a "reasoning" process and featured *kumina* and other related practices could serve to create dialogical spaces in Jamaica and beyond, spaces in which communities might discuss the forms of renewal and respect they would like to see moving forward. Thus began Tambufest in 2018.

Tambufest is a space of *performed* ritual practice, which is to say that in showcasing *kumina*, among other Afro-Jamaican ritual traditions, we are not seeking to produce a mass myal event. Instead, we are curious as to whether it is possible to cooperatively activate the conditions for the relational space of myal and whether, in that space, we can glean insights into how we learn to surrender to one another and to a different way of reckoning collective belonging and accountability. While it is true that one aspect of Tambufest has to do with attaching value and legitimacy to *kumina* and other practices in a context in which they are often either unknown or stigmatized, it is also true that the performance of ritual practice generates a sphere of improvisation and play. Here, I am invoking improvisation in the way Margaret Drewal (1992) has written about Yoruba ritual, whereby it signals "moment-to-moment maneuvering based on acquired in-body techniques to achieve a particular effect and/or style of performance" (7). For Drewal, "improvisation is transformational" (7) because it is a process of participatory play. It constitutes a creative and agential process of negotiation and argumentation, both within and among the performing groups and between these groups and their audiences, thereby destabilizing the idea that ritual is static, something to be preserved and protected.

There is also an aspect of Tambufest that might be understood as the protection of a heritage perceived to be endangered. Not as many practitioners know the "bongo language" as in previous times, and some songs have fallen out of ceremonial rotation while others that, as one elder put it, "are not appropriate to this culture," have been brought in. The eldest women who were keepers of the tradition have passed on, and practitioners worry about *kumina* becoming "watered down" without the strong leadership of elders. "We don't want it fi die out," one person said, either because younger people are no longer interested in *kumina* or because those who are interested are not sufficiently supported. Continuity, in other words, is a concern for practitioners, but this is not a continuity defined by static modes of preservation. It is, instead, something more akin to a process Mary Louise Pratt (2022) has found to be "defined not by the collective maintenance of practices, stories, and beliefs over time but by the shared work of world-making conducted by the group over time. Practices, stories, and beliefs play a fundamental role in this work, but they are not the work itself" (9).

It is to this work that I would like to turn now, or more specifically, to the labor of producing Tambufest. *Kumina* may, as practitioners say, bring peace and healing, may create the conditions for relation, but it also takes work. And this is not only the work of drumming, singing, dancing, playing the grater, or caring for people in myal, but also the work of preparation—building a stage, gathering food, contracting performers, hanging lights, renting portable toilets, hiring security guards and a master of ceremonies, arranging travel (for students, for performers), inviting those who will reason with us, and dealing with all the various things (both small and large) that go wrong before an event. Surrender is not spontaneous but is effortful and intentional; it emerges out of already existing relations even as it also expands the relational field.

2018

The first Tambufest was held at Lynval's Lawn in Port Morant, St. Thomas. Junior asked Alain Van Achte, his colleague at the Broadway show *The Lion King*, to record and mix the sound so they could release a CD afterward. Two of my graduate students, Leniqueca Welcome and Jake Nussbaum, were invited to come along to video record the festival and to broadcast it live over internet radio, respectively. The four undergraduate students who had come to Jamaica with me that summer to conduct research on human rights and sexuality also traveled with us to St. Thomas. As Alain and Jake were setting up the microphones, members of the *kumina* collective arrived. Early and Patrick sat down on the drums for a sound check, with Kiddie behind Early on the *kata* sticks. Fine Spear stood at the microphone as lead singer, with Dwayne beside him, and Kerrieann was on the other side dancing, next to Cornell.

When we were ready to start, the Kingston Drummers—who had also played at the commemorative drum circles at Roktowa and Liberty Hall—began their set, and those who had been milling around took seats. After their performance, we screened *Four Days in May*, and Carol Lawes, Junior's longtime friend and "auntie," moderated the discussion. Being in St. Thomas rather than Kingston meant that not everyone fully understood the ins and outs of what had happened in 2010, but those who did spoke up about how partisan politics, and specific politicians, were the cause not only for moments of spectacular violence, such as the Tivoli Incursion, but also for the ongoing gang wars that plague downtown Kingston and other communities. After the discussion, the *kumina* began in earnest. Leniqueca positioned herself on the ground to the side of the circle. Junior and John-I were finding places to store the extra electrical cables on the side of the venue. Alain was still adjusting the microphones, and Muggy was wandering around with another video camera. Rocky began moving extra drums out of the way. Then Kiddie sat on the *(ki)bandu*, his sock foot damping the drum, and Patrick played the *kata* sticks behind him. Doma entered the frame dancing the circle; Kerrieann, too, handed off the grater to someone else and started dancing in place. Fine Spear rose up to take over the lead singing of "Come wi just a come." The man who was playing the shaker during the early sound check began dancing, as did a few women in one of the corners. He was attempting to engage them but they were not taking him on. Apple's little boy positioned himself between her and the *kyas* drum; he stayed mostly still but took in the subtle rocking of his mother's legs. It was early in the night, and the sweat hadn't yet started to pour.

A little later, Leniqueca moved to a place where she could shoot over the back of the *kyas* drummer. Now Cornell was on the *bandu* and the energy was starting to heat up. Patrick was behind him playing the *kata* sticks, and also leading the song. People came to the side of the group and stood, many filming with their own phones. Leniqueca moved again; now she was behind three women dancing, their bodies responding to the *bandu*, which Dwayne was by then playing. Kerrieann was sweating through her jean jacket. I remember she wouldn't take it off because she had only a bandeau top on underneath and she didn't want people staring. Eventually, Junior gave her a T-shirt to wear with her long skirt. Later still, Early was drumming. Doma started to lead the song "Oh, Donna Oh," and a couple of people poured glasses from the bottle of rum that sits in front of the drummers. A woman crossed between Doma and Leniqueca's camera. Her body quickened with the rhythm but she continued to sing. She quickened again, and then again. She picked up the rum and sprayed it from her mouth in the four directions. The playing continued, and she seemed to shake it off. The circle appeared to move inward, and Early was intensifying the tempo, until with a flourish, towel in his mouth, he ended the song with a final break.

A while later, the vibe cooled out a little, and Early directed his twin daughters to play the drums with him behind on the *kata* sticks. They were maybe about sixteen, both wearing long-sleeve Neymar soccer jerseys over their skinny jeans, and both sporting sequined embroidered sneakers, one of which they each had to remove to begin to play. A crowd formed around them to watch. They were steady, slower, talking with each other across the drums. Doma, their mother, was singing. They marked the end of one song with the drums and began to get up, but someone in the crowd shouted, "Neymar, no, give us another." They started again. The twin on the *bandu* looked serious. At one point, her shoulders dipped, someone in the group shouted encouragement, and she offered an intense flourish, at the end of which she raised her head and smiled. She turned around to look at her father and seemed to ask if it would be OK for her to stop. He clearly said no, and she turned back around, smiling again, and continued to play. Now her body was less stoic. She was focused, unfazed by the many camera lights in her face, and responsive to her mother's singing. A bit later she looked back again, as if to ask, "Now?" This time, the answer was yes. She smiled, looked up, and said something to her mother, and within twenty seconds she wrapped it up. She and her sister quickly put their shoes back on as Aisha, the emcee for the evening, announced that the live streaming had ended and the evening was over. Junior, Rocky, and I quickly debriefed, after which point they helped Alain dismantle the recording equipment before we all headed back to Kingston.

2019

I am waiting at the airport in Kingston to pick up two of the graduate students who have been most involved with the Center for Experimental Ethnography (CEE) and CAMRA at Penn. CAMRA is the graduate student–run Collective for the

Advancement of Multi-Modal Research Arts, which serves graduate students across several of Penn's twelve schools and also mentors undergraduate students interested in integrating film, performance, sound, or other forms of creative practice into the research they are conducting. Similarly, the CEE is a hub for faculty and graduate students who have a creative practice at the heart of their research process, and among its many mandates is to support a wide range of student and faculty initiatives. Farrah Rahaman, a graduate student in the Annenberg School, and Gordon Divine "Dee" Asaah, who has since received his PhD from the Graduate School of Education, were invited to travel down to help with documentation of Tambufest 2019. We were not the only ones documenting the festival, however. A Jamaican woman who is based in the United States and who had traveled to St. Thomas with the Kingston Drummers had asked us whether it would be OK for her to film the evening. Because we realized we wouldn't be able to control who was filming due to the ubiquity of cell phones, and because she wasn't proposing to set up professional equipment with the intent to sell the recording, we decided to allow it.

The daughter of a good friend of Carol Lawes, Joelle Powe, who was then a student at Bard interested in anthropology and filmmaking, was also meeting us at the airport so we could drive to St. Thomas together. As we drove along the south coast toward Port Morant, Dee, who is originally from Cameroon, kept marveling at the landscape. "The red dirt," he said, "looks just like home." "The roads," he continued, "just like home." The goats, the fruit trees, the people, "just like home." His father had passed on the year before, and he had been unable to travel for the funeral, so he was looking forward to hearing the drums, which, he later also said, sounded "just like home."

When we arrived at Lynval's Lawn, the finishing touches were being placed on the stage. The stage itself was an innovation from the previous year, a result of complaints by the dancers that because attendees were congregating around the drums, they were unable to complete the circle around them. Indeed, Junior, Rocky, and other members of the collective felt that the 2018 iteration had been a bit "chaotic," in part because we had not anticipated how different holding a *kumina* in a public venue would be from holding a ceremony in more conventional spaces: Here, participants would be attuned to the structures guiding their engagement in the ceremony, and the focus of the *kumina* circle would not allow for the constitution of an "audience," per se. Because we had set up chairs at Lynval's Lawn, we created the conditions for "audience" in "front" of the drummers, and because we had hung a screen on which to project the film, a screen we didn't have time to strike before the *kumina* began, we created a "backstage" of sorts. People congregated in that backstage, which prevented dancers from moving counterclockwise around the drums, which meant that we lost the *kumina* circle, as well as the energy created by and through the movement in the circle. Without the circle, the body cannot become unbounded. Building a stage, therefore, served the purpose of mitigating the risk of unwanted incursions into the ceremonial space, and it also allowed for the free movement of the dancers.

In 2019, too, we decided to give "Lifetime Achievement Awards" to elders who had maintained the practice over many years and who had supported younger practitioners. Elders are living archives—of languages, lineages, and songs—but they don't always attend ceremonies; some abstain because they feel *kumina* has changed too much from what it was "first time." Our stealth mission with the awards was thus also to encourage them to come to the festival, so that younger ones could learn from them and their presence. That year, we recognized Virgil "Manzie" Ellis and Miss Ivy Stewart with plaques and a small amount of money.

The evening proceeded much as it had in 2018, though this time without the film. Vendors who had heard about Tambufest 2018 came and set up tables. Someone Rocky knew from St. Thomas (whom Junior also later realized he knew from New York) was present and wanted to be involved, so we invited him to pour libations to open the event. He was followed by a poet, and then Rocky, Junior, and I gathered on stage to speak about the history and importance of *kumina* and about our roles in relation to Tambufest. The Kingston Drummers played a set, we took a short break to set up the *kumina* circle, and then the *kumina* began.

Later that evening, because of intensifying noise in front of the entrance to the pavilion at Lynval's Lawn, Junior and a couple friends went outside to see what was happening. They came to realize that people had set up gambling tables, among other activities, and that a fight was breaking out that turned into a big commotion. We didn't have any security outside, and this fight jeopardized not only our ability to maintain the safety of those participating in Tambufest but also the energy we were trying to produce with the festival. These kinds of behaviors and activities ran counter to the way we were seeking to build community. After the *kumina* ended, I drove Joelle back to Kingston; Junior, Rocky, and everyone else packed up the recording equipment and dismantled the stage; and then Junior took Farrah, Dee, and Alain to a hotel in Portland, since we had planned to do a screening and discussion of *Four Days in May*, followed by more *kumina*, a couple of days later on the beach in the community of Prospect, Port Antonio.

Junior, Rocky, and I had planned to hire someone to edit the footage Farrah and Dee (and Joelle) were shooting so that we could create some promotional reels for the festival. However, after Tambufest ended, Farrah said she wanted to take a solo stab at editing, and the result is available online.[13] There are many things to notice about Farrah's editing decisions here. First, the clip captures the energy of a community event, one that features a practice with which attendees are likely familiar even though they may not be directly involved, but in which they nevertheless take part since it is what's going on in one of the main gathering places in the area on a Saturday night. Notably, the clip is also doubly mediated. By this, I mean that while our students are shooting, they are also capturing people in the audience who are themselves recording. This is characteristic not only of our moment, but of the ways Caribbean people participate in Black public spheres across diasporic locations (Thompson 2015). And, finally, as a dancer myself, I love that when V and Apple are seated on the edge of the stage when Patrick begins singing, you can see the kernel of what the movement will become even as they are resting, and that what propels them to rise up is that this kernel grows and grows until sitting can no longer accommodate it. We would later use this clip in fundraising efforts.

2020

In March, we gathered members of the St. Thomas Kumina Collective to discuss the planning for that year's festival. We began by debriefing. A number of people felt that though the stage helped maintain the *kumina* circle, it still wasn't big enough. Many of those who gathered in 2019 joined the circle of dancers, which meant that there wasn't enough room for everyone, and some people began dancing in front of the stage, creating issues similar to those in 2018. Junior resolved to build two additional panels in order to enlarge the stage and to make it round rather than rectangular, and we decided to have a rope around it that could deter people from climbing on. We also decided to move the stage from under the overhang so that there would be more room for others to join. We agreed to extend the time of the festival by starting it earlier in the afternoon and in hopes of attracting a larger audience, and to create a family vibe by bringing in additional performing groups, such as the Kaya Jonkonnu group from Port Maria and a group from Manchioneal that performs the Bruckins tradition. We thought we might also hire a storyteller who could entertain the children. We brainstormed about films we could show, focusing on offerings that would allow for a reasoning about similar practices and histories across the Caribbean. We decided on our lifetime achievement awardees for 2020; we determined that we would open a bar and invite vendors to sell at the festival so that we could start making some money to pay the performers more and cover our costs; and we resolved to bring someone in as a "stage manager" to keep things moving during the event. Finally, because people from key *kumina* areas outside Port Morant had not been well represented at the previous two Tambufests, we decided to hold five promotional events beginning in June in Seaforth, Dalvey, Old Pera, Bath, and Morant Bay. Late that night, Junior got on a plane back to New York, and a couple of days after, I was set to return to Philadelphia. After several canceled flights and not a little panic, I finally got home. The next day we locked down. Because of the global pandemic, there would be no Tambufest in 2020.

2021

It was July, and though we couldn't produce the festival due to the COVID curfews still in effect, we resolved to have a small gathering early in the day in John's Town, St. Thomas, in the yard of Kerrieann's shop, next to her house. Rocky, Fine Spear, Apple, Bradley (and their two kids), Cornell (and his two boys), Kiddie, and a few others came, including Junior's partner Laurie Lambert. It was a treat to have Bradley there, since he usually misses Tambufest because he travels to Colorado every summer on the US farmwork program. The play was casual and relaxed, intimate. Bradley led several songs until Kerrieann joked that he had to stop singing church hymns. When she wasn't playing the grater, Apple held her sleeping baby on her chest as she moved with the rhythm. Because it was the middle of the day and we were in the middle of a yard, people were around, going about the business of their days. Kerrieann's daughter and other folk were watching from the shop's back veranda, and as her movements became more vigorous and playful, they egged her on, laughing and shouting. Toward the end of the afternoon, someone brought Kerrieann's mother, Miss Ivy, whom we had honored in 2019 and who had suffered a stroke not long after, to the yard. We played for her, and she responded by moving what she still could (she eventually passed on in April 2023). We talked a little about the following year, and we tried to remind ourselves of what we had decided on during the meeting in March 2020. After a few hours, I headed back to Kingston, and Junior and Laurie returned to Port Antonio.

2022

In the hope that we could provide a monetary foundation for Tambufest 2022, we set up a GoFundMe campaign during the spring, which raised a little over US$5,000, money that went primarily to the performers (and their transportation). That year the rest of the costs were paid out of pocket—our own pockets.[14] Because of the previous experiences in 2019 at Lynval's Lawn, Junior and Rocky had started thinking about other potential venues for the festival, spaces where we would have more control over who was coming in and out and where we could be relatively assured of the safety of performers and guests. During the early spring of 2021, Junior and Laurie had decamped to Jamaica to spend the remaining months of COVID insecurity there. Later in the fall, Bradley, Rocky, and others got a job playing a *kumina* in the community of Arcadia, St. Thomas, where Manzie is from. On Junior's way to that ceremony, he stopped to visit Mark Cover, who had opened a seaside tavern in Long Bay called Cover's Bar and Grill just before the pandemic began. Junior had known Mark before; they had co-organized (with another friend, Silas) a Drum Festival at Folly in Port Antonio in 2009, where the Kingston Drummers performed alongside other *kumina* groups. As Junior and Mark were talking, they came up with the idea that it would be nice to host an evening of drumming, to bless the place and invite people back. Junior continued on to Arcadia and discussed this with the drummers, and they set a date for early 2022. When the evening of the event arrived, people came from the community (a few tourists even showed up), and everyone ate, drank, and joined the circle of dance. When Junior and Rocky talked about it afterward, they decided to move Tambufest to Cover's.

The seaside venue is beautiful, but farther to travel for the St. Thomas people. And that year, the roads were torn up all the way from Kingston to St. Thomas going one way, and from Port Antonio to St. Thomas going the other. Travel was slowgoing (and dust saturated) for everyone, which meant we were worried about attendance since we knew people would intend to come and then decide not to brave the roads. The festival itself grew to include a few additional drumming collectives and community cultural groups: the Kaya Jonkonnu group from Port Maria, the Charles Town Maroon Drummers, Lynval's African Descendants, and the Manchioneal Cultural Group. The latter, a group that focuses on the Bruckins and Dinki-mini traditions, is only a short distance from Long Bay. We also invited Devon Taylor (who directs the Jamaica Birthright Beach Movement [JABBEM]) and Miss Cynthia Miller (who led the fight against the corporate development of Winnifred Beach) to talk about access to public beaches. During the festival itself, this discussion was particularly robust, in part because the issues regarding public access to beaches are especially important in that section of eastern Jamaica.

Because Cover's is a fully outdoor venue, there was much more to be done in terms of building the stage; renting tents, chairs, and portable toilets; building a kitchen, hiring security guards, finding places for people to stay, and managing the various moving parts. Because I had a group of undergraduate students in Jamaica as part of a different project, I was out of commission for the last week and a half of planning and coordinating for Tambufest. On top of that, my own family had arrived—my son had been enlisted to assist the videographer, Courtney Panton—and I was juggling them alongside my class. Rocky also was out because he had contracted COVID when he went to Sumfest, the reggae festival, after finishing his med school exams for the year. This meant that Junior bore the brunt of all the final logistics such as transporting the sound equipment to the venue, buying the materials for and overseeing the construction of the stage, setting up the lighting, hiring and facilitating the videographer, and dealing with all the decorations. By the day of the festival, we were both broke, he was exhausted, and I was burnt out from coordinating the students' activities and processing their experiences. Despite the fact that the perennial issue with the stage manifested again—this time, because everybody wanted to be on it—the festival went off more or less smoothly. However, it wasn't until the *kumina* at the end of the night that I was able to be fully present.

A beautiful moment caught my eye. Members of the *kumina* collective were onstage, mostly with their backs to the "audience" since their focus was inward on the drums. Dwayne was on the *bandu*, and Manzie and Fine Spear were singing. Apple was dancing in front with her son, who was maybe six or seven at the time. They were facing each other at the beginning of the clip, circling around each other. Apple was holding her skirt, and her son stopped dancing to ask her a question (the microphone almost picked it up, but not quite). Apple never stopped moving, and she didn't specifically answer his question, but then as her son heard the drum break, he was right back into the movement. She approached him and retreated, leaned forward and back. He moved backward and circled himself. Then she approached, arms outstretched, and he approached too. She encouraged him to follow her lead to dip to one side, then to the other—they almost touched but not quite. He jerked his head to one side and faced away from her, then turned back around and assumed the normative posture of the dance, hips forward and pelvis moving circularly, shoulders and elbows back, feet flat and inching forward (insofar as this is possible in sneakers). They both broke with the drum, and then suddenly they were in perfect unison, circling around themselves to the left, right elbow up, with the exact same effort quality, at the exact same pace, and in the exact same place in their kinespheres. They were clearly being moved by the same spirit, which created a unison of unbounded bodies in time.

Apple was teaching her son how to tune in, how to feel the spirit through dance. She was teaching him to surrender—to the drums, to the spectral presences being called by the drums—and she was clearly enjoying it. Her son was not always completely smooth in his movements, but he always knew when the break was coming, and his body marked it with certainty. And while Apple didn't verbally answer the question he had for her earlier, his demonstration of sensory perception and attunement indicated that he assimilated the lesson she was actually giving him, through her body.

2023

It is January, and we are in Bath, St. Thomas. My friend Nadia Ellis is with us because she, too, is interested in the affective experiences of embodied knowledge elicited in and through *kumina*. In Bath, Bradley has agreed to take the lead in organizing a small *kumina* event where we can discuss the importance of being screened for prostate cancer. The Caribbean region as a whole is reported to have the highest prostate cancer mortality rate worldwide. Prostate cancer is the most common cancer in Jamaica, accounting for close to a third of all cancers diagnosed, and it is the leading cancer-related cause of death in the country (Morrison et al. 2014). In Jamaica, there is no formal national screening program for prostate cancer, and though PSA testing has been available since 1989, an under-resourced health system, a dearth of urologists, and hesitations about digital rectal testing among Jamaican men who associate it with homosexuality mean that diagnoses are often made at a more advanced state of the cancer's progression, by which time it has often already metastasized.

The more immediate cause for our convening around prostate health, however, was Junior's prostatectomy, which he had immediately after Tambufest 2022. Junior wanted to organize a *kumina* that would center on sharing information about the disease. He hoped that his own experience might diminish the stigma associated with testing, and that it would encourage other men in the community to be proactive about what is locally known as "stoppage of water." We decided to gather on a Saturday, on the main road outside the Bath health center. We would begin by playing drums, Rocky would offer a tutorial about the prostate gland and prostate cancer, Junior would share his own experience, and we would open the floor for questions and discussion, distribute the food and soup Bradley had arranged, and then finish with more drumming, dancing, and singing.

Bradley had posted flyers around the community, so as we began to gather to set up the area, men started to arrive in ones and twos. Cornell, Doma and Early, Kerrieann, Rocky, Fine Spear, Apple, and a few others began to play and sing. Eventually Rocky signaled that it was time to break for the discussion. He passed out photocopies of pages from his medical school textbooks that showed the anatomy of the male reproductive system, and he asked those gathered whether they knew where their prostates were and what its function was. He then began to describe what happens when it becomes cancerous. He outlined the symptoms, and one of the men who joined us spoke about his own experience of these symptoms. Rocky talked about the diagnostic tests used to determine whether a man has prostate cancer, and he discussed the various stages of its progression in the body. This led to an elaboration of the various treatments available and their possible effects and side-effects. Junior then shared his own experience of diagnosis, surgery, and recovery. He told everyone that he thought Tambufest 2022 might have been his last one, and that though he had some complications after the surgery that were frightening, he was happy to have done it so that he could still share space with everyone gathered. Because he hadn't told many of those gathered about what he had been going through the previous year, they were surprised and moved. The younger men present were clearly engaged and taking it in.

People asked questions, and Rocky discussed the resources available in community health centers, while also acknowledging that for serious treatment, one would have to travel to Kingston. One particularly vocal member of the community, who had arrived halfway through the discussion, balked at the description of the digital test. Junior took him to the side to reason with him privately as the rest of us broke for food. As people finished eating, the drummers sat down again to bring us back to the *kumina*, which ended in the early evening. That summer, during Tambufest 2023, we enlisted one of the only urologists in Jamaica who specializes in prostate cancer to follow up on this smaller-group gathering by leading a reasoning on the topic, and again Junior offered his testimony. We also invited someone to update those gathered on the previous year's conversations about beach access, as well as Marcus Goffe, who talked about the issues many small farmers and Rastafari have had with obtaining licenses to cultivate ganja for export for medicinal markets. The iteration and reiteration of these conversations in some ways parallels the kind of repetition understood to characterize ritual practices like *kumina*. Repetition, in this sense, is not duplication. It is, instead, an embodiment of creativity, an ongoing dynamic experimentation with form and representation (Drewal 1992).

In the lead-up to Tambufest 2023, we were still struggling to find funding other than our own pockets. We were grateful to have received a Fellows Grant from the Crossroads Project, a collaborative research initiative directed by Judith Weisenfeld, Anthea Butler, and Lerone Martin, based at Princeton University, and supported by the Henry Luce Foundation. This grant supported the lion's share of expenses related to the festival itself. We received additional funds in the form of a discretionary grant from the John K. Wilson Foundation (which we had also received the previous year to support some transportation and housing), and the Center for Experimental Ethnography covered Junior's expenses and fee.

As in 2022, we invited the Kaya Jonkonnu group, the Charles Town Maroon Drummers, the Kingston Drummers, and the Manchioneal Cultural Group, and we added the Islington Cultural Group to the roster. We invited a new emcee as well, on the recommendation of a mutual friend. That year, we also attempted a new solution to the problem of the stage. Junior suggested that the drummers remain on the main stage, surrounded by a few singers and a few dancers, so that they could be seen and mic'd properly. He also thought we should raise a pole on the grounds so that attendees could also dance the *kumina* circle. During the festival, this innovation meant that the people who gathered were free to dance without discombobulating the St. Thomas Kumina Collective dancers, and that other performers could also join the circle on the grounds. This was especially important because in 2023, word had spread about the festival to the extent that people traveled from across the country, and even from various cities in the United States, just to spend the day at Tambufest.

THE VULNERABILITY OF PRAXIS

What can Tambufest teach us about the practice of anthropology? The intentions behind the festival, as with other community-based spaces of care, creativity, and spirituality, are to promote reflection and joy, to think from circularity rather than linearity, to create channels of accountability to one another, and to transparently engage with our histories and our future, at one and the same time. Throughout the long night of the festival, dancers surrender to the drums, drummers surrender to the ancestors, some audience members surrender to sleep, and others join the circle of dance, moving collectively in and toward a relational, iterative practice of being and belonging. By bringing together representatives of different *kumina* groups, the St. Thomas Kumina Collective attempts to refuse divisions among practitioners that had been unwittingly (though perhaps inevitably) introduced by nationalist institutions like the Jamaica Cultural Development Commission (JCDC) through the competitive logics of the festival program. And by tapping into transnational networks of practitioners and promotors, Tambufest constitutes one iteration of a broader, multiscalar complex of traditional and popular cultural production through which we try to engage the violences of modern political formations in order to imagine alternative futures.

Our aim, in brief, is to tap into that space of memory, that inheritance that knows that the body—individually and collectively—is unbounded. If Tambufest is a living, community space that celebrates and honors the past, present, and future resources of the community, it is also a way to practice a kind of radical sovereignty, something Laura Harjo (2019) defines as a set of everyday, community-based practices through which people recognize their own power to act and to self-determine, a multimodal and multispatial sphere of energy, relationality, and decolonial love that creates the conditions for bringing into being a futurity that isn't enclosed in the infrastructures of governance or management, of museums or universities.

The question might be raised as to whether my involvement with Tambufest and with members of the *kumina* community constitutes research. There are many things about and in relation to Tambufest that one might readily recognize as research, or potential research. One might decide to conduct oral histories with elder practitioners of *kumina* so as to glean insights into their spiritual genealogies, their networks of practice, and their philosophical and epistemological taken-for-granteds (which we have started to do). One might do ethnomusicological research on *kumina* or the other music and dance forms that are highlighted during the festival. One might be interested in how to produce a community-based event that foregrounds cultural heritage. One might even probe the ways different audiences apprehend what is on offer at Tambufest, interrogating the potentially different perspectives that emerge from overseas tourists, from Kingstonians, from diasporic visitors, and from those who hail from the area where the festival is held. For me, however, my involvement with Tambufest is more accurately an experiment in feeling in solidarity—what Édouard Glissant (1997) would have called a "giving-on-and-with," grounded in vulnerability and oriented toward study and self-determination.

Years ago, Ruth Behar (1996) suggested that anthropologists should be "vulnerable observers." She encouraged us to conceptualize anthropology as a disturbing yet necessary form of witnessing, one central dilemma of which has to do with our relationships to the work we do. How do we deal with our own involvement with our material, she asked? In what ways do we analyze our implication within global geopolitical and historical processes of inequality? How are we complicit in reproducing these processes, and how might we work to transform them? Behar was calling on us to risk exposure, as scholars and practitioners, in ways that would deeply historicize and contextualize our research. One aspect of this vulnerability is recognizing that there is a difference between being *part of* a community and being *in* community with people.

In my own case, I do not have to be convinced to appreciate the African heritage embodied and embedded in *kumina*, but I am not a practitioner of *kumina*; I am not a member of a *kumina* family. I am not compelled to know the secrets of the more private work some practitioners do to address individuals' concerns, or in producing a detailed mapping of particular lineages, or in parsing the meaning of the ki-Kongo words in particular songs. And though I am interested in the ways people understand the extent to which *kumina* might or might not be different from Revival, or from Pocomania, or from maroon practices, it is not my intention to provide a definitive map of these differences (or the lack thereof). Nor is it important for me to make transparent and legible certain rhythms or movements, or even the things people do when they're in myal, or to myself affiliate with a *kumina* lineage. I had never imagined I would write about such classically anthropological fodder, and I continue to refuse the mode of transparency in relation to these kinds of questions. In fact, writing this chapter has been a considerable challenge.

Junior, who himself was not born into a *kumina* family but who understands it as similar to other ritual practices in Jamaica and elsewhere in the African diaspora, helps us to understand that while we must appreciate the specificity of why particular practices emerge and concentrate in particular areas, and how they are elaborated through particular lineages, we can also conceptualize the relational field of *kumina* as encompassing other traditions, other spaces, and other lineages. Junior's grandfather, for example, was a well-respected *gerreh* drummer in the Hanover-Westmoreland region, so his mother would have grown up familiar with those rhythms. Yet, when he used to play *kumina* drums for his mother, she would move in ways that recalled a Bongo-nation spirit, even though her embodied inheritance would have been *gerreh*. Neither are the ancestors available only to practitioners in rural St. Thomas. While we were recording an episode of a series called *Bush Music: A Kumina Podcast*, Junior told a story about a rehearsal he had for his drumming group in New York City. He had gotten the group together to practice for an upcoming performance, and as he began playing the *kumina* drums and dancing the circle, he went into myal—in the middle of Brooklyn! *Kumina*, though situated, is also in a way porous, and its porosity enables these forms of boundary crossing.[15]

Junior insists that *kumina* is similarly in me. He contends that my father, who is from rural St. Catherine, not far from the camp of a well-known *kumina* queen, would have heard the drums playing at night—even if it was in his sleep—and that this would also thus be part of my own inheritance. "I've known you forever," he says. "When you get around the ceremony, the way you move and respond to it, it is *in* you." Rocky asked me one year why I "stay so far" from the circle. "Don't you love the *kumina*?" he asked. I do love it, actually. And if I could just lie on the ground and be enveloped by the drums, if the singing could wash over and around me, if I could raise up and dance it when I am moved (by the spirit? by my own ancestors?), I would. But I know what it looks like for my light-skinned, mixed-race, half-foreign body to stand up with Black Jamaicans in their (our) inheritance, and I don't want my relationship to *kumina* and its practitioners to be misconstrued by people outside our immediate Tambufest community, people who don't know me, who don't know my own history as a dancer, who wouldn't necessarily assume that I am also Jamaican. Not that it matters, but this is nonetheless one marker of my own vulnerability in relation to the relation we are creating.

Junior brought me into Tambufest because we have been working together and supporting each other's projects since the days I was dancing with the Urban Bush Women and he was our percussionist, over thirty years ago. Although I initially considered myself merely to be a kind of support staff for Tambufest, helping with the organizing and the fundraising, bringing the weight and prestige of the big American university to small corners of eastern Jamaica, Junior insisted I take greater ownership of it, to invest myself in its success, to see it as one iteration of the dream he has had since he was a teenager of creating space for community engagement in and through Jamaican ritual traditions. And although Junior, Rocky, and I talk through every plan and challenge, playing out possible scenarios from a range of vantage points, the decisions are not mine to make.

At the same time, Tambufest benefits from the resources to which I have access. As we find ways for Tambufest to travel—to New York City, for example, where we offered a version of it in the context of a conversation that was organized by Jennifer Jones at City University of New York Graduate Center's James Gallery in May 2024; or to South Africa, where we mounted another iteration of it called "Talk + Tambu" at the Johannesburg Institute for Advanced Studies in March 2025—I am inevitably transforming *kumina*. In cocreating a performative spiritual space in which I was not raised, I am part of constituting a new way of making *kumina* happen, which means that we are many moons away from modes of anthropological research in which researchers were presumed to remain detached from their object of observation. We are instead in the murky territory of a researcher actively and collaboratively shaping the performance of a practice understood to belong exclusively to its traditional practitioners, even as it has also been reconstituted as nationalist patrimony. Outside the relational community of Tambufest, the implications of this influence are uncomfortable for me, and I cannot know how my presence and work are perceived and adjudicated by those other than the members of the collective who have invited me into their worlds, for whatever reason.

Vulnerability, however, is not mine alone.[16] We intentionally make ourselves vulnerable to myal in the *kumina* circle. The drummers, in removing their shoes to play, create the conditions for this vulnerability. Our bodies are vulnerable in other ways too—to COVID, to prostate cancer. We are vulnerable to the effects of government development projects: Will we be able to maintain access to the beaches that are our birthright? Will we be able to get to Portland without a flat tire, without wrecking the car's alignment, without inhaling so much construction dust we cough for days? We are vulnerable to the inevitable failures of collective praxis in terms of dashed expectations, uneven workloads, and the difficulty of making sure everyone is on the same page and arriving on time, literally and metaphorically. And we are vulnerable to the petty and disappointing betrayals that emerge in generalized conditions of scarcity.

We are also vulnerable to one another as we struggle to represent what we have been doing. Junior and I have agonized over every word of this chapter together, which has been critically important but also occasionally onerous. We have had to jog each other's memories and have sometimes remembered things differently; we have sometimes also disagreed about interpretation or focus; we have different things at stake and different relationships to "writing about it." Nevertheless, we are, with Rocky, a kind of interpretive community—and therefore a research community that also extends to members of the St. Thomas Kumina Collective more broadly. To some, this might look like "activist anthropology," or "public" or "engaged" anthropology."[17] As someone who was drawn to anthropology from a career as a performer, I would be more inclined to identify the community we are building and the processes we are enacting as "critical ethnography," a mode that emerges from the twinning of critique and ethics in performance studies, and in which "the primary interests are restorative justice, critical analysis," and ethical engagement (Madison 2019, xi). Critical ethnography is also a mode of relation, of being together in time and space, of asking questions and seeking answers, of building stages and laughing and dancing, of falling in and out of one another's rhythms, and of agreeing to continue. In the introduction, I asked what twenty-first-century anthropological scholarship could look like if it invited vulnerability. This reflection is one answer to that question.

CODA

THE LABOR OF SOVEREIGNTY

We could think about the process of producing Tambufest as a form of choreography. Here, I'm thinking of choreography not in terms of the delineation of set sequences of movement in dance but in the way Aimee Cox (2015) has positioned it, as strategic and performative practices employed by those who have been marginalized by the juridical terms of Being that aim to unsettle these terms' foundations. Within this sense of choreography, improvisation emerges as key, both in terms of redefining what it means to care and protect and in relation to the ways we might draw from our inheritances in order to push them in new directions.[1] When I was performing with the Urban Bush Women, sometimes we would improvise in rehearsal to generate new material, new movement vocabularies, or new sequences. Sometimes we improvised to experiment or, as those involved with contact improvisation would say, to explore negative space. Improvisation is a mode of practice that requires responsiveness rather than reaction, attunement instead of anxiety, deep and considered breath not shallow and impulsive contraction. It insists that we remain in the present rather than anticipating the future (or dwelling on the past), but also that we stay true to the mission of holding each other and shifting our weight. Improvisation also celebrates the ingenuity of individuals within the context of a group. The body, in improvisation, is a catalyst for the development of shared exorbitance, as ephemeral or lasting as that may be. The Coptics have also held this understanding of the body.

I mentioned in chapter 2 that the story of the Coptics remains unresolved in Jamaica. There were, indeed, people who wouldn't talk with us. Videos about the Coptics and the movement of ganja that were available on the internet last year, last month, last week have since been removed. Quite a bit of secrecy still surrounds whether and how the community's activities continue. And the political problem raised by the Coptics in the United States—the legalization of ganja—is a problem still being wrestled with in Jamaica. In the 1980s, this problem was framed in terms of freedom of religious practice. The *60 Minutes* report on the Coptics features Florida assistant state attorney Henry Adorno, discussing First Amendment provisions:

> If a court were to rule that the Coptics do have a First Amendment right, then I think that would be the opening of the floodgates for possible legalization of marijuana in Florida. I, as a prosecutor, would then have to go around and decide who to arrest for possession of marijuana. They obviously would then come up with the defense, "Well, I'm a Coptic," or "I have, you know, I believe that marijuana is my sacrament," which would then muddle the criminal system to no end in trying to defend or trying to prosecute a case where the defense is First Amendment grounds.

By now, forty years later, much has evolved in terms of decriminalizing ganja, both in the United States and in Jamaica, and with the development of the medical marijuana industry, new openings have emerged for its legal cultivation and sale. However, it is still the case that those who have been persecuted the most for ganja are still virtually unable to capitalize on it, despite the long-term mobilization of Rastafari and other small-scale ganja growers, and notwithstanding the government's 2015 revision of the Dangerous Drugs Act and establishment of the Cannabis Licensing Board, which has created a legal process for growers. While Jamaica is known internationally for its ganja, eight of the largest fifteen cannabis companies globally are based in Canada,[2] which legalized medical cannabis production in 2001. In Jamaica, although the Life Science Cannabis Research Group was founded at the University of the West Indies, the expansion of the industry remains controversial, with the loudest opposition coming from churches.

The Coptics in Jamaica did not see legalization as a foundational tenet of the church, in part because the Coptics believed that ganja is inherently legal since it is a gift from God, a vehicle for consciousness. Its subsequent decriminalization is viewed skeptically. As Alan Meyerson put it, ganja "was part of an underground economy that was undermining the economic and political sources of wealth." He thus saw its legalization as a means of control, corruption, and profiteering. "As you see now, the corporations have taken it over," he continued, "and it's a shame because the people who have really fought and suffered for it, they're not getting the full benefit." In the Coptic view, restricting its flow restricts the "spirit of upliftment," the consciousness that would "undermine the political, corporate, religious world." This is the consciousness, after all, that infuses their testimonies, the consciousness of building a new world through new relations, both material and spiritual.

I began this book with a discussion of the ways proponents of eugenics mined the body for evidence of inherent racial inferiority, and in chapter 3 we saw that folklorists shared a similar approach, understanding Africanity as something that would leave a trace that could be quantified and translated into civilizational hierarchies. The context for the focus on collection, classification, quantification, and comparison was, of course, early-twentieth-century policing of segregation and the development of American empire throughout the region (and beyond), but this evidentiary fetishization also haunts the contemporary anthropological landscape, both literally through the vast collections of human remains held in many anthropology departments and ethnographic museums, and figuratively through drives toward "big data" and large language learning models.

My own interest in these processes reflects, in part, my location as a mixed-race Jamaican American and, in part, my position as a professor at the University of Pennsylvania, where these social scientific histories have sedimented in particular ways that produce the conditions of possibility for contemporary events. When I first arrived at Penn in 2006, I experienced the Penn Museum as a site of constant and ongoing violence. I avoided walking through the galleries on my way to my office, especially the Africa gallery, and this feeling sometimes extended to the department, where the portraits of all previous faculty (which students unaffectionately called the "Wall of Mancestors") ran the length of the hallway outside my office. While there had also been members of the anthropological community at Penn, such as Frank Speck, who encouraged Native American interlocutors and research assistants to pursue their PhDs and to copublish

(Bruchac 2018), and while the Museum has recently completed a renovation of its Africa section that now foregrounds the history of the slave trade, the long-term effects of the trafficking in persons and imperial looting still haunt decolonization efforts. They also enable what Eve Tuck and K. Wayne Yang (2012, 1) have called "settler moves to innocence," which is perhaps a generous reading of the unethical treatment of the remains of individuals killed during the 1985 bombing by the City of Philadelphia of the MOVE headquarters in West Philadelphia.

As has now been extensively reported (see, e.g., B. Dickey 2022; Strong 2021), Janet Monge, who was herself trained by Alan Mann, filmed a discussion of forensic identification featuring the MOVE bombing, using Katricia Africa's remains for a massive open online class at Princeton called "Adventures in Forensic Anthropology." During the class, Dr. Monge and a student handled Katricia Africa's bones with the Morton Collection in the background, which made manifest the enduring violence of human remains collecting. Once awareness of this class circulated, and with it the fact that the Africa family and the city had been unaware that the Museum was still holding remains from the 1985 bombing, a wave of protests ensued (Nussbaum 2024). Both Princeton and Penn hired law firms to investigate Dr. Monge's actions, and while they found that Monge had acted in poor judgment, she was not legally liable for violating policies regarding the handling and public showing of human remains, because no such policy existed at the Penn Museum.[3]

This is the series of events that led the American Anthropological Association (AAA) to establish the Commission on the Ethical Treatment of Human Remains, which I cochaired with Professor Michael Blakey of William and Mary College. In establishing this commission, the AAA was responding to an urgent call across the field of anthropology for institutional and professional accountability related to ancestral remains in education and research collections, with special attention to standards and guidelines concerning respectful care for all ancestors as well as for ancestral belongings. This specifically includes but is not limited to African Americans and Native Americans whose remains and belongings are housed in research collections at museums and academic institutions in the United States and elsewhere. The commission was tasked with reviewing and assessing the current status of laws, policies, and professional society standards and guidelines with a view to eliminating the gap between the current status and model standards. Toward this end, we conducted listening sessions with colleagues and descendant communities domestically and internationally.

Our mandate was to draft a report for the AAA that could guide anthropologists, museums, and other institutions in ethically and respectfully handling ancestral remains, burial places, and belongings from burials by engaging with lineal descendants, ancestral communities, descendant communities, and communities of care (understanding that not all communities of care have the same relationships to ancestors).[4]

Tens of thousands of ancestors continue to reside in museums and anthropology departments across the world, raising the question of whether there is any future scientific insight to be gleaned from these remains that could satisfactorily transform the white supremist rationale that originally legitimated grave robbing and the experimentation on Black and Indigenous bodies. For my archaeology, bioarchaeology, and biological anthropology colleagues on the commission, there is virtually no research that can legitimately be conducted on ancestral remains collections, since in the vast majority of cases, those whose remains are in these collections could not have given informed consent. What research my colleagues do conduct is requested and led by descendant communities, and this they consider to be a service rather than research per se. They also understand themselves to be providing evidence that will support the oral histories and origin stories these communities already pass down generationally, and they therefore position the investigations they conduct as forms of restitution in a movement toward justice.

This kind of work is oriented toward envisioning an anthropological practice grounded in equality and a notion of being and becoming that moves us beyond the conceptualization of a liberal subject that is transparent, knowable, and reducible to the bits of trace evidence whose collection has supported physical, psychic, and intellectual dehumanization. What I hope I have shown in these pages is that a focus on embodiment, on the ways our bodily inheritances always potentially exceed juridical mobilizations of personhood, allows us to explore the knowledge the body holds and transmits through its active and relational worldliness, rather than through its measurements, features, traits, or whatever else those committed to evolutionary and eugenicist evaluations of moral, corporal, and intellectual fitness found in the bodies they saw as objects. I also hope to have demonstrated that the body and its movements (both individual and collective) give evidence both in and through their materiality and through other realms, opening up additional portals for both sovereignty and accountability.

During the fall of 2021 when I was giving a virtual talk at Indiana University, a graduate student asked, "If the anthropological house is burning, is there anything we should grab as we run out the door?"[5] If we are committed to expanding the tools of anthropology to include a broader range of sensory perception and more phenomenological forms of evidence, then the criteria with which our understanding is evaluated will also have to shift. What if the depth of our analyses were demonstrated in our ability to gauge what role we should be playing at any given moment, with an awareness that that role is fluid, and that it is likely to change to meet the needs of the moment rather than the needs of tenure? What if our interventions were measured by our own levels of attunement to what is being transmitted to us with equal intention by extrahuman means?[6] What if we positioned the research relation, like any relationship, as a leap of faith, one whose ultimate shape is not predetermined but co-constituted? Then we would, as Elaine Castillo (2022) has argued in her extended reflection on the art of reading, be required to recognize our inheritances.

In railing against the idea that reading (especially the work of writers of color) should produce empathy and that "other people" tell particular stories while "white stories" are universal, Castillo exhorts us to understand that those "white stories" written by white authors are stories made possible by ignoring and erasing the legacies of settler colonialism, Indigenous dispossession, slavery, and overseas imperialism. We are implicated in one another's stories, she argues, implicated "like perpetrators, witnesses, and inheritors of a great crime, the other word for which might be our history" (73–74). For Castillo, it is an attachment to inheritance, rather than to freedom, that should undergird our work: "Understanding who we are from the perspective of inheritance, not freedom or exceptionalism, means knowing ourselves as fundamentally made possible by—and fundamentally reliant upon—other people, both living and dead, some we may know intimately and some we may never know" (71–72). Thinking from inheritance requires of us to "encounter our bondages—and our boundedness"; it asks of us to express "our smallness, our ordinariness, our contingency, our vulnerability and reliance" (72, 73). It is only in so doing, as Castillo reveals in a discussion of the etymology of the word *mana* across Austronesian languages, that we might realize our sacred, impersonal life force.

This realization, it should by now be obvious, requires work. If, as it is sometimes said, process is product, it is also true that process is neither effortless nor predetermined. There is rigor in recognizing our inheritances, in developing the kind of bodily attunement that creates the conditions for surrender, that allows one to intuit the drum break, to know when to spin and with what quality, to align oneself with the flow of spirit. It takes work to surrender, just as it takes work to cultivate the exorbitance it takes to release ourselves from the structures of imperialism and colonization, and this work is necessarily durational.

I should admit that after not quite a year back, I stopped going to the dance class I mentioned in the introduction to this book. Some months in, after I had rehabilitated my own bodily memory, there were moments of rapture during the combinations at the end of class. These were moments when everything aligned, when my foot or my hip or my shoulder met the beat at precisely the right moment but also had that extra split second to reach beyond the beat, when a spin or a leap or a fall seemed absolutely effortless and bled seamlessly into the next spin or leap or fall, when it felt like the music I was hearing was actually emanating from inside of me, when it no longer felt as though I was the oldest person in the room but instead felt as if I could go on and on and on forever. But ultimately, it wasn't going anywhere. Unlike others in the class, I wasn't preparing for an upcoming performance, a tour, or some other event, and without that teleology, one that had previously structured my experience of class when I was dancing professionally, I wasn't sure what I was striving for. In those moments, the rapture wasn't enough. I could not fully surrender to the quotidianity of what the class sometimes—but not every time—produced. We could think of this as a failure on my part to release myself from colonial logics of progress and developmentalism, as an inability to inhabit the moment without placing it in relation to some future moment, as an unwillingness to stay in the zone of practice. And all of that is likely true on some level. But it is also true that these, too, are my bodily inheritances, and pushing against them—consciously or preobjectively—takes a stamina and patience I don't always have, given everything else that is always going on. Yet, in striving to remember that rapture, to create the conditions for it in ways that are familiar to me, I am sovereign-ing. We do not choose our inheritances, but we can choose how to mobilize them.

Acknowledgments

As is the case with all books, this one benefited from the many conversations—some decades long—that I have been privileged to have had with so many smart, generous, and fun people. Ideas, concepts, and interventions always develop collectively, and Alissa Trotz, Nadia Ellis, Tracy Robinson, Faith Smith, Annie Paul, John Jackson, Lotti Silber, and Wayne Modest will all find bits and pieces of their own obsessions, questions, and concerns in the analytic thrusts of this book. I also thank the Practicing Refusal Collective for asking me to clarify my attachments to "sovereignty" as a concept, practice, and affect. Alexis Goffe, sometime partner in crime, found and passed along the Ethiopian Zion Coptic Church incorporation files from the Jamaican Parliament for me, as well as the telegram from Seaga to Reagan. And I thank Kamari Clarke for always being on the decolonial journey with me.

I owe a debt of extraordinary gratitude to Kathryn Mariner, Llerena Searle, and their wonderful colleagues at the University of Rochester for hosting me as the 2023 Lewis Henry Morgan lecturer. By patiently reminded me what I signed up for—delivering them at least three chapters and a loose introduction very early on in my sabbatical year—Kate and Llerena kick-started this book. They also enlisted Faith Smith, Maya Berry, and Kristin Doughty to offer feedback on my then-nascent chapters, which was formative. I had never had a manuscript workshop before, and the experience was truly mind-blowing. I want to single out Maya Berry in particular, because she saw, felt, and understood what I was doing in the third chapter better than I did, and her perceptive questions helped me to see it more clearly. Her attunement to the work literally brought me to tears and made me unable to speak.

A million thank-yous to Sharon Hayes, to whom I was explaining what then seemed a rather disorganized project, and in explaining it to her it finally took on a shape that made sense to me. Ana-Maurine Lara read and commented on an early version of the introduction, and her suggestions helped me to clarify problems at a key juncture. Kesha Fikes similarly read chapters and made important interventions that were right on time. Paul Mitchell offered detailed comments on chapter 1, and he has been a cotraveler in relation to the physical anthropology collection at the Penn Museum. Amade M'charek solicited an earlier (and shorter) version of this discussion for the edited volume "Evidence on Display," which she is coediting with Lisette Jong. Danilyn Rutherford, as always, remains a patient and incisive reader, and Alissa Jordan provided support and affirmation when I wasn't sure it had all come together. Ana-Maurine Lara's work always circulates in my head, even (and perhaps especially) when I am not conscious of it. As always, the graduate students with whom I have the pleasure to work in the classroom and in the field push me to think harder and better. I am especially grateful to those who have had their hands in the projects that populate this book, including Hakimah Abdul-Fattah, Gordon "Dee" Asaah, Latoya Briscoe, Xiao Ke, Paul Mitchell, Jake Nussbaum, Farrah Rahaman, Katleho Kano Shoro, Melissa Skolnick-Noguera, and Leniqueca Welcome, whose beautiful collage serves as the cover of this book, for which I am particularly grateful. This book is also better because of the probing questions of audiences at Columbia University, the University of Michigan, the New School, the University of North Carolina, Rochester University, the annual meetings of the American Anthropological Association, and the University of Johannesburg, and because of the support and insights of those at my own institution, such as Nikhil Anand, David Eng, Sharon Hayes, Alissa Jordan, Tim Rommen, and Grace Sanders Johnson.

The Center for Experimental Ethnography crew always inspires me, as do the folk at the Center for the Study of Race:Gender:Class and the Johannesburg Institute for Advanced Study at the University of Johannesburg, especially Victoria Collis-Buthelezi, James MacDonald, and Gabrielle Goliath. I am forever thankful for their hospitality and engagement. The St. Thomas Kumina Collective keeps my head and heart open, and I'm grateful for the ongoing trust and relationship. I am also grateful for the devotion of the army of people it takes to realize Tambufest year after year. Patrick White and David Nissenbaum inaugurated our journey into the world of the Ethiopian Zion Coptic Church, and Alan Meyerson joined that journey at a key moment. We are indebted to their openness, their guidance in navigating us toward additional brethren, and their willingness to engage our various questions. As usual, Jerry Small opened his archive of experience and comrades to us, and Sonia Clarke and others along the route to Bogue helped guide our appreciation of the Coptics' activities in St. Elizabeth. Trenton Streck-Havill, the Museum and archives specialist at the Otis Archives of the National Museum of Health and Medicine in Silver Spring, Maryland, was more than gracious in his facilitation of my visits to the army base where the archives for the 1926 anthropometric study in Jamaica are housed.

Research funds from the University of Pennsylvania, a Guggenheim Fellowship, and a grant from the Crossroads Fund (a collaborative research initiative directed by Judith Weisenfeld, Anthea Butler, and Lerone Martin, based at Princeton University and supported by the Henry Luce Foundation) provided the financial wherewithal to realize the various ambitions of the communities for whom this book might matter, and allowed us to experiment. By "us," I mean the research and production partnership that is myself and Junior "Gabu" Wedderburn, the ongoing gift that is friendship, co-conspiracy, coauthorship, and love. As always, John Jackson is my right and left hand, and my heart. What we have been able to build at Penn is a testament to the unexpected turns life takes over decades walking alongside each other. But what we have been able to build at home is our biggest triumph. This book is the last book I will write with children in the house, and it will be my greatest joy to follow Oliver's and Marleigh's adventures in the years to come, some of which will, I hope, lead them back home, whatever that means to them.

Notes

INTRODUCTION. SOVEREIGN-ING: THE BODY AS METHOD

1. Here, I am referencing Georges Bataille (2017), who argued that sovereignty should be grounded in immediacy rather than future-thinking, consumption rather than production, and the desire for nothingness rather than attachment. To refuse conventionally iterated sovereignty for Bataille's sovereignty *"in the storm"* (342) is to seek a life *"beyond utility"* (198) and beyond the engulfment of recognition. What he called the *"human quality"* should not be sought in the language of either democratic rights and responsibilities or socialist collectivity, but in the one "who refuses *the given*" (343). This iteration of sovereignty also refuses the world of "projects" and eschews the expectation embedded in the temporality of the future anterior or the notion of progress or the politics of recognition.

2. Heritability has, in fact, been a key term in thinking about notions of class, race, and behavior in Jamaica (J. Alexander 1977; Austin-Broos 1994). While this is not the immediate referent for my thinking about inheritance in this book, it does inform my understanding of how these notions circulate, and how they are attached to particular bodies in particular moments.

3. On recognition and elimination, see Wolfe 2006 and Morgensen 2011; on Black people as dispossessed and depoliticized, see Spillers 1987; on dominant settler reckonings of time and place, see Bruyneel 2007; Rifkin 2017; and Harris 1993.

4. For an extended discussion of the prehistories of nondomination and autonomy, see Graeber and Wengrow 2021.

5. See Curiel 2007, 2021; Espinosa Miñoso 2017; and Aguila-Way 2014. For overviews of Latin American autonomous feminisms, see also Laó-Montes 2016 and Martínez-Cairo and Buscemi 2021. For analyses of the Red Thread Organization in Guyana, see Trotz 2007, 2010, 2021; and Peake and Trotz 1999. For reflections on Sistren Women's Theatre Collective in Jamaica, see Ford-Smith 1999; and Ford-Smith with Sistren 1994. And for a literary analysis of Grenadian feminist reflections on the revolution, see Lambert 2020.

6. I'm thinking here with Irina Silber (2010, 2022) and Courtney Desiree Morris (2023).

7. As Aileen Moreton-Robinson (2015) has argued, "The possessive logics of patriarchal white sovereignty discursively disavow and dispossess the Indigenous subject

of an ontology that exists outside the logic of capital, by always demanding our inclusion within modernity on terms that it defines" (191).

8. See, especially, Stoller 1994, which argues against those scholars of collective memory who read possession as text rather than as bodily practice and sensory experience. See also Covington-Ward 2016 and Masquelier 2001.

9. I thank Ana-Maurine Lara for this insight, which she offered on reading an earlier draft of this discussion.

10. For a somewhat different perspective on what they identify as "theopolitics," see also McAllister and Napolitano 2020, 2021

11. I thank Danilyn Rutherford for this insight.

12. On sovereignty as interdependence, see Cattelino 2023. For an analysis that similarly positions Idle No More (2013–14) as a form of countersovereignty, grounded in deep relationality with other humans, water, and land, see Melamed 2015.

13. David Scott (2013) understands this intervention by Brathwaite as a humanist incursion into Caribbean studies, which had been, to that point, predominantly social scientific. This incursion was meant both to displace the centrality of structuralist and Marxist interpretations of plantation economies, and to reorient critical attention from top-down analyses of the problems of the postcolonial state to bottom-up engagements with popular action and worldviews.

14. This attunement to chaos also suffuses Antonio Benítez-Rojo's (1996) rendering of the relation between the plantation and the sea, and of the Caribbean region as a meta-archipelago in which processes of infinite differentiation and repetition correlate. The Caribbean, for Benítez-Rojo, is fractal, a "spiral galaxy tending outward—to the universe—that bends and folds over its own history, its own inwardness" (36). Here, again, we see the elaboration and embrace of what seems unpredictable but is nonetheless governed by dynamic regularities, an attunement to the different positions from which histories of contact, conquest, creolization, and *cimarronaje* emerge and are experienced. At the same time, the territorial proliferation of plantation-based sugar production for export allows us insights into the dynamics of a "changing same" throughout the region. The repetition of the sugar plantation, Benítez-Rojo shows us, is dynamically conditioned by its relation with other forms of social and economic organization, and by the generational temporalities of its establishment in different Caribbean territories. Like Glissant, Benítez-Rojo demands a move away from teleologies and toward (unresolvable) process, away from the certain identities of nationalism and toward chaos. "I start from the belief that Caribbeanness is a system full of noise and opacity," he writes; "[it is] a nonlinear system, an unpredictable system, in short a chaotic system beyond the total reach of any specific kind of knowledge or interpretation of the world" (295).

15. Waves are an obvious example here, but so are plantations (Benítez-Rojo 1996) and sand (Agard-Jones 2012).

16. The National Library of Jamaica notes that oral histories conducted with maroons demonstrate that the First Maroon War actually began in 1655, which is when England took imperial control of Jamaica from Spain. "The English," in "History Notes: Information on Jamaica's Culture and Heritage," National Library of Jamaica, accessed January 8, 2025, https://nlj.gov.jm/history-notes-jamaica/.

17. Here, I am of course thinking of Lorde 1984 and M. Alexander 2005. For more recent work, see J. Allen 2011; Gill 2018; Berry 2021, 2025; Castor 2017.

18. Here, I am drawing from Barker 2005; Sturm 2017; Rutherford 2018; Cattelino 2008, 2023; A. Simpson 2014; and Dennison 2012.

19. See also Farquhar and Lock 2007.

20. The New Melanesian Ethnography is perhaps the most iconic of this type of interrogation (Geertz 1975; Marriott 1976; Strathern 1988; Mosko 2015), but this topic has also been addressed by Africanists (Covington-Ward 2016; Comaroff 1985; Wariboko 2018; Oladipo 1992), Caribbeanists (E. James 2008; Jordan forthcoming), and scholars of Indigenous Australia (Moreton-Robinson 2015; Myers 1979). Indeed, many scholars have turned to African diasporic religions to show how an Afro-diasporic self is "removable, external, and multiple" (Strongman 2019, 10; see also Covington-Ward and Jouili 2021) and have argued that a distinction between the material and immaterial components of a person cannot be mapped onto Cartesian dualisms. This of course would be the legacy of continental beliefs among the Yoruba, for example, who hold that a person is made of the material body (which includes the feelings and psychic life that are governed by the internal organs); a life-giving element (which is immortal and intangible, and which can leave the body and assume tangible form, perform activities, and return to the body); and an individuality element (which is unique to the person) (Oladipo 1992). Indeed, across many African communities, personhood is understood as processual, communal, and relational, something that is recognized and conferred by others as a result of growing into responsibility and accountability within the community (Hoekema 2008; Mbiti 1970; Wariboko 2018).

21. Many Indigenous South Americans, for example, perceived the body as "populated by extra-human intentionalities endowed with their own perspectives" (Viveiros de Castro 1998, 472) and therefore as continuously and actively made through the sharing of bodily substances. Black bodies, too, were permeable not only to the whims of estate owners and managers but also to "the spiritual hosts that had animated [them] prior to [their] capture by the West and its philosophy" (Strongman 2019, 4).

22. On fungibility, see Spillers 1987; Hartman 1997; and Z. Jackson 2020; on carnality and corporeality, see Povinelli 2006. It is worth noting that Indigenous populations in South America, too, perceive of the body as "populated by extra-human intentionalities endowed with their own perspectives" (Viveiros de Castro 1998, 472), and therefore as continuously made. Kinship, Viveiros de Castro argued, was "a process of active assimilation of individuals through the sharing of bodily substances, sexual

and alimentary—and not as a passive inheritance of some substantial essence" (480–81).

23. For review articles, see Lock 1993; Farnell 1999; Desjarlais and Throop 2011; Van Wolputte 2004; and R. Morris 1995. See also Crossland 2009, 2012; and for a critique of poststructuralist approaches to the body, see T. Turner 1994, 1995. An entire literature on embodied cognition has emerged in philosophy, coming from ecological psychology, neuroscience, philosophy, linguistics, and robotics, which rejects the computational dynamics of cognitive science and emphasizes a study of the body's interactions with environment as the basis for cognition. These scholars argue that the body learns and produces knowledge, and their interest is in how our bodies shape our thoughts (see, for example, Lakoff and Johnson 1981). Thomas Csordas (2008) has argued against this position, arguing that embodied experience cannot be interpreted through cognitive and linguistic models—it is not "body language" nor "non-verbal communication."

24. This, of course, represents an argument against Saussurian structuralism as it was taken up by Lévi-Strauss, which locates deep cultural structures like myth, language, and cosmologies in the categories of mind.

25. Terence Turner (1994, 1995) would not have seen himself as a phenomenologist, and indeed his critique of poststructuralism revolved around a view of the body as passive and naked prior to its construction by discourse(s), a construction that then directed attention to the management and control of individual desires, rather than to the broader spheres of material, political, and pragmatic action in which people were engaged. However, I am citing him here to include his insights into bodily plurality and the "multifold ways [the body] is constituted by relations with other bodies" (1994, 28).

26. For more on refusal in anthropology, see Thomas 2024.

27. By "improvisation," I mean here to invoke the eschewal of universalisms, totalizations, and characterizations that push us to situate our perspectivity in relation to concrete temporal and material contexts (Drewal 1992; Covington-Ward 2016; and Farnell 1999).

28. Nigerian poet and theater scholar Esiaba Irobi (2006) has argued that phenomenology can, in any case, be fully expressed only "through a bodily participatory experience" (7), with participation here understood as a practice that exceeds linear and material conceptualizations of time and space. By claiming that thought in African continental communities is validated through symbolic action and transmitted through performed structures such as proverbs, myths, ceremonies, rituals, and festivals, Irobi argues that those Africans who were trafficked to the so-called New World were "mobile libraries of their culture's total intelligence" (5). The body, as he puts it, thus "functions as a somatogenic instrument as well as a site of multiple discourses which absorbs and replays, like music recorded on vinyl, epistemologies of faith and power grooved into it by history" (3).

29. Even within this juridical framework, however, evidence, or valorizations of differ- ent kinds of evidence, is not static. For more on this in relation to race, see, for ex- ample, Chinn 2000.

30. See, for example, several contributions to the volume *How Do We Know?* (Chua, High, and Lau 2008), most particularly Emma Varley's. See also Hastrup 2004.

31. "What can dance do for the world?" is a question choreographer Reggie Wilson, di- rector of the Fist and Heel Performance Group, asks in every class, workshop, and gathering. Reggie and I cotaught a kinesthetic anthropology class together when he was a fellow with the Center for Experimental Ethnography, and we realized that we have been asking the same questions on parallel paths.

CHAPTER 1. TRACES

A version of this chapter will appear in Amade M'charek and Lisette Long, eds., forthcoming, *Evidence on Display* (Amsterdam: University of Amsterdam Press).

1. See Carby (2019) for an analysis of how every Jamaican family has a Black branch and a white branch.

2. For an analysis of German racial atlases, see Mak 2020; on Dutch racial science and anthropometry in colonial Indonesia, see Sysling 2016; and on various collections of images in South Africa, see Campt 2017. As Campt (2017) writes, these kinds of collections were "made to identify, classify, isolate and distinguish" through physical attributes (75).

3. Harvard was, at the time, the center of eugenics education, offering four separate courses.

4. In *Race Crossing*, Davenport and Steggerda acknowledge Mr. D. H. Hall, Second Assistant Colonial Secretary; Dr. B. M. Wilson, Superintending Medical Officer; Mr. P. J. O'Leary Bradbury, Director of Education; Mr. Frank Cundall, Director of the Jamaica Institute (Institute of Jamaica); Dr. B. E. Washburn, Rockefeller Foun- dation, Director of the Jamaica Hookworm Commission; Dr. Crutchley, Director of the Gordon Town branch of the Jamaica Hookworm Commission; Mr. A. J. New- man, Principal of Mico College; Rev. J. F. Gartshore; Mr. Graham, the Chief of the Kingston Fire Department; Miss Ethel Henderson, Director of the City Crèche in Kingston; Mr. Harrell, Inspector General (Police); and Inspector Knolls, Sargeant- Major Higgins, and Corporal Ford (Police).

5. Sydney Rhoden is the only assistant named in the book. Steggerda stayed in touch with Rhoden, or perhaps it is more accurate to say that Rhoden wrote Steggerda from time to time looking for work—first should Steggerda return to Jamaica and later because he had emigrated to New York City. Davenport and Steggerda had first hired as assistant Sydney Carby, but after Steggerda returned from the holidays in winter 1926, Carby had taken another job. Box 16, Folder 8, Steggerda Collection, Otis Historical Archives [OHA], National Museum of Health and Medicine (hereaf- ter cited as Steggerda Collection).

6. This possibly betrays an assumption that "White" meant British, and therefore purportedly signified an uncomplicated genetic pedigree (an assumption that is itself unfounded), but it also ignores local gradations of whiteness, such as that between "White Jamaican" and "Jamaica White," the latter referring to someone who is apparently white, or nearly white, but likely has some mixture in their genealogy.

7. Steggerda Collection.

8. Rockefeller also had antihookworm projects in Egypt, India, Ceylon, the Malay states, and elsewhere (Webb 2020, 103–23). For more on the Rockefeller Foundation's health campaigns in the Caribbean, see Palmer 2010.

9. Washburn had particularly novel approaches to eradicating hookworm in Jamaica that combined public health with popular expressive cultural practices. He traveled from community to community, giving lectures with magic lantern slides, lectures that were extraordinarily popular, drawing audiences of up to one thousand people. He developed a number of didactic parables and plays that featured characters who would have been locally familiar, parables and plays that reflected the depth of his own ethnographic intuition (at a moment when folklore was being collected across the island), as it were. For more on this initiative in Jamaica, and to read the "Health Stories and Plays," see Jones 2013 and Washburn 1929.

10. Memo from Steggerda to director of Jubilee Hospital, and memo from Davenport to Steggerda, December 14, 1926, Box 8, Folder 8, Steggerda Collection.

11. The area of skin between the eyebrows and above the nose.

12. The point where the nasal septum and upper lip meet.

13. The lowest point of the midline of the lower jaw.

14. The visible portion of the outer ear.

15. The point where the hairline and the middle line of the forehead intersect.

16. The most anterior point of the suture that joins the nasal part of the frontal bone and the nasal bones.

17. The midpoint of the oral fissure where the lips close.

18. See "Metal Case Containing an Eye Color Chart and 20 Artificial Eyes Used to Verify Racial Identity," United States Holocaust Memorial Museum, accessed January 10, 2025, https://collections.ushmm.org/search/catalog/irn4728.

19. Box 2, Folder 7, Steggerda Collection.

20. Indeed, demographer G. W. Roberts noted that emigration from Jamaica reached a high between 1911 and 1921, before coming to a halt between 1921 and 1943 because of US quota restrictions and a tightening of Latin American immigration policies (G. Roberts 1968; see also Putnam 2013).

21. The transcripts of these interviews are housed in the Documentation Centre of the Sir Arthur Lewis Institute for Social and Economic Studies at the University of the West Indies, Mona Campus (Life in Jamaica in the Early Twentieth Century: A Presentation of Ninety Oral Accounts, Sir Arthur Lewis Institute for Social and Economic Research), but some have also been published in *Standing Tall: Affirmations of the Jamai-*

can Male, 24 Self-Portraits (Brodber 2003). While I focus on the economic and political dimensions of the material in the interviews here, the selection published in the 2003 volume is framed by Barry Chevannes as an addition (and a corrective) to the family studies so prevalent in the Caribbean social science research beginning in the 1950s. For a more detailed discussion of the Brodber interviews, see also Thomas 2020.

22. Steggerda Collection, especially Boxes 1–4, 14.

23. By this, they meant in their underclothes, which is what is represented in their photographs (OHA 316, Steggerda Collection).

24. Box 5, Folder 2, Steggerda Collection.

25. Box 5, Folder 3, Steggerda Collection.

26. Box 5, Folder 5, Steggerda Collection.

27. Box 3, Folder 3, Steggerda Collection.

28. It is not unsurprising that while Steggerda was collecting anthropometric measurements on Jamaican people, he was also collecting plant samples, which he taped to pieces of paper. For each plant—for example, broom weed, black sage, butter cup, bitter bush, black mint, cersee, chicken net, cow foot, dandelion, dog tongue, elder, fever grass, and on and on to white sage—he gives the scientific name, mode of preparation, and what it's used for. In other words, Steggerda followed the lead of early collectors, folklorists, and ethnobotanists like Hans Sloane (who was a physician on a slave plantation in Jamaica during the eighteenth century). Box 14, Steggerda Collection.

29. See, for example, Mak 2020; Sysling 2016.

30. The HRAF was founded in 1949 at Yale University with support from Harvard University, the University of Pennsylvania, the University of Oklahoma, and the University of Washington (and, later, the University of Chicago, the University of North Carolina, and the University of Southern California). It emerged from the work of scientists at Yale's Institute of Human Relations during the 1930s, as they collected data globally regarding cultural materials and behavioral traits. It is a sort of clearinghouse of microethnographic details that is designed to enable easy searching across cultures for common attributes, such as particular forms of religious practice or languages. For more, see "About HRAF," Human Relations Area Files, accessed January 10, 2025, https://hraf.yale.edu/about/.

31. This analysis reflects the view of craniometrists, who held "that the cranial sutures of Negroes closed at an earlier period in individual growth than those of the white man, thus placing a rigid osseous limit on their mental growth" (Stocking 1968, 55).

32. Box 12, Folders 1 and 2, Steggerda Collection.

33. Box 1, Folders 16 and 17, Steggerda Collection.

34. Two reviews, primarily descriptive, also appeared in German journals, one penned by the person who trained Josef Mengele.

35. Steggerda's research with Maya community members in Pisté, three kilometers from Chichen Itza, focused on agriculture, anthropometry, social history, and census taking.

It later became the basis for an ethnographic research project in the 1990s directed by Quetzil Castaneda, and this ended up yielding an interactive exhibition for the community, described here: Quetzil E. Castañeda, "Chilam Balam Ah P'izté' Project in Memory and History: Antecedents and Agenda," OSEA-CITE: Open School of Ethnography and Anthropology, accessed January 10, 2025, http://www.osea-cite.org/history/chilam.php.

36. Morris Steggerda to Dr. Blakeslee, director of the Department of Genetics in Cold Spring Harbor, July 17, 1940, Folder "Steggerda, Morris, 1940," Charles Benedict Davenport Papers, American Philosophical Society.

37. While these statements from the United Nations Economic, Social, and Cultural Organization were meant to replace essentializing notions of racial difference with an understanding of race as socially and historically constructed, many have argued that they also ended up obscuring the ways racism has structured the modern world by advancing a "seemingly nonracial discourse of 'international development'" grounded in equitable potentiality across the globe (Gil-Riaño 2023, 7). According to this view, the legacies of imperialism and slavery were to be overcome through hard work and aspiration to capitalist accumulation rather than through a worldwide redistribution of wealth, materially and socially. Geneticist William Provine's account of these UNESCO statements provides a cautionary tale about the attempt to "fight racism worldwide by promulgating science and truth" (Provine 1986, 874). Provine demonstrates that these statements generated so much argumentation among geneticists and physical anthropologists that one of the critics of the original statement came to argue that while UNESCO was making an attempt to "'justify a particular ethical position on scientific grounds,'" in fact that position should be "'based upon moral grounds, with science merely an ally of secondary importance'" (Provine 1986, 877).

38. Morris Steggerda to Milislav Demerec, June 8, 1942, Folder "Steggerda, Morris, 1940," Charles Benedict Davenport Papers, American Philosophical Society.

39. For elaborations of this assertion, see Baker 1998; Thomas, Manning, and Pallares 2021; J. Jackson and Depew 2017; J. Jackson 2001.

40. Draper funded the publication of this book and personally delivered a copy to Wilhelm Frick.

41. There is also speculation that Draper may have played a role in the assassination of US president John F. Kennedy, and before his death from prostate cancer in 1972, he donated to right-wing political organizations like the World Anti-Communist League, an alliance founded in 1952 in the Republic of China but expanded in 1966 in Taiwan. The League worked to oppose communist regimes (the organization changed its name in 1990 to the World League for Freedom and Democracy), which tied it to right-wing authoritarian regimes throughout East Asia and Latin America during the Cold War. For more on how this brand of anticommunism impacted countries like Jamaica, see Thomas 2019.

42. The Pioneer Fund still exists and, as recently as 2018, funded the work of a psychologist at the University of Arizona. See Colleen Flaherty, "Pioneering Eugenics in

2018?," *Inside Higher Ed*, September 9, 2018, https://www.insidehighered.com/news
/2018/09/10/arizona-psychologist-faces-scrutiny-grants-organization-founded
-support-research.

43. Jamaican planter Edward Long, in his *History of Jamaica* (1774), created lists of racial vocabulary in Jamaica, and Moreau de St. Méry (1797) famously documented racial combinations in Saint Domingue. Recent scholarship has thought critically about the legacies of these categories. See, for example, Walker 2017; Wheeler 2000.

44. For a discussion of this anthropological research, see Thomas 2011, chapter 2.

45. See, for example, the exhibit *You Name It*, by Sasha Huber, at Autograph UK. "Who Was Renty Taylor," Autograph, November 10, 2022, https://autograph.org.uk/blog /texts/who-was-renty-taylor-honouring-and-recalling-7-stories-of-black-liberation -struggles/

46. Box 2, Folder 7, and Box 3, Folders 1 and 3, Steggerda Collection.

47. On the affective economy of archives, see Cvetkovich 2003.

48. Whereas Peggy Phelan (1993) famously argued that "performance becomes itself through disappearance" (146), Rebecca Schneider (2001) has countered that, actually, "performance remains."

49. See also Peacock and Holland 1994; Ahearn 2001; and Ochs and Capps 1996.

CHAPTER 2. TESTIMONIES

1. This definition comes from "Circumstantial Evidence," Cornell Law School Legal Information Institute, accessed January 10, 2025, https://www.law.cornell.edu/wex /circumstantial_evidence.

2. See, for example, Paul's letters to the Corinthians, especially I Corinthians, chapter 15.

3. Géraldine Mossière (2021) has argued for a gradual and reflexive, rather than disruptive, understanding of conversion among Pentecostal practitioners, noting that the former produces an approach to personhood that can "be thought of in terms of continuity, fluidity, and dividuality, especially as it involves personal and intimate contact with and incorporation of the Holy Spirit" (192). In the context in which she is working (among women migrants in Quebec), the testimony is a calling that helps them reinterpret events in their lives in relation to a slow teleology toward accepting the call, which they ultimately experience as a co-constitution of personhood (with the Holy Spirit) rather than an individually focused experience. For analysis of the relationship between testimony and identity construction, see Faimau 2017.

4. Hence, the Quaker SPICES: simplicity, peace, integrity, community equality, and stewardship.

5. There are, of course, other anthropological modes of attention to testimony, and here I am thinking of the robust body of literature on testimony as a mode of political reparation (which includes the important critiques of truth and reconciliation commissions that have emerged in many contexts); the deconstruction and vindication of *testemunhos*, a genre of solidarity work that emerged perhaps most forcefully in Latin

America during the 1970s and 1980s; and the analyses of what it means to be an expert witness as an anthropologist. While I do not investigate these modes in this chapter, they do inform my approach to testimony as a genre, to what it reveals and what it silences, and to its gendered dimensions in particular. See, especially, Ross 2002; Das 2007; Doughty 2016; Stephen 2017; Clarke 2020; and Loperena, Mora, and Hernández-Castillo 2020.

6. In her article "Coptic Ingratitude," Ritch (1979c, 8) claims that it was then–Minister of National Security Dudley Thompson who told her that the Coptics owned ganja estates in Colombia.

7. Later in May, Blake Hannah (1980b, 5) also reported on their motion to dismiss charges against them in Miami for transporting a "dangerous drug." Their motion was centered around the argument that ganja should not be considered a Schedule One substance and presented testimony from those who had used ganja medicinally during chemotherapy treatment, or for glaucoma. Blake Hannah saw this as potentially a watershed decision that could open a route to the decriminalization of ganja (1980b).

8. Horace, Bartilow, interview with the author, October 31, 2021.

9. I also discuss some of the elements of press involvement in the destabilization campaign against Michael Manley in the third chapter of *Political Life in the Wake of the Plantation* (Thomas 2019).

10. Bartilow interview.

11. Bartilow interview.

12. This anti-Coptic sentiment is also reflected in Williams 1981a.

13. For details on the defendants' various court cases, see "Cases," Ethiopian Zion Coptic Church, accessed January 10, 2025, https://www.ethiopianzioncopticchurch.org/cases/.

14. Williams (1981b) showed in this article, through interviews with ganja farmers, that this "rub-off" was definitely more substantial than Seaga was portraying it, allowing farmers to access significant foreign exchange, which then enabled them to build houses and educate their children, and generating significant incomes for politicians, lawyers, doctors, diplomatic staffers, policemen, soldiers, company directors, businessmen, engineers, contractors, and so forth. The article outlined how pervasive ganja involvement was up and down the societal ladder and how rampant corruption characterized not only politicians but also members of the security forces.

15. Telegram from Prime Minister Edward Seaga to US President, March 19, 1981 (passed along March 31, 1981), Central Intelligence Agency, approved for release April 1, 2009, RDP84B00049R001202970016–1, accessed October 15, 2022, https://www.cia.gov/readingroom/document/cia-rdp84b00049r001202970016–1.

16. For more on Operation Buccaneer III, see Thomas 2019, chapter 3. See also Central Intelligence Agency, "Jamaica: Drug Industry in Transition," GI 85–10268, November 1985, https://www.cia.gov/readingroom/docs/CIA-RDP86T00586R000500540006–1.pdf.

17. It is possible that the original publication date of this document was 1978, and sections of it also appear in a 1978 letter to the *Miami Herald*. It can be found online

("History," Ethiopian Zion Coptic Church, accessed January 11, 2025, https://www
.ethiopianzioncopticchurch.org/history/) and both the history and the text of the
letter are online at "History of the Ethiopian Zion Coptic Church," Schaffer Library of Drug Policy, accessed January 11, 2025, https://www.druglibrary.org/olsen
/rastafari/wells2.html

18. With the mention of "Brother Editor," it is clear that at least this section of the history was drawn from the 1978 letter to the *Miami Herald*.

19. Here, Brother Wally uses a spelling other than the more common "*kumina*," also
used by early American scholars of the tradition (see chapter 3).

20. See, for example, Abu-Lughod 1993; Mintz 1974.

21. The invocation of the "plant of renown" is from Ezekiel 34:29 (KJV): "I will raise up
for them a plant of renown, and they shall be no more consumed with hunger in the
land, neither bear the shame of the heathen any more." Many Christians understand
the "plant of renown" as Jesus, and this passage as one of the most important proph-
ecies of the Old Testament, speaking to deliverance and the restoration of Israel.

22. I believe Brother Tony meant to say Augustino Neto, the former president of Angola
who led the popular movement toward independence and who was then head of the
Popular Movement for the Liberation of Angola. That movement was under siege
by South African forces, which invaded in 1975 to drive out Soviet and Cuban forces
during the Angolan Civil War, which followed independence, earlier in 1975.

23. Here, he is referring to the alleged attempt on Manley's life.

24. Michael Manley left office in 1980, not 1976. *Nyah* is an honorific given to elder Rastafari and leaders, and Keith Gordon, Nyah Keith, was by that time the leader of the
community.

25. Here, of course, Tony is referring to Edward Seaga.

26. See, for example, stories in the New Testament about Jesus healing lepers (Luke 5:13,
17:12–24; Mark 1:40–42; Matthew 8:3). In the Gospel of Matthew, Jesus is quoted as
saying, "Heal the sick, raise the dead, cleanse those who have leprosy, drive out demons. Freely you have received; freely you give" (Matthew 10:8, New International
Version). In the Old Testament, Leviticus chapters 13 and 14 discuss diagnosis, isolation, and purification of persons with leprosy.

27. June 20–August 17, 2023, https://open.spotify.com/show/59S2jAmnvdbLQHCE
Gnjuvp.

28. Of course, there are several Biblical examples of this kind of disobedience to juridical authority, even though the Apostle Paul, in Romans, professes respect for the
authority of the state.

29. This celebration took place beginning on August 6, 1978, also Independence Day in
Jamaica.

30. Garrison communities are territorially rooted homogeneous voting communities in
which political support is exchanged for contracts and other social welfare benefits.
These exchanges have been institutionalized, and even codified, as part of general

procedures for the distribution of paid work and social services among constituencies downtown, with the vote-benefits nexus mediated through the relationship between the politician and a local don. This relationship became part of a more general ideological struggle during the 1970s, and it subsequently transformed as the elaboration of the transnational trades in cocaine and weapons supplanted a previously smaller-scale trafficking in ganja. This has strengthened the role of dons vis-à-vis politicians, as dons' increasing involvement in both illicit and legitimate businesses has provided politicians with financial support, in addition to the military support offered during election periods. This is also what has perpetuated a kind of permanent war in which Kingston figures centrally as a spatially, racially, and politically polarized place, both discursively and symbolically (see Thomas 2019).

31. Here, Patrick is referring to Galatians 3:10, which in the King James Version of the Bible, reads: "For as many as are of the works of the law are under the curse: for it is written, Cursed is every one that continueth not in all things which are written in the book of the law to do them."

32. For more on the International Peacemakers Association, see Thomas 2019, chapter 2.

33. David didn't have specific feedback, and indeed when we laid out with him our ideas about how to organize the film, he reiterated that he trusted us, and that he saw his role as facilitating the work, but he didn't feel the need to direct it in any way. In early 2025, when Junior and I visited with him in Jamaica, he reiterated these points but also said he felt the movement couldn't be understood in academic terms.

CHAPTER 3. EMBODIMENTS

1. For overviews of this position with respect to ritual, see Crosson 2019b and Johnson 2011. For an exegesis of agency as a "non-sovereign experience," see Krause 2015 (5).

2. Martinican novelist Maryse Condé (1992) rewrote the story of Tituba, offering a speculative reading of her experiences in Barbados, on the long journey to Massachusetts, and the subsequent trials.

3. See, for example, Ong 1987; Comaroff and Comaroff 1993, 2001; Lincoln and Lincoln 2015; Good 2020; Klima 2001, 2019; Ng 2020.

4. This society was founded in 1888 by Newell, but Daniel Garrison Brinton (discussed in chapter 1) served as its president in 1889. This fact should underscore the similarities in approach between physical and cultural anthropology at the time.

5. Herskovits had begun correspondence with Price-Mars after the publication of Ainsi and met him in 1928 en route to Suriname. Subsequently, Price-Mars assisted Herskovits in selecting a field site and reviewed his books (Yelvington 2006; Magloire and Yelvington 2005).

6. Elsewhere (Thomas 2004), I have discussed the broader effects of and transitions within this kind of cultural politics in Jamaica, arguing that these "folk nationalisms" were, by the 1990s, supplanted by a form of modern Black nationalism.

7. Price-Mars 1928, 10. Price Mars was not alone in seeking to jump-start radical politics during and after the occupation. As field secretary for the NAACP (National Association for the Advancement of Colored People), James Weldon Johnson mobilized a governmental mission to Haiti in 1920. Alongside W. E. B. Du Bois, Johnson was extremely critical of the US occupation, linking the overseas imperialist pursuit with the intensification of domestic racism, and therefore establishing Haiti as a pillar of African American political consciousness during that period. This pan-African sensibility was buttressed by African American artists such as Langston Hughes, William E. Scott, Paul Robeson, and Aaron Douglas, who also traveled to Haiti during this period, inspired by a sense of diasporic unity and uplift. While there, however, as Krista Thompson (2007) has shown us, many of these artists unexpectedly came face to face with their own diasporic difference. We must remember, too, that it was not only political leaders, activists, and artists who were traveling throughout the circum-Caribbean during the first decades of the twentieth century but also "ordinary" people seeking a better life away from home during this crucial period in which the geopolitical arrangements that had been hegemonic were suddenly in flux after World War I. Lara Putnam (2013) has argued that acknowledging the circulations that resulted from this movement—of people, of information and media, of cultural practices including religion, of popular culture, of consciousness and solidarity movements—must transform our understanding not only of how ordinary people imagined the world in which they traveled (and their place in it) but also of the ways they made that world.

8. Yvonne Daniel (2005) has given an account of what it feels like to go into myal, and Karen McCarthy Brown (1991) presents readers with Lourdes's (Mama Lola's) own descriptions of this.

9. This is Stewart's (2005) word for a community of deities or invisible beings.

10. For a beautiful elaboration of these connections, see Lewin 2000.

11. Simpson's use of this term likely reflects the Hollywood fascination with Afro-Atlantic ritual practices that deepened after the US military occupation of Haiti. Zora Neale Hurston also used the term, most probably for the same reason. See Warner-Lewis (2016) for a critique of Joseph Moore's (and by extension, Simpson's) linguistic arrival to this term.

12. But see Stewart (2005) on the lack of sufficient governmental "support" for *kumina* as folk culture: "Entertaining performances of African religious practices in staged competitions, coupled with the distribution of champion ribbons and certificates, are, in the end, dramatic displays of Jamaican social stratification and colonialist consciousness. The negligible economic compensation offered to performers especially suggests that the Jamaican government's reductionist treatment of African-derived religion is no less than a recolonization of an imagined and symbolic 'Africa,' one that must be viewed as self-imposed if it is to be overcome in the future" (176). For a similar analysis, see Thomas 2004.

13. See "Tambufest 2019," Vimeo, uploaded by Deborah Thomas, September 17, 2024, https://vimeo.com/1010438148.

14. Because Penn students had been involved in previous festivals, my faculty research account also provided support for the students' participation, logistics and marketing, and Junior's expenses. Junior and I also used our own funds to cover costs for 2018 and 2019.

15. I thank Nadia Ellis for pushing me to think more about this, and for offering this insight.

16. On collective vulnerability, see Cox 2015.

17. See, for example, the conversation between Keisha-Khan Perry and Daniel Goldstein in Goldstein and Perry 2017; or the one between Bianca Williams and Sophie Chao in Cory-Alice André-Johnson, "What Does Anthropology Sound Like?: Activism," *AnthroPod* (blog, Society for Cultural Anthropology), January 20, 2020, https://culanth.org/fieldsights/what-does-anthropology-sound-like-activism; also see the website of the Center for a Public Anthropology, founded by Rob Borofsky, at https://www.publicanthropology.org.

CODA. THE LABOR OF SOVEREIGNTY

1. The process of ethnography—both research and writing—is also both improvisational and processual, as has effectively been discussed by Malkki and Cerwonka 2007.

2. The other seven companies are based in the United States. See Chris Kolmar, "The 15 Largest Cannabis Companies in the World," Zippia, the Career Expert, April 9, 2023, https://www.zippia.com/advice/largest-cannabis-companies/.

3. Tucker Law Group, "Report of the Independent Investigation into the Demonstrative Display of MOVE Remains at the Penn Museum and Princeton University," Penn Museum, August 20, 2021, https://www.penn.museum/documents/pressroom /MOVEInvestigationReport.pdf.

4. "Protocol, The Commission for the Ethical Treatment of Human Remains," 2022, https://americananthro.org/news/aaa-commission-on-the-ethical-treatment-of -human-remains-issues-final-report/. Sabrina C. Agarwal et al., *The Commission for the Ethical Treatment of Human Remains, American Anthropological Association: Final Report*, American Anthropological Association, June 2024, https://www .americananthro.org/wp-content/uploads/tcethr-report-2024-06.pdf.

5. The student was referring to Ryan Jobson's (2020) year-in-review essay for the *American Anthropologist*, "The Case for Letting Anthropology Burn."

6. I thank Maya Berry, who raised these questions in response to an earlier draft of this manuscript.

Bibliography

PRIMARY SOURCES

Charles Benedict Davenport Papers. American Philosophical Society, Philadelphia.
Life in Jamaica in the Early Twentieth Century: A Presentation of Ninety Oral Accounts. Documentation Centre of the Sir Arthur Lewis Institute for Social and Economic Studies. University of the West Indies, Mona, Jamaica.
Morris Steggerda Collection (316). Otis Historical Archives, National Museum of Health and Medicine, Silver Spring, MD.

SECONDARY SOURCES

Abel, Christopher. 1995. "External Philanthropy and Domestic Change in Colombian Health Care: The Role of the Rockefeller Foundation, ca. 1920–1950." In *Hispanic American Historical Review* 75 (3): 339–76.
Abrahams, Roger. 1983. *The Man-of-Words in the West Indies: Performance and the Emergence of Creole Culture*. Baltimore: Johns Hopkins University Press.
Abu-Lughod, Lila. (1993) 2008. *Writing Women's Lives: Bedouin Stories*. 15th anniversary edition. Berkeley: University of California Press.
Abu El-Haj, Nadia. 2007. "The Genetic Reinscription of Race." *Annual Review of Anthropology* 36:283–300.
Agard-Jones, Vanessa. 2012. "What the Sands Remember." GLQ: *A Journal of Lesbian and Gay Studies* 18 (2–3): 325–46.
Agard-Jones, Vanessa. 2013. "Bodies in the System." *Small Axe* 17 (3): 182–92.
Aguila-Way, Tania. 2014. "The Zapatista 'Mother Seeds in Resistance' Project: The Indigenous Community Seed Bank as a Living, Self-Organizing Archive." *Social Text* 118 32 (1): 67–92.
Ahearn, Laura. 2001. "Language and Agency." *Annual Review of Anthropology* 30:109–37.
Alexander, Jack. 1977. "The Culture of Race in Middle-Class Kingston, Jamaica." *American Ethnologist* 4 (3):413–435.
Alexander, M. Jacqui. 2005. *Pedagogies of Crossing: Meditations on Feminism, Sexual Politics, Memory, and the Sacred*. Durham, NC: Duke University Press.
Alfred, Taiaiake. 1999. *Peace, Power, Righteousness: An Indigenous Manifesto*. New York: Oxford University Press.

Allen, Garland E. 2011. "Eugenics and Modern Biology: Critiques of Eugenics, 1910–1945." *Biological Faculty Publications and Presentations* 5. https://openscholarship.wustl .edu/cgi/viewcontent.cgi?params=/context/bio_facpubs/article/1001/&path _info=Eugenics__Annals_of_Eugenics_.pdf.

Allen, Jafari. 2011. *¡Venceremos! The Erotics of Black Self-Making in Cuba*. Durham, NC: Duke University Press.

Alleyne, Mervyn. 1988. *Roots of Jamaican Culture*. London: Pluto Press.

Anderson, Warwick. 2012. "Racial Hybridity, Physical Anthropology, and Human Biology in the Colonial Laboratories of the United States." *Current Anthropology* 53, supp. 5: S95–S107.

Arendt, Hannah. 1998. *The Human Condition*. 2nd edition. Chicago: University of Chicago Press.

Austin-Broos, Diane. 1994. "Race/Class: Jamaica's Discourse of Heritable Identity." *New West Indian Guide* 68 (3–4): 213–33.

Baker, Lee D. 1998. *From Savage to Negro: Anthropology and the Construction of Race, 1896–1954*. Berkeley: University of California Press.

Baker, Lee D. 2000. "Daniel G. Brinton's Success on the Road to Obscurity, 1890–1899." *Cultural Anthropology* 15 (3): 394–423.

Baker, Lee D. 2010. *Anthropology and the Racial Politics of Culture*. Durham, NC: Duke University Press.

Barker, Joanne. 2005. "For Whom Sovereignty Matters." In *Sovereignty Matters: Locations of Contestation and Possibility in Indigenous Struggles for Self-Determination*, edited by Joanne Barker, 1–31. Lincoln: University of Nebraska Press.

Bataille, Georges. 2017. *The Accursed Share*. Vols. 2 and 3. New York: Zone Books.

Beckwith, Martha Warren. 1924. *Jamaica Anansi Stories*. New York: American Folklore Society.

Beckwith, Martha Warren. 1929. *Black Roadways: A Study of Jamaican Folk Life*. Chapel Hill: University of North Carolina Press.

Behar, Ruth. 1996. *The Vulnerable Observer: Anthropology That Breaks Your Heart*. Boston: Beacon Press.

Beliso-De Jesús, Aisha. 2015. *Electric Santería: Racial and Sexual Assemblages of Transnational Religion*. New York: Columbia University Press.

Benítez-Rojo, Antonio. 1996. *The Repeating Island: The Caribbean and the Postmodern Perspective*. 2nd edition. Durham, NC: Duke University Press.

Berry, Maya J. 2021. "Black Feminist Rumba Pedagogies." *Dance Research Journal* 53 (2): 27–48.

Berry, Maya J. 2025. *Defending Rumba in Havana: The Sacred and the Black Corporeal Undercommons*. Durham, NC: Duke University Press.

Berry, Maya J., Claudia Chávez Argüelles, Shanya Cordis, Sarah Ihmoud, and Elizabeth Velásquez Estrada. 2017. "Toward a Fugitive Anthropology: Gender, Race, and Violence in the Field." *Cultural Anthropology* 32 (4): 537–65.

Besson, Jean. 2016. *Transformations of Freedom in the Land of the Maroons*. Kingston, Jamaica: Ian Randle.

Bilby, Kenneth M. 2006. *True Born Maroons*. Kingston, Jamaica: Ian Randle.

Bilby, Kenneth M., and Fu-Kiau Kia Bunseki. (1983) 2015. "Kumina: A Kongo-Based Tradition in the New World." In *A Reader in African-Jamaican Music, Dance and Religion*, edited by Markus Coester and Wolfgang Bender, 473–528. Kingston, Jamaica: Ian Randle.

Blackmon, Douglas. 1999. "How the South's Fight to Uphold Segregation Was Funded by North." *Wall Street Journal*, June 11. https://www.wsj.com/articles/SB929056013324992946?mod=Searchresults_pos1&page=1.

Blake Hannah, Barbara. 1980a. "The Coptics Brethren of Star Island, White Rastas." *Sunday Gleaner Magazine*, May 11.

Blake Hannah, Barbara. 1980b. "Letter from New York: More About the 'White Rastas.'" *Jamaica Gleaner*, May 25.

Blakey, Michael. 1987. "Skull Doctors: Intrinsic Social and Political Bias in the History of American Physical Anthropology, with Special Reference to the Work of Aleš Hrdlička." *Critique of Anthropology* 7 (2): 7–35.

Boas, Franz. 1907. "Heredity in Anthropometric Traits." *American Anthropologist* 9 (3): 453–69.

Boggs, Grace Lee. 2012. "Reimagine Everything." *Race, Poverty, and the Environment* 19 (2): 44–45.

Bonilla, Yarimar. 2015. *Non-Sovereign Futures: French Caribbean Politics in the Wake of Disenchantment*. Chicago: University of Chicago Press.

Bonilla, Yarimar. 2017. "Unsettling Sovereignty." *Cultural Anthropology* 32 (3): 330–39.

Bradley, Rizvana. 2023. *Anteaesthetics: Black Aesthesis and the Critique of Form*. Stanford, CA: Stanford University Press.

Brathwaite, Edward Kamau. 1971. *The Development of Creole Society in Jamaica, 1770–1820*. Oxford: Clarendon Press.

Brathwaite, Edward Kamau. 1975. "Caribbean Man in Space and Time." *Savacou* 11–12:1–11.

Brathwaite, Edward Kamau. 1978. "Kumina: The Spirit of African Survival." *Jamaica Journal* 12 (2): 44–63.

Brathwaite, Edward Kamau. 1999. *ConVERSations with Nathaniel Mackey*. Staten Island, NY: We Press.

Brodber, Erna. 2003. *Standing Tall: Affirmations of the Jamaican Mule; Twenty-Four Self-Portraits*. Mona, Jamaica: University of the West Indies Press.

Brown, Vincent. 2008. *The Reaper's Garden: Death and Power in the World of Atlantic Slavery*. Cambridge, MA: Harvard University Press.

Brownson, Lucy. 2023. "Odds, Ends, and Archival Exclusion: Ephemeral Archives and Counter-History in the English Country House." *Journal of the Archives and Records Association* 44 (3): 308–29.

Bruchac, Margaret. 2018. *Savage Kin: Indigenous Informants and American Anthropologists*. Tucson: University of Arizona Press.

Bruyneel, Kevin. 2007. *The Third Space of Sovereignty: The Postcolonial Politics of U.S.–Indigenous Relations*. Minneapolis: University of Minnesota Press.

Butler, Judith. 2005. *Giving an Account of Oneself*. New York: Fordham University Press.

Byrd, Jodi. 2011. *The Transit of Empire: Indigenous Critiques of Colonialism*. Minneapolis: University of Minnesota Press.

Campbell, Horace. 1987. *Rasta and Resistance*. Trenton, NJ: Africa World Press.

Campt, Tina. 2017. *Listening to Images*. Durham, NC: Duke University Press.

Carby, Hazel. 2019. *Imperial Intimacies: A Tale of Two Islands*. New York: Verso.

Carnegie, Charles V. 2002. *Postnationalism Prefigured: Caribbean Borderlands*. New Brunswick, NJ: Rutgers University Press.

Castillo, Elaine. 2022. *How to Read Now*. New York: Viking.

Castle, W. E. 1930. "Race Mixture and Physical Disharmonies." *Science* 71 (1850): 603–6.

Castor, N. Fadeke. 2017. *Spiritual Citizenship: Transnational Pathways from Black Power to Ifá in Trinidad*. Durham, NC: Duke University Press.

Cattelino, Jessica. 2008. *High Stakes: Florida Seminole Gaming and Sovereignty*. Durham, NC: Duke University Press.

Cattelino, Jessica. 2023. "Sovereign Interdependencies." In *Sovereignty Unhinged: An Illustrated Primer for the Study of Present Intensities, Disavowals, and Temporal Derangements*, edited by Deborah A. Thomas and Joseph Masco. Durham, NC: Duke University Press.

Cavarero, Adriana. 2000. *Relating Narratives: Storytelling and Selfhood*. Translated by Paul A. Kottman. New York: Routledge.

Cep, Casey. 2020. "William Faulkner's Demons," *New Yorker*, November 23. https://www.newyorker.com/magazine/2020/11/30/william-faulkners-demons.

Chevannes, Barry, ed. 1998. *Rastafari and Other African-Caribbean Worldviews*. New Brunswick, NJ: Rutgers University Press.

Chinn, Sarah E. 2000. *Technology and the Logic of American Racism: A Cultural History of the Body as Evidence*. New York: Continuum.

Chopra, Ruma. 2018. *Almost Home: Maroons Between Slavery and Freedom in Jamaica, Nova Scotia, and Sierra Leone*. New Haven, CT: Yale University Press.

Chua, Liana, Casey High, and Timm Lau, eds. 2008. *How Do We Know? Evidence, Ethnography, and the Making of Anthropological Knowledge*. Cambridge: Cambridge Scholars Press.

Clarke, Kamari. 2020. "Toward Reflexivity in the Anthropology of Expertise and Law." Forward to Special Section on Cultural Expertise. *American Anthropologist* 122 (3): 584–87.

Comaroff, Jean. 1985. *Body of Power, Spirit of Resistance: The Culture and History of a South African People*. Chicago: University of Chicago Press.

Comaroff, Jean, and John L. Comaroff. 2001. "Millennial Capitalism: First Thoughts on a Second Coming." In *Millennial Capitalism and the Culture of Neoliberalism*, edited by Comaroff and Comaroff, 1–56. Durham, NC: Duke University Press.

Comaroff, Jean, and John L. Comaroff, eds. 1993. *Modernity and Its Malcontents: Ritual and Power in Post-colonial Africa*. Chicago: University of Chicago Press.

Condé, Maryse. 1992. *I, Tituba*. Charlottesville: University of Virginia Press.

Conklin, Alice L. 2013. *In the Museum of Man: Race, Anthropology, and Empire in France, 1850–1950*. Ithaca, NY: Cornell University Press.

Coombes, Annie E. 1994. *Reinventing Africa: Museums, Material Culture and Popular Imagination in Late Victorian and Edwardian England*. New Haven, CT: Yale University Press.

Coon, Carleton. 1939. *The Races of Europe*. New York: Macmillan Company.

Coon, Carleton. 1962. *The Origin of Races*. New York: Alfred A. Knopf.

Cooper, Davina, Nikita Dhawan, and Janet Newman, eds. 2020. *Reimagining the State: Theoretical Challenges and Transformative Possibilities*. New York: Routledge.

Cordis, Shanya. 2019. "Settler Unfreedoms." *American Indian Culture and Research Journal* 43 (2): 9–23.

Coulthard, Glen. 2014. *Red Skin, White Masks: Rejecting the Colonial Politics of Recognition*. Minneapolis: University of Minnesota Press.

Cousins, Thomas. 2023. *The Work of Repair: Capacity After Colonialism in the Timber Plantations of South Africa*. New York: Fordham University Press.

Covington-Ward, Yolanda. 2016. *Gesture and Power: Religion, Nationalism, and Everyday Performance in Congo*. Durham, NC: Duke University Press.

Covington-Ward, Yolanda, and Jeanette S. Jouili, eds. 2021. *Embodying Black Religions in Africa and Its Diasporas*. Durham, NC: Duke University Press.

Cox, Aimee M. 2015. *Shapeshifters: Black Girls and the Choreography of Citizenship*. Durham, NC: Duke University Press.

Crossland, Zoë. 2009. "Of Clues and Signs: The Dead Body and Its Evidential Traces." *American Anthropologist* 111 (1): 69–80.

Crossland, Zoë. 2012. "Materiality and Embodiment." In *The Oxford Handbook of Material Culture Studies*, edited by Dan Hicks and Mary C. Beaudry, 386–405. New York: Oxford University Press.

Crosson, J. Brent. 2019a. "What Possessed You? Spirits, Property, and Political Sovereignty at the Limits of 'Possession.'" *Ethnos* 84 (4): 546–56.

Crosson, J. Brent. 2019b. "Catching Power: Problems with Possession, Sovereignty, and African Religions in Trinidad." *Ethnos* 84 (4): 588–614.

Crosson, J. Brent. 2020. *Experiments with Power: Obeah and the Remaking of Religion in Trinidad*. Chicago: University of Chicago Press.

Csordas, Thomas J. 1990. "Embodiment as a Paradigm for Anthropology." *Ethos* 18 (1): 5–47.

Csordas, Thomas J. 1993. "Somatic Modes of Attention." *Cultural Anthropology* 8 (2): 135–56.

Csordas, Thomas. 1994. "Introduction: The Body as Representation and Being-in-the-World." In *Embodiment and Experience: The Existential Ground of Culture and Self*, edited by Csordas, 1–26. Cambridge: Cambridge University Press.

Csordas, Thomas J. 2008. "Intersubjectivity and Intercorporeality." *Subjectivity* 22 (1): 110–21.

Cummings, Ronald. 2018. "Maroon In/Securities." *Small Axe* 22 (3): 47–55.

Curiel, Ochy. 2007. "Crítica poscolonial desde las prácticas políticas del feminismo antirracista." *Nomádas* 26:92–101.

Curiel, Ochy. 2021. "Decolonial Feminism in Abya Yala." *Multitudes* 84 (3): 78–86.

Cvetkovich, Ann. 2003. *An Archive of Feelings: Trauma, Sexuality, and Lesbian Public Cultures*. Durham, NC: Duke University Press.

Daily Gleaner. 1976. "Coptic Members Complain of Police Persecution." April 30.

Daily Gleaner. 1980a. "Listening Post." March 17.

Daily Gleaner. 1980b. "Coptics Say $2M Equipment Seized by JDF." September 26.

Daily Gleaner. 1980c. "Listening Post." October 13.

Daily Gleaner. 1980d. "Listening Post." December 19.

Daily Gleaner. 1981a. "Listening Post." April 23.

Daily Gleaner. 1981b. "Illegal Airstrip." May 5.

Daily Gleaner. 1981c. "Probe Urged into Coptics, Drugs." May 29.

Daily Gleaner. 1981d. "Police Probing Coptics." May 30.

Daniel, Yvonne. 2005. *Dancing Wisdom: Embodied Knowledge in Haitian Vodou, Cuban Yoruba, and Bahian Candomblé*. Urbana: University of Illinois Press.

Das, Veena. 2007. *Life and Words: Violence and the Descent into the Ordinary*. Berkeley: University of California Press.

Davenport, Charles B. 1928. "Race Crossing in Jamaica." *Scientific Monthly* 27:225–38.

Davenport, Charles B., and Morris Steggerda. 1929. *Race Crossing in Jamaica*. Washington, DC: Carnegie Institution of Washington.

Davis, Jenny. 2018. *Talking Indian: Identity and Language Revitalization in the Chickasaw Renaissance*. Tucson: University of Arizona Press.

De la Cadena, Marisol. 2015. *Earth Beings: Ecologies of Practice Across Andean Worlds*. Durham, NC: Duke University Press.

De la Cadena, Marisol and Mario Blaser, eds. 2018. *A World of Many Worlds*. Durham, NC: Duke University Press.

Dennison, Jean. 2012. *Colonial Entanglement: Constituting a Twenty-First-Century Osage Nation*. Chapel Hill: University of North Carolina Press.

Desjarlais, Robert and C. Jason Throop. 2011. "Phenomenological Approaches in Anthropology." *Annual Review of Anthropology* 40:87–102.

Dickey, Bronwen. 2022. "She Was Killed by the Police: Why Were Her Bones in a Museum?" *New York Times Magazine*, October 19.

Dickey, Christopher. 1980. "'Ganja' Bouys Jamaica." *Washington Post*, November 10. https://www.washingtonpost.com/archive/politics/1980/11/10/ganja-bouys-jamaica/b646c8b3-bc78-42ee-929c-a85c1bb0a273/.

Doughty, Kristin Conner. 2016. *Remediation in Rwanda: Grassroots Legal Forums*. Philadelphia: University of Pennsylvania Press.

Drewal, Margaret. 1992. *Yoruba Ritual: Performers, Play, Agency*. Bloomington: Indiana University Press.

Ellis, Nadia. 2015. *Territories of the Soul: Queered Belonging in the Black Diaspora*. Durham, NC: Duke University Press.

Elman, Cheryl, Robert McGuire, and Barbara Wittman. 2014. "Extending Public Health: The Rockefeller Sanitary Commission and Hookworm in the American South." *American Journal of Public Health* 104 (1): 47–58.

Escobar, Arturo. 2020. *Pluriversal Politics: The Real and the Possible*. Translated by David Frye. Durham, NC: Duke University Press.

Espinosa Miñoso, Yuderkys. 2017. "De por qué es necesario un feminismo descolonial: Diferenciación, dominación co-constitutiva de la modernidad occidental y el fin de la política de identidad." *Revista Solar* 12 (1): 141–71.

Fabian, Ann. 2010. *The Skull Collectors: Race, Science, and America's Unburied Dead*. Chicago: University of Chicago Press.

Faimau, Gabriel. 2017. "Religious Testimonial Narratives and Social Construction of Identity: Insights from Prophetic Ministries in Botswana." *Cogent Social Sciences* 3 (1). https://doi.org/10.1080/23311886.2017.1356620.

Farnell, Brenda. 1999. "Moving Bodies, Acting Selves." *Annual Review of Anthropology* 28:341–73.

Farquhar, Judith and Margaret Lock, eds. 2007. *Beyond the Body Proper: Reading the Anthropology of Material Life*. Durham, NC: Duke University Press.

Federici, Silvia. 1975. *Wages Against Housework*. Bristol, UK: Falling Wall Press and Power of Women Collective.

Feldman, Allen. 1991. *Formations of Violence: The Narrative of the Body and Political Terror in Northern Ireland*. Chicago: University of Chicago Press.

Ferreira da Silva, Denise. 2007. *Toward a Global Idea of Race*. Minneapolis: University of Minnesota Press.

Ferreira da Silva, Denise. 2017a. "1 (life) ÷ 0 (blackness) = ∞ - ∞ or ∞/∞: On Matter Beyond the Equation of Value." *E-flux Journal*, no. 79 (February). https://www.e-flux.com/journal/79/94686/1-life-o-blackness-or-on-matter-beyond-the-equation-of-value/.

Ferreira da Silva, Denise. 2017b. "Unpayable Debt: Reading Scenes of Value Against the Arrow of Time." In *Documenta 14 Reader*, edited by Quinn Latimer and Adam Szymczyk, 81–112. Munich: Prestal Verlag.

Ferreira da Silva, Denise. 2021. "Tangible Possibility." Lecture at the Institute of Contemporary Art, Miami. YouTube. Posted September 8. https://www.youtube.com/watch?v=79UWUHtCW6g.

Ferreira da Silva, Denise. 2022. *Unpayable Debt*. London: Sternberg Press.

Ford-Smith, Honor. 2013. "Ring Ding in a Tight Corner: Sistren, Collective Democracy, and the Organization of Cultural Production." In *Feminist Genealogies, Colonial Legacies, Democratic Futures*, edited by Chandra Mohanty and M. Jacqui Alexander, 213–58. New York: Routledge.

Ford-Smith, Honor, with Sistren. 1994. *Lionheart Gal: Life Stories of Jamaican Women*. Toronto: Sister Vision Press.

Forsythe, Dennis. 1979. "Talk of Ingratitude." *Jamaica Gleaner*, September 8.

Freitas, Décio. 1978. *Palmares: A Guerra dos escravos*. Rio de Janeiro: Graal.

Fullwiley, Duana. 2007. "The Molecularization of Race: Institutionalizing Human Difference in Pharmacogenetics Practice." *Science as Culture* 16 (1): 1–30.

Furani, Khaled. 2022. "*Khalifah* and the Modern Sovereign: Revisiting a Qur'anic Ideal from Within the Palestinian Condition." *Journal of Religion* 102 (4): 482–506.

Furnivall, J. S. 1945. "Some Problems of Tropical Economy." In *Fabian Colonial Essays*, edited by Rita Hinden, 161–84. London: George Allen and Unwin.

Furnivall, J. S. 1948. *Colonial Policy and Practice: A Comparative Study of Burma and Netherlands India*. Cambridge: Cambridge University Press.

Geertz, Clifford. 1975. "On the Nature of Anthropological Understanding." *American Scientist* 63:47–53.

Gil-Riaño, Sebastián. 2023. *The Remnants of Race Science: UNESCO and Economic Development in the Global South*. New York: Columbia University Press.

Gill, Lyndon. 2018. *Erotic Islands: Art and Activism in the Queer Caribbean*. Durham, NC: Duke University Press.

Gleaner Parliamentary Reporter. 1976a. "House Ends Recess." January 15.

Gleaner Parliamentary Reporter. 1976b. "Housing Trust Changes Proposed." February 19, 19.

Glissant, Édouard. 1997. *Poetics of Relation*. Ann Arbor: University of Michigan Press.

Goldstein, Daniel M., and Keisha-Khan Y. Perry. 2017. "Activist Anthropology: A Conversation Between Daniel M. Goldstein and Keisha-Khan Y. Perry." *American Anthropologist*, March 27. https://www.americananthropologist.org/online-content/activist-anthropology-a-conversation-between-daniel-m-goldstein-and-keisha-khan-y-perry.

Gómez, Pablo F. 2017. *The Experimental Caribbean: Creating Knowledge and Healing in the Early Modern Atlantic*. Chapel Hill: University of North Carolina Press.

Good, Byron J. 2020. "Hauntology: Theorizing the Spectral in Psychological Anthropology." *Ethos* 47 (4): 411–26.

Goodman, Alan, Deborah Heath, and M. Susan Lindee, eds. 2003. *Genetic Nature/Culture: Anthropology and Science Beyond the Two-Culture Divide*. Berkeley: University of California Press.

Government of Jamaica. 1976. The Ethiopian Zion Coptic Church (Incorporation and Vesting) Act. No. 11–1976. https://www.ethiopianzioncopticchurch.org/pdfs/jamaica_1976.pdf?

Graeber, David, and David Wengrow. 2021. *The Dawn of Everything: A New History of Humanity*. New York: Farrar, Straus and Giroux.

Gross-Wyrtzen, Leslie, and Alex A. Moulton. 2023. "Toward 'Fugitivity as Method': An Introduction to the Special Issue." *ACME: An International Journal for Critical Geographies* 22 (5): 1258–72.

Hale, John. (1702) 1914. "A Modest Enquiry into the Nature of Witchcraft." In *Narratives of the Witchcraft Cases, 1648–1706*, edited by George L. Burr, 395–423. New York: Charles Scribner's Sons.

Hall, Louis Karoniaktajeh. 2023. *The Mohawk Warrior Society: A Handbook on Sovereignty and Survival*, edited by Kahentinetha Rotiskarewake, Philippe Blouin, Matt Peterson, and Malek Rasamny. Oakland, CA: PM Press.

Harden, Blaine. 1985. "Marijuana Is Not a Jamaican Staple Crop, Seaga Says." *Washington Post*, February 2. https://www.washingtonpost.com/archive/politics/1985/02/02/marijuana-is-not-a-jamaican-staple-crop-seaga-says/02a5108f-2255-4b0d-a40f-cc06bc9688af/.

Harjo, Laura. 2019. *Spiral to the Stars: Mvskoke Tools of Futurity*. Tucson: University of Arizona Press.

Harris, Cheryl. 1993. "Whiteness as Property." *Harvard Law Review* 106 (8): 1710–91.

Hartman, Saidiya. 1997. *Scenes of Subjection: Terror, Slavery, and Self-Making in Nineteenth-Century America*. New York: Oxford University Press.

Hartman, Saidiya. 2008. "Venus in Two Acts." *Small Axe* 12 (2): 1–14.

Hastrup, Kirsten. 2004. "Getting It Right: Knowledge and Evidence in Anthropology." *Anthropological Theory* 4 (4): 455–72.

Herskovits, Melville J. 1927. "Variability and Racial Mixture." *American Naturalist* 61 (672): 68–81.

Herskovits, Melville J. 1930. "The Negro in the New World: The Statement of a Problem." *American Anthropologist* 32 (1): 145–55.

Herskovits, Melville J. (1937) 1971. *Life in a Haitian Valley*. New York: Doubleday.

Herskovits, Melville J. (1941) 1990. *The Myth of the Negro Past*. Boston: Beacon Books.

Hoekema, David A. 2008. "African Personhood: Morality and Identity in the 'Bush of Ghosts.'" *Soundings: An Interdisciplinary Journal* 91 (3–4): 255–86.

Hogarth, Rana A. 2017. *Medicalizing Blackness: Making Racial Difference in the Atlantic World, 1780–1840*. Chapel Hill: University of North Carolina Press.

Hogarth, Rana A. 2021. "Race, Place, and Power in the Production of Medical Knowledge: Perspectives from the Greater Caribbean." *History Compass* 19. https://doi.org/10.1111/hic3.12694.

Hurston, Zora Neale. (1938) 1990. *Tell My Horse: Voodoo and Life in Haiti and Jamaica*. New York: Harper and Row.

Hutton, Clinton A. 2015. *Colour for Colour, Skin for Skin: Marching with the Ancestral Spirits into War Oh at Morant Bay*. Kingston, Jamaica: Ian Randle.

Ife, Fahima. 2021. *Maroon Choreography*. Durham, NC: Duke University Press.

Irobi, Esiaba. 2006. "The Philosophy of the Sea: History, Economics and Reason in the Caribbean Basin." *Worlds and Knowledges Otherwise* 1 (3). https://globalstudies.trinity.duke.edu/sites/globalstudies.trinity.duke.edu/files/documents/v1d3_EIrobi.pdf.

Jackson, John P. 2001. "'In Ways Unacademical': The Reception of Carleton S. Coon's *The Origin of Races*." *Journal of the History of Biology* 34:247–85.

Jackson, John P., and David J. Depew. 2017. *Darwinism, Democracy, and Race: American Anthropology and Evolutionary Biology in the Twentieth Century*. New York: Routledge.

Jackson, Shona. 2012. *Creole Indigeneity: Between Myth and Nation in the Caribbean*. Minneapolis: University of Minnesota Press.

Jackson, Zakiyyah Iman. 2020. *Becoming Human: Matter and Meaning in an Antiblack World*. New York: New York University Press.

Jaffe, Rivke. 2024. *The Rule of Dons: Criminal Leaders and Political Authority in Urban Jamaica*. Durham, NC: Duke University Press.

James, Erica Caple. 2008. "Haunting Ghosts: Madness, Gender, and *Ensekirite* in Haiti in the Democratic Era." In *Postcolonial Disorders*, edited by Mary-Jo DelVecchio Good, Sandra Hyde, and Byron Good, 132–56. Berkeley: University of California Press.

James, Selma. (1974) 2012. "Sex, Race, and Class." In *Sex, Race, and Class: The Perspective of Winning—A Selection of Writings, Writings, 1952–2011*. Oakland, CA: PM Press.

James, Selma. 2021. *Our Time Is Now: Sex, Race, Class, and Caring for People and Planet*. Oakland, CA: PM Press.

Jekyll, Walter. (1907) 1966. *Jamaican Song and Story: Annancy Stories, Digging Sings, Dancing Tunes and Ring Tunes*. New York: Dover Press.

Jennings, Herbert Spencer. 1924. "Heredity and Environment." *Scientific Monthly* 19:225–38.

Jobson, Ryan. 2020. "The Case for Letting Anthropology Burn: Sociocultural Anthropology in 2019." *American Anthropologist* 122 (2): 259–71.

Johnson, Paul Christopher. 2011. "An Atlantic Genealogy of 'Spirit Possession.'" *Comparative Studies in Society and History* 53 (2): 393–425.

Johnson, Paul Christopher. 2014a. "Toward an Atlantic Genealogy of 'Spirit Possession.'" In *Spirited Things: The Work of 'Possession' in Afro-Atlantic Religions*, edited by Johnson, 23–45. Chicago: University of Chicago Press.

Johnson, Paul Christopher, ed. 2014b. *Spirited Things: The Work of 'Possession' in Afro-Atlantic Religions*. Chicago: University of Chicago Press.

Johnson, Paul Christopher. 2019. "Possession's Native Land." *Ethnos* 84 (4): 660–77.

Jones, Margaret. 2013. *Public Health in Jamaica, 1850–1940*. Mona, Jamaica: University of the West Indies Press.

Jordan, Alissa. Forthcoming. *Atlas of Nanm: Bodily Openings and Encounters in Haiti*. Philadelphia: University of Pennsylvania Press.

Kauanui, J. Kēhaulani. 2008. *Hawaiian Blood: Colonialism and the Politics of Sovereignty and Indigeneity*. Durham, NC: Duke University Press.

Keel, Terence. 2018. *Divine Variations: How Christian Thought Became Racial Science*. Stanford, CA: Stanford University Press.

Kindley, Evan. 2020. "William Faulkner's Southern Guilt." *New Republic*, August 18. https://newrepublic.com/article/158710/william-faulkner-civil-war-biography-review-southern-white-guilt.

King, Tiffany L. 2019. *The Black Shoals: Offshore Formations of Black and Native Studies.* Durham, NC: Duke University Press.

Kitchin, Arthur. 1980. "A People's Temple?" *Jamaica Gleaner,* May 19.

Kivland, Chelsey. 2020. *Street Sovereigns: Young Men and the Makeshift State in Urban Haiti.* Ithaca, NY: Cornell University Press.

Klima, Alan. 2001. *The Funeral Casino: Meditation, Massacre, and Exchange with the Dead in Thailand.* Princeton, NJ: Princeton University Press.

Klima, Alan. 2019. *Ethnography #9.* Durham, NC: Duke University Press.

Krause, Sharon R. 2015. *Freedom Beyond Sovereignty: Reconstructing Liberal Individualism.* Chicago: University of Chicago Press.

Krogman, Wilton Marion. 1976. "Fifty Years of Physical Anthropology: The Men, the Material, the Concepts, the Methods." *Annual Review of Anthropology* 5:1–14.

Kuipers, Joel. 2013. "Evidence and Authority in Ethnographic and Linguistic Perspective." *Annual Review of Anthropology* 42:399–413.

Lakoff, George, and Mark Johnson. 1981. *Metaphors We Live By.* Chicago: University of Chicago Press.

Lambert, Laurie. 2020. *Comrade Sister: Caribbean Feminist Revisions of the Grenada Revolution.* Charlottesville: University of Virginia Press.

Laó-Montes, Agustín. 2016. "Afro-Latin American Feminisms at the Cutting Edge of Emerging Political-Epistemic Movements." *Meridians* 14 (2): 1–24.

Lara, Ana-Maurine 2020. *Queer Freedom: Black Sovereignty.* Albany: State University of New York Press.

Leacock, Eleanor. 1978. "Women's Status in Egalitarian Society: Implications for Social Evolution." *Current Anthropology* 19:247–76.

Lewin, Olive. 2000. *Rock It Come Over: The Folk Music of Jamaica.* Mona, Jamaica: University of the West Indies Press.

Lewis, Jovan. 2020. *Scammer's Yard: The Crime of Black Repair in Jamaica.* Minneapolis: University of Minnesota Press.

Lewis, Jovan. 2023. "Fugitive Repair." ACME: *An International Journal for Critical Geographies* 22 (5): 1388–97.

Lewis, Jovan. 2024. "Black Life Beyond Injury: Relational Repair and the Reparative Conjuncture." *Political Geography* 108 (January). https://www.sciencedirect.com/science/article/abs/pii/S0962629823001415.

Lewis, Rupert, and Patrick Bryan, eds. 1991. *Garvey: His Work and Impact.* Trenton, NJ: Africa World Press.

Lincoln, Martha, and Bruce Lincoln. 2015. "Toward a Critical Hauntology: Bare Afterlife and the Ghosts of Ba Chúc." *Comparative Studies in Society and History* 57 (1): 191–220.

Lock, Margaret. 1993. "Cultivating the Body: Anthropology and Epistemologies of Bodily Practice and Knowledge." *Annual Review of Anthropology* 22:133–55.

Lombardo, Paul A. 2016. "Anthropometry, Race, and Eugenic Research: 'Measurements of Growing Negro Children' at the Tuskegee Institute, 1932–1944." In *The Uses of*

Humans in Experiment: Perspectives from the 17th to the 20th Century, edited by Erika Dyck and Larry Stewart, 215–39. Leiden, Netherlands: Brill.

Long, Edward. 1774. *The History of Jamaica*. London: T. Lowndes.

Loperena, Chris. 2020. "Adjudicating Indigeneity: Anthropological Testimony in the Inter-American Court of Human Rights." *American Anthropologist* 122 (3): 595–605.

Loperena, Chris, Mariana Mora, and R. Aída Hernández-Castillo. 2020. "Cultural Expertise? Anthropologist as Witness in Defense of Indigenous and Afro-Descendant Rights." Introduction to Special Section on Cultural Expertise. *American Anthropologist* 122 (3): 588–94.

Lorde, Audre. 1984. "Uses of the Erotic: The Erotic as Power." In *Sister Outsider*, 53–59. Berkeley, CA: Crossing Press.

Lumsden, Joy. 1987. "Robert Love and Jamaican Politics." PhD diss., University of the West Indies.

MacMillan, Ken. 2006. *Sovereignty and Possession in the English New World: The Legal Foundations of Empire, 1576–1640*. Cambridge: Cambridge University Press.

Madison, D. Soyini. 2019. *Critical Ethnography: Method, Ethics, and Performance*. 3rd edition. Thousand Oaks, CA: Sage.

Magloire, Gérarde, and Kevin A. Yelvington. 2005. "Haiti and the Anthropological Imagination." *Gradhiva* 1 (1): 127–52.

Mak, Geertje. 2020. "A Colonial-Scientific Interface: The Construction, Viewing, and Circulation of Faces via a 1906 German Racial Atlas." *American Anthropologist* 122 (2): 327–41.

Malkki, Liisa, and Allaine Cerwonka. 2007. *Improvising Theory: Process and Temporality in Ethnographic Fieldwork*. Stanford, CA: Stanford University Press.

Manning, Aleia, and Jesus Pallares, dirs. 2021. *The Controversial Carleton Coon: Legacies of Scientific Racism in American Anthropology*. Short documentary film screened during *Rotten Foundations, Dangerous Footholds*, Slought, Department of Anthropology, University of Pennsylvania, Philadelphia, December 9–21.

Marks, Jonathan. 1996. "Science and Race." *American Behavioral Scientist* 40 (2): 123–33.

Marriott, McKim. 1976. "Hindu Transactions: Diversity Without Dualism." In *Transaction and Meaning: Directions in the Anthropology of Exchange and Symbolic Behavior*, edited by Bruce Kapferer, 109–42. Philadelphia: University of Pennsylvania Press.

Martínez-Cairo, Bárbara, and Emanuela Buscemi. 2021. "Latin American Decolonial Feminisms: Theoretical Perspectives and Challenges." *Amérique Latine Histoire et Mémoire* 42:1–13.

Masquelier, Adeline. 2001. *Prayer Has Spoiled Everything: Possession, Power, and Identity in an Islamic Town of Niger*. Durham, NC: Duke University Press.

Matory, J. Lorand. 2018. *The Fetish Revisited: Marx, Freud, and the Gods Black People Make*. Durham, NC: Duke University Press.

Mauss, Marcel. 1935. "Techniques of the Body." *Journal de psychologie normal et pathologique* 32:271–93.

Maynard, Robyn, and Leanne B. Simpson. 2022. *Rehearsals for Living*. Chicago: Haymarket Books.

Mbiti, John S. 1970. *African Religions and Philosophy*. London: Heinemann.

McAllister, Carlota, and Valentina Napolitano. 2020. "Introduction: Incarnate Politics Beyond the Cross and the Sword." *Social Analysis* 64 (4): 1–20.

McAllister, Carlota, and Valentina Napolitano. 2021. "Political Theology/Theopolitics: The Thresholds and Vulnerabilities of Sovereignty." *Annual Review of Anthropology* 50:109–24.

McCarthy Brown, Karen. 1991. *Mama Lola: A Vodou Priestess in Brooklyn*. Berkeley: University of California Press.

M'charek, Amade. 2013. "Beyond Fact or Fiction: On the Materiality of Race in Practice." *Cultural Anthropology* 28 (3): 420–42.

M'charek, Amade. 2014. "Race, Time and Folded Objects: The HeLa Error." *Theory, Culture and Society* 31 (6): 29–56.

M'charek, Amade. 2020. "Tentacular Faces: Race and the Return of the Phenotype in Forensic Identification." *American Anthropologist* 122 (2): 369–80.

M'charek, Amade. 2023. "Curious About Race: Generous Methods and Modes of Knowing in Practice." *Social Studies of Science* 53 (6): 826–49.

M'charek, Amade, Katharina Schramm, and David Skinner. 2014. "Technologies of Belonging: The Absent Presence of Race in Europe." *Science, Technology, and Human Values* 39 (4): 459–67.

Melamed, Jodi. 2015. "Racial Capitalism." *Critical Ethnic Studies* 1 (1): 76–85.

Merleau-Ponty, Maurice. 1962. *Phenomenology of Perception*. New York: Routledge.

Mintz, Sidney. 1974. *Worker in the Cane: A Puerto Rican Life History*. New York: W. W. Norton.

Mitchell, Paul W. 2022. "The Making and Unmaking of Cranial Race Science: The Origins and Afterlives of Human Skull Collections, 1768–1851." PhD diss., University of Pennsylvania.

Moore, Joseph G. 1953. "Religion of Jamaican Negroes: A Study of Afro-American Acculturation." PhD diss., Northwestern University.

Moreau de Saint-Méry, M. L. E. 1797. *Description topographique, physique, civile, politique, et historique de la partie française de l'isle Saint-Domingue*. Philadelphia: published by author.

Moreton-Robinson, Aileen, ed. 2007a. *Sovereign Subjects: Indigenous Sovereignty Matters*. London: Allen and Unwin.

Moreton-Robinson, Aileen. 2007b. "Introduction." In *Sovereign Subjects: Indigenous Sovereignty Matters*, edited by Moreton-Robinson, 1–11. London: Allen and Unwin.

Moreton-Robinson, Aileen. 2007c. "Writing Off Indigenous Sovereignty: The Discourse of Security and Patriarchal White Sovereignty." In *Sovereign Subjects: Indigenous Sovereignty Matters*, edited by Moreton-Robinson, 86–102. London: Allen and Unwin.

Moreton-Robinson, Aileen. 2015. *The White Possessive: Property, Power, and Indigenous Sovereignty*. Minneapolis: University of Minnesota Press.

Moreton-Robinson, Aileen. 2017. "Relationality: A Key Presupposition of an Indigenous Social Research Paradigm." In *Sources and Methods in Indigenous Studies*, 69–77. New York: Routledge.

Morgensen, Scott L. 2011. "The Biopolitics of Settler Colonialism: Right Here, Right Now." *Settler Colonial Studies* 1 (1): 52–76.

Morris, Courtney Desiree. 2023. *To Defend This Sunrise: Black Women's Activism and the Authoritarian Turn in Nicaragua*. New Brunswick, NJ: Rutgers University Press.

Morris, Rosalind C. 1995. "All Made Up: Performance Theory and the New Anthropology of Sex and Gender." *Annual Review of Anthropology* 24:567–92.

Morrison, Belinda F., William D. Aiken, and Richard Mayhew. 2014. "Current State of Prostate Cancer Treatment in Jamaica." *Ecancermedicalscience* 8:456. https://www.ncbi.nlm.nih.gov/pmc/articles/PMC4154943/.

Morton, Samuel George. 1839. *Crania Americana, or, A Comparative View of the Skulls of Various Aboriginal Nations of North and South America*. Philadelphia: J. Dobson.

Mosko, Mark S. 2015. "Unbecoming Individuals: The Partible Character of the Christian Person." *HAU: Journal of Ethnographic Theory* 5 (1): 361–93.

Mossière, Géraldine. 2021. "The Anthropology of Christianity and the Dividual Self: Spiritual Flow, Physical Mobility, and Embodied Callings." *Studies in Religion/Sciences Réligeuses* 50 (2): 189–209.

Muñoz, José Estéban. 2001. "Gesture, Ephemera, and Queer Feeling: Approaching Kevin Aviance." In *Dancing Desires: Choreographing Sexualities on and off the Stage*, edited by Jane Desmond, 423–42. Madison: University of Wisconsin Press.

Murphy, Joseph M. 1994. *Working the Spirit: Ceremonies of the African Diaspora*. Boston: Beacon Press.

Myers, Fred. 1979. "Emotions and the Self: A Theory of Personhood and Political Order Among Pintupi Aborigines." *Ethos* 7 (4): 343–70.

Ndikung, Bonaventure Soh Bejeng. 2022. "Corpoliteracy: Envisaging the Body as Slate, Sponge, and Witness." Eindhoven, Netherlands: Van Abbemuseum.

Nelkin, Dorothy, and M. Susan Lindee. 2004. *The DNA Mystique: The Gene as a Cultural Icon*. Ann Arbor: University of Michigan Press.

Nelson, Alondra. 2016. *The Social Life of DNA: Race, Reparations, and Reconciliation After the Genome*. New York: Beacon Press.

Newton, Melanie J. 2013. "Returns to a Native Land: Indigeneity and Decolonization in the Anglophone Caribbean." *Small Axe* 17 (2):108–122.

Newton, Melanie J. 2022. "Counterpoints of Conquest: The Royal Proclamation of 1763, the Lesser Antilles, and the Ethnocartography of Genocide." *William and Mary Quarterly* 79 (2): 241–82.

Ng, Emily. 2020. *A Time of Lost Gods: Mediumship, Madness, and the Ghost After Mao*. Oakland: University of California Press.

Nussbaum, Jacob. 2024. "Beyond Time: Radical Experiments with Politics and Performance in Philadelphia." PhD diss., University of Pennsylvania.

Ochs, Elinor, and Lisa Capps. 1996. "Narrating the Self." *Annual Review of Anthropology* 25:19–43.

Oladipo, Olusegun. 1992. "The Yoruba Conception of a Person: An Analytico-Philosophical Study." *International Studies in Philosophy* 24 (3): 15–24.

Ong, Aihwa. 1987. *Spirits of Resistance and Capitalist Discipline: Factory Women in Malaysia*. Albany: State University of New York Press.

Palmer, Steven. 2009. "Migrant Clinics and Hookworm Science: Peripheral Origins of International Health, 1840–1920." *Bulletin of the History of Medicine* 83 (4): 676–709.

Palmer, Steven. 2010. *Launching Global Health: The Caribbean Odyssey of the Rockefeller Foundation*. Ann Arbor: University of Michigan Press.

Palmié, Stephan. 2002. *Wizards and Scientists: Explorations in Afro-Cuban Modernity and Tradition*. Durham, NC: Duke University Press.

Paton, Diana. 2015. *The Cultural Politics of Obeah: Religion, Colonialism and Modernity in the Caribbean World*. Cambridge: Cambridge University Press.

Patterson, Orlando. 1982. *Slavery and Social Death: A Comparative Study*. Cambridge, MA: Harvard University Press.

Peacock, James L., and Dorothy C. Holland. 1994. "The Narrated Self: Life Stories in Process." *Ethos* 21 (4): 367–83.

Peake, Linda and D. Alissa Trotz. 1999. *Gender, Ethnicity and Place: Women and Identities in Guyana*. New York: Routledge.

Pearson, Karl. "Review." 1930. *Nature* 3177 (126): 427–29.

Pemberton, Rita. 2003. "A Different Intervention: The International Health Commission/Board, Health, Sanitation in the British Caribbean, 1914–1930." *Caribbean Quarterly* 49 (4): 87–103.

Pettit, Philip. 1997. *Republicanism: A Theory of Freedom and Government*. Cambridge: Cambridge University Press.

Phelan, Peggy. 1993. *Unmarked: The Politics of Performance*. London: Routledge.

Povinelli, Elizabeth. 2006. *The Empire of Love: Toward a Theory of Intimacy, Genealogy, and Carnality*. Durham, NC: Duke University Press.

Pratt, Mary Louise. 2022. *Planetary Longings*. Durham, NC: Duke University Press.

Price, Charles. 2022. *Rastafari: The Evolution of a People and Their Identity*. New York: New York University Press.

Price, Richard. 1972. *Maroon Societies: Rebel Slave Communities in the Americas*. New York: Doubleday.

Price, Richard. 2011. *Rainforest Warriors: Human Rights on Trial*. Philadelphia: University of Pennsylvania Press.

Price-Mars, Jean. 1928. *Ainsi parla l'oncle: Essais d'ethnographie*. New York: Parapsychology Foundation.

Priest, Dana. 1987. "Jamaicans Oppose Marijuana Eradication Push." *Washington Post*, March 15. https://www.washingtonpost.com/archive/politics/1987/03/15/jamaicans-oppose-marijuana-eradication-push/cadba140-4c7f-4ca0-8b3b-ca5d186a4484/.

Provine, William B. 1986. "Geneticists and Race." *American Zoologist* 26 (3): 857–87.

Putnam, Lara. 2013. *Radical Moves: Caribbean Migrants and the Politics of Race in the Jazz Age*. Chapel Hill: University of North Carolina Press.

Quashie, Kevin. 2021. *Black Aliveness, or, A Poetics of Being*. Durham, NC: Duke University Press.

Redman, Samuel J. 2016. *Bone Rooms: From Scientific Racism to Human Prehistory in Museums*. Cambridge: Harvard University Press.

Richman, Karen. 2014. "Possession and Attachment: Notes on Moral Ritual Communication Among Haitian Descent Groups." In *Spirited Things: The Work of "Possession" in Afro-Atlantic Religions*, edited by Paul Christopher Johnson, 207–23. Chicago: University of Chicago Press.

Riddle, Oscar. 1947. "Biographical Memoir of Charles Benedict Davenport, 1866–1944." National Academy of Sciences of the United States of America, Biographical Memoirs, Volume 25, 4th Memoir.

Rifkin, Mark. 2017. *Beyond Settler Time: Temporal Sovereignty and Indigenous Self-Determination*. Durham, NC: Duke University Press.

Ritch, Dawn. 1979a. "Business as Usual." *Jamaica Gleaner*, April 26.

Ritch, Dawn. 1979b. "Need for Legislation." *Jamaica Gleaner*, August 4.

Ritch, Dawn. 1979c. "Coptic Ingratitude." *Jamaica Gleaner*, August 30.

Roberts, Dorothy. 2011. *Fatal Invention: How Science, Politics, and Big Business Re-Create Race in the Twenty-First Century*. New York: The New Press.

Roberts, G. W. 1968. "Demographic Aspects of Rural Development: The Jamaican Experience." *Social and Economic Studies* 17 (3): 276–82.

Roberts, Neil. 2015. *Freedom as Marronage*. Chicago: University of Chicago Press.

Rosaldo, Michelle Z. 1984. "Toward an Anthropology of Self and Feeling." In *Culture Theory: Essays on Mind, Self, and Emotion*, edited by Richard Shweder and Robert LeVine, 137–57. Cambridge: Cambridge University Press.

Ross, Fiona. 2002. *Bearing Witness: Women and the Truth and Reconciliation Commission in South Africa*. London: Pluto Press.

Rutherford, Danilyn. 2012. *Laughing at Leviathan: Sovereignty and Audience in West Papua*. Chicago: University of Chicago Press.

Rutherford, Danilyn. 2018. *Living in the Stone Age: Reflections on the Origins of a Colonial Fantasy*. Chicago: University of Chicago Press.

Ryman, Cheryl. 1984. "Kumina: Stability and Change." *ACIJ Research Review* 1: 81–128.

Salesa, Damon Ieremia. 2011. *Racial Crossings: Race, Intermarriage, and the Victorian British Empire*. Oxford: Oxford University Press.

Schneider, Rebecca. 2001. "Performance Remains." *Performance Research* 6 (2): 100–108.

Schuler, Monica. 1980. *"Alas, Alas, Kongo": A Social History of Indentured African Immigration into Jamaica, 1841–1865*. Baltimore: Johns Hopkins University Press.

Scott, David. 2002. "The Sovereignty of the Imagination: An Interview with George Lamming." *Small Axe* 6 (2): 72–200.

Scott, David. 2004. *Conscripts of Modernity: The Tragedy of Colonial Enlightenment*. Durham, NC: Duke University Press.

Scott, David. 2013. "On the Question of Caribbean Studies." *Small Axe* 17 (2): 1–7.

Seaga, Edward. 1969. "Revival Cults in Jamaica." *Jamaica Journal* 3 (2): 3–13.

Sebastião de Souza, Vanderlei. 2016. "Science and Miscegenation in the Early Twentieth Century: Edgard Roquette-Pinto's Debates and Controversies with US Physical Anthropology." *História, Ciências, Saúde–Manguinhos* 23 (3): 1–17.

Shaw, Rosalind. 2002. *Memories of the Slave Trade: Ritual and the Historical Imagination in Sierra Leone*. Chicago, IL: University of Chicago Press.

Siegel, James. 2005. *Naming the Witch*. Stanford, CA: Stanford University Press.

Silber, Irina Carlota. 2010. *Everyday Revolutionaries: Gender, Violence, and Disillusionment in Postwar El Salvador*. New Brunswick, NJ: Rutgers University Press.

Silber, Irina Carlota. 2022. *After Stories: Transnational Intimacies of Postwar El Salvador*. Stanford, CA: Stanford University Press.

Simpson, Audra. 2007. "On Ethnographic Refusal: Indigeneity, 'Voice' and Colonial Citizenship." *Junctures* 9:67–80.

Simpson, Audra. 2014. *Mohawk Interruptus: Political Life Across the Borders of Settler States*. Durham, NC: Duke University Press.

Simpson, Audra. 2016. "Consent's Revenge." *Cultural Anthropology* 31 (3): 326–33.

Simpson, Audra. 2020. "The Sovereignty of Critique." *SAQ* 119 (4): 685–99.

Simpson, George Eaton. 1970. *Religious Cults of the Caribbean: Trinidad, Jamaica, and Haiti*. Rio Piedras: Institute of Caribbean Studies, University of Puerto Rico.

Simpson, Leanne B. 2017. *As We Have Always Done: Indigenous Freedom Through Radical Resistance*. Minneapolis: University of Minnesota Press.

Skaria, Ajay. 2022. "The Subaltern and the Minor: For Qadri Ismail." *Critical Times* 5 (2): 275–309.

Smith, Faith. 2013. "Good Enough for Booker T to Kiss: Hampton, Tuskegee, and Caribbean Self-Fashioning." *Journal of Transnational American Studies* 5 (1). http://doi.org/10.5070/T851019717.

Smith, Faith. 2023. *Strolling in the Ruins: The Caribbean's Non-Sovereign Modern in the Early Twentieth Century*. Durham, NC: Duke University Press.

Smith, M. G. 1965. *The Plural Society in the British West Indies*. Berkeley: University of California Press.

Spillers, Hortense J. 1987. "Mama's Baby, Papa's Maybe: An American Grammar Book." *Diacritics* 17 (2): 64–81.

St. Aubyn Gosse, Dave. 2022. *Alexander Bedward, The Prophet of August Town: Race, Religion and Colonialism*. Kingston: University of the West Indies Press.

Stengers, Isabelle. 2010. *Cosmopolitics*. Vol. 1. Translated by R. Bononno. Minneapolis: University of Minnesota Press.

Stephen, Lynn. 2017. "Bearing Witness: Testimony in Latin American Anthropology and Related Fields." *Journal of Latin American and Caribbean Anthropology* 22 (1): 85–109.

Stephens, Michelle. 2013. "What Is an Island?: Caribbean Studies and the Contemporary Visual Artist." *Small Axe* 17 (2): 8–26.

Stewart, Dianne. 2005. *Three Eyes for the Journey: African Dimensions of the Jamaican Religious Experience*. Oxford: Oxford University Press.

Stocking, George. 1968. "The Persistence of Polygenist Thought in Post-Darwinian Anthropology." In *Race, Culture, and Evolution: Essays in the History of Anthropology*, 42–68. Chicago: University of Chicago Press.

Stoller, Paul. 1994. "Embodying Colonial Memories." *American Anthropologist* 96 (3): 634–48.

Strathern, Marilyn. 1988. *The Gender of the Gift: Problems with Women and Problems with Society in Melanesia*. Berkeley: University of California Press.

Strong, Krystal. 2021. "A Requiem for Delisha and Tree Africa." *Anthropology News*, October 25. https://www.anthropology-news.org/articles/a-requiem-for-delisha -and-tree-africa/.

Strongman, Roberto. 2019. *Queering Black Atlantic Religions: Transcorporeality in Candomblé, Santería, and Vodou*. Durham, NC: Duke University Press.

Sturm, Circe. 2002. *Blood Politics: Race, Culture, and Identity in the Cherokee Nation of Oklahoma*. Berkeley: University of California Press.

Sturm, Circe. 2017. "Reflections on the Anthropology of Sovereignty and Settler Colonialism: Lessons from Native North America." *Cultural Anthropology* 32 (3): 340–48.

Sysling, Fenneke. 2016. *Racial Science and Human Diversity in Colonial Indonesia*. Singapore: National University of Singapore Press.

Taylor, Diana. 2003. *The Archive and the Repertoire: Performing Cultural Memory in the Americas*. Durham, NC: Duke University Press.

Temin, David Myer. 2023. *Remapping Sovereignty: Decolonization and Self-Determination in North American Indigenous Political Thought*. Chicago: University of Chicago Press.

Teo, Thomas. 2004. "The Historical Problematization of 'Mixed Race' in Psychological and Human-Scientific Discourses." In *Defining Difference: Race and Racism in the History of Psychology*, edited by A. S. Winston, 79–108. Washington DC: American Psychological Association.

Teo, Thomas. 2022. "What Is a White Epistemology in Psychological Science? A Critical Race-Theoretical Analysis." *Hypothesis and Theory* 13 (April): 1–10.

Thomas, Deborah A. 2004. *Modern Blackness: Nationalism, Globalization, and the Politics of Culture in Jamaica*. Durham, NC: Duke University Press.

Thomas, Deborah A. 2011. *Exceptional Violence: Embodied Citizenship in Transnational Jamaica*. Durham, NC: Duke University Press.

Thomas, Deborah A. 2019. *Political Life in the Wake of the Plantation: Sovereignty, Witnessing, Repair*. Durham, NC: Duke University Press.

Thomas, Deborah A. 2020. "Displacements: The Jamaican 1950s." *Small Axe* 24 (3): 53–64.

Thomas, Deborah A. 2021. Remarks delivered at a screening of *The Controversial Carleton Coon: Legacies of Scientific Racism in American Anthropology*, directed by Aleia Manning and Jesus Pallares. *Rotten Foundations, Dangerous Footholds*, Slought, Department of Anthropology, University of Pennsylvania, Philadelphia, December 9–21.

Thomas, Deborah A. 2024. "Refusal (and Repair)." *Annual Review of Anthropology* 53:93–109.

Thomas, Deborah A., and Joseph Masco, eds. 2023. *Sovereignty Unhinged: An Illustrated Primer for the Study of Present Intensities, Disavowals, and Temporal Derangements*. Durham, NC: Duke University Press.

Thompson, Krista. 2007. "Preoccupied with Haiti: The Dream of Diaspora in African American Art, 1915–1942." *American Art* 21 (3): 74–97.

Thompson, Krista. 2015. *Shine: The Visual Economy of Light in African Diasporic Aesthetic Practice*. Durham, NC: Duke University Press.

Threadcraft, Shatema. 2015. "Embodiment." *The Oxford Handbook of Feminist Theory*, edited by Lisa Disch and Mary Hawkesworth, 207–26. New York: Oxford University Press.

Trotz, D. Alissa. 2007. "Red Thread: The Politics of Hope in Guyana." *Race and Class* 49 (2): 71–130.

Trotz, D. Alissa. 2010. "Who Does the Counting? Gender Mainstreaming, Grassroots Initiatives, and Linking Women Across Space and 'Race' in Guyana." In *The International Handbook of Gender and Poverty: Concepts, Research, Policy*, edited by Sylvia Chant, 655–60. Cheltenham, UK: Edward Elgar.

Trotz, D. Alissa, ed. 2021. *The Point Is to Change the World*. London: Pluto Press.

Tuck, Eve, and K. Wayne Yang. 2012. "Decolonization Is Not a Metaphor." *Decolonization: Indigeneity, Education, and Society* 1 (1): 1–40.

Tucker, Veta Smith. 2000. "Purloined Identity: The Racial Metamorphosis of Tituba of Salem Village." *Journal of Black Studies* 30 (4): 624–34.

Tucker, William H. 2002. *The Funding of Scientific Racism: Wickliffe Draper and the Pioneer Fund*. Urbana: University of Illinois Press.

Tuhiwai Smith, Linda. 2012. *Decolonizing Methodologies: Research and Indigenous Peoples*. London: Zed Books.

Turner, Bryan. 1984. *The Body and Society: Explorations in Social Theory*. New York: Basil Blackwell.

Turner, Terence. 1994. "Bodies and Anti-Bodies: Flesh and Fetish in Contemporary Social Theory." In *Embodiment and Experience*, edited by Thomas Csordas, 27–47. Cambridge: Cambridge University Press.

Turner, Terence. 1995. "Social Body and Embodied Subject: Bodiliness, Subjectivity, and Sociality Among the Kayapo." *Cultural Anthropology* 10 (2): 143–70.

Van Wolputte, Steven. 2004. "Hang On to Your Self: Of Bodies, Embodiment, and Selves." *Annual Review of Anthropology* 33: 251–69.

Varley, Emma. 2008. "Enmities and Introspection: Fieldwork Entanglements and Ethnographic Reflexivity." In *How Do We Know? Evidence, Ethnography, and the Making of Anthropological Knowledge*, edited by Liana Chua, Casey High, and Timm Lau, 133–55. Cambridge: Cambridge Scholars Press.

Viveiros de Castro, Eduardo. 1998. "Cosmological Deixis and Amerindian Perspectivism." *Journal of the Royal Anthropological Institute* 4 (3): 469–88.

Wagley, Charles. 1957. "Plantation America: A Culture Sphere." In *Caribbean Studies: A Symposium*, edited by Vera Rubin. Kingston, Jamaica: Institute of Social and Economic Studies.

Wagner-Pacifici, Robin. 2005. *The Art of Surrender: Decomposing Sovereignty at Conflict's End*. Chicago: University of Chicago Press.

Walker, Tamara. 2017. *Exquisite Slaves: Race, Clothing, and Status in Colonial Lima*. Cambridge: Cambridge University Press.

Wariboko, Nimi. 2018. "Colonialism, Christianity, and Personhood." In *A Companion to African History*, edited by William H. Worger, Charles Ambler, and Nwando Achebe, 59–75. Hoboken, NJ: Wiley-Blackwell.

Warner-Lewis, Maureen. 1977. *The Nkuyu: Spirit Messengers of the Kumina*. Mona, Jamaica: Savacou.

Warner-Lewis, Maureen. 2003. *Central Africa in the Caribbean: Transcending Time, Transforming Cultures*. Mona, Jamaica: University of the West Indies Press.

Warner-Lewis, Maureen. 2016. "Kumina Fieldwork: Findings and Revisions." *Jamaica Journal* 36 (3): 22–31.

Washburn, B. E. 1929. *Jamaica Health Stories and Plays*. Kingston, Jamaica: Government Printing Office.

Webb, James L. A. 2020. *The Guts of the Matter: A Global History of Human Waste and Infectious Intestinal Disease*. Cambridge: Cambridge University Press.

Weeks, Kathi. 2011. *The Problem with Work: Feminism, Marxism, Antiwork Politics, and Postwork Imaginaries*. Durham, NC: Duke University Press.

Weiss, Erica. 2016. "Refusal as Act, Refusal as Abstention." *Cultural Anthropology* 31 (3): 351–58.

Weiss, Gail. 1999. *Body Images: Embodiment as Intercorporeality*. New York: Routledge.

Wheeler, Roxann. 2000. *The Complexion of Race: Categories of Difference in Eighteenth-Century British Culture*. Philadelphia: University of Pennsylvania Press.

Whitely, Victor. 1979. "Ganja Only Source of Unity." *Jamaica Gleaner*, August 28.

Wilder, Gary. 2017. "The Promise of Freedom and the Predicament of Marronage: On Neil Roberts's *Freedom as Marronage*." *sx Salon*, February. https://smallAxe.net/sxsalon/reviews/promise-freedom-and-predicament-marronage-neil-robertss-freedom-marronage.

Williams, Lloyd. 1981a. "The Coptics—A Country Within Jamaica," *Sunday Gleaner*, April 26.

Williams, Lloyd. 1981b. "Ganja: Big Men Faceless but Influential," *Sunday Gleaner*, July 5.

Wolfe, Patrick. 2006. "Settler Colonialism and the Elimination of the Native." *Journal of Genocide Research* 8 (4): 387–409.

Wynter, Sylvia. n.d. "Black Metamorphosis." Unpublished manuscript.

Wynter, Sylvia. 1970. "Jonkonnu in Jamaica: Toward the Interpretation of Folk Dance as a Cultural Process." *Jamaica Journal* 4 (2): 34–48.

Wynter, Sylvia. 1977. "'We Know Where We Are From:' The Politics of Black Culture from Myal to Marley." Paper presented at the joint meetings of the African Studies Association and the Latin American Studies Association, Houston, TX, November.

Wynter, Sylvia. 2003. "Unsettling the Coloniality of Being/Power/Truth/Freedom: Towards the Human, After Man, Its Overrepresentation." In "Coloniality's Persistence," edited by Greg Thomas. Special issue, *CR: The New Centennial Review* 3 (3): 257–338.

Wynter, Sylvia. 2022. *We Must Learn to Sit Down Together and Talk About a Little Culture: Decolonising Essays, 1967–1984*. London: Peepal Tree Press.

Yelvington, Kevin. 2006. "The Invention of Africa in Latin America and the Caribbean: Political Discourse and Anthropological Praxis, 1920–1940." *Afro-Atlantic Dialogues: Anthropology in the Diaspora*, edited by Yelvington, 35–82. Santa Fe: School for Advanced Research Press.

Yerby, Erin. 2016. "Spectral Bodies of Evidence." In *Speculation, Heresy, and Gnosis in Contemporary Philosophy of Religion: The Enigmatic Absolute*, edited by Joshua Ramey and Matthew S. Haar Farris, 91–104. Lanham, MD: Rowman and Littlefield.

Young, Iris Marion. 2001. "Two Concepts of Self-Determination." In *Human Rights: Concepts, Contests, Contingencies*, edited by Austin Sarat and Thomas R. Kearns, 25–44. Ann Arbor: University of Michigan Press.

Index

archives: affective, 69; elders as, 185; embodied, 166; ephemera in, 68–69; "haptic temporalities," 67; normative frames of crime disturbed by, 179; photographic, 33; photographic, South Africa, 66–67; of surrender, 12; visual, 165. *See also* autobiographies; human remains collections

Arendt, Hannah, 73

Armstrong, Richard, 166

Armstrong, Samuel Chapman, 166

Army Alpha Test, 46

arrival stories, 152

arrivants: English as, 10

Asaah, Gordon Divine "Dee," 184

Asselar Man, 35

Australian context, 13

autobiographies, 45, 67–77; dispossession of self by narrative, 73, 75; genealogical histories in, 65, 71–74; narratives of achievement, 69–70; placing of self geographically, historically, and familially, 74; from vantage point of observer, 73–74. *See also* ephemera

autonomy, 5, 7–9; relational, 8–9, 30; without authority, 18, 166

Bacon, Alice, 166

Bad Friday (film), 78–79

Baker, Lee D., 166

Baldus de Ubaldis, 22

Bartilow, Horace, 91–92

Bataille, Georges, 209n1

Bearing Witness: Four Days in West Kingston, 179

Beckwith, Martha, 166–68

Bedward, Alexander, 47–48, 83

Behar, Ruth, 194

Being, 5, 8, 24, 69, 83, 198

Bell, Deanne, 178

Benedict, Ruth, 62

Benítez-Rojo, Antonio, 210n14

Bennett, Enid, 94

Bilby, Kenneth, 172, 173

Bishop, Maurice, 134

"Black Metamorphosis" (Wynter), 16

Black people: aestheticized as outside of history, 66–67; bodies as archive of modernity's violences and antecedents, 22; depoliticization and dispossession of, 7, 209n3; interiority denied to, 19–20; mental inferiority attributed to, 59–60, 63; sovereignty of, 16

Black Roadways: A Study of Folk Life in Jamaica (Beckwith), 166–68

Black Star Line, 86

Blake Hannah, Barbara, 89, 90, 218n7

Blakey, Michael, 62, 201

Blumenbach, Johann Friedrich, 31–32

Boas, Franz, 51, 62

"bodiliness," 21

body: abstraction of resisted, 30; agency of, 161–62; Black, as archive of modernity's violences and antecedents, 22; body-lands, 10, 17; of the church, 152; collective, fitness of measured, 66; control of through reason, 19; *corpus mysticum*, 22; embodied cognition, 212n23; as exorbitant to European categories, 5; and flesh, 20–21; as index of political community, 22; interiority denied to Black, 19–20; as medium, 161–62; as object, 20, 202; plurality of, 212n25, 212n28; and political subjectivity, 4–5; as populated by the extra-human, 211n20, 211n21, 211n22; as porous and unstable, 19–20, 63; as "racial apparatus," 20; reading innate racial difference on, 27, 30–33; as "scalar intertext," 19; sovereignty carried by, 13; of state, fictive, 22–23; as subordinated to mindsoul, 19; unaffected by material reality in myal, 178; unboundedness of, 166, 171–78, 190, 193; vulnerability of, 196. *See also* embodiment; possession

Bogle, Paul, 100

Bowie, Joe, 1–2

Bradley, Rizvana, 20–21

maroons, 9, 165; First Maroon War, 211n16; historical role in quelling rebellions, 16; Leeward and Windward treaty of 1739, 15; "resistance" embodied by, 15–16

Maroon Wars (Jamaica), 15, 16

Martin, Rudolph, 43

Marxism, 91

Mauss, Marcel, 20

McIntyre, Dianne, 2

Mead, Margaret, 62

memory: collective, 68, 193; colonial, 162; corporeal and affective, 3; and ephemera, 69; and folklore, 169; mimesis, 162

mental capacity, attempts to measure, 28, 36, 59–60, 63, 65, 76, 166–67, 215n31

Merleau-Ponty, Maurice, 20

"messianic impossibility," 18

Meyerson, Alan, 119–42, 149, 200; African travel, 150–51; as aide-de-camp to Brother Keith, 139–40; on end of Coptic Church, 140–42; feedback from, 153–60

Mico Teacher's College (Jamaica), 39; autobiographical accounts of students, 67–77

Middle Passage, 14

Mill, John Stuart, 7–8

Miller, Miss Cynthia, 188

mind, as site of objectification, 20

mind-soul: Cartesian, 19, 22–23; Greek and Roman formulations of, 22; soul as mind-force of governance, 22–23

"minor," figure of, 17

missionaries, 166

Mississippi State Sovereignty Commission, 64

misterios, 17

Mitchell, Paul W., 32

"mixed" populations, 28

modernity, 9–10, 16, 148, 210n7; violent elaboration of, 19–22, 25

Mohawk Interruptus (Simpson), 13

Mohawk Warrior Society, The: A Handbook on Sovereignty and Survival (Hall), 14

Monge, Janet, 201

Montagnais-Naskapi communities, 8

Moore, Joseph G., 172

Morant Bay Rebellion (1865), 100

Moreton-Robinson, Aileen, 13, 209–10n7

Morgan, Denroy, 103

Morgan, Thomas Hunt, 61

Morton, Samuel G., 32–34, 64

Morton Collection, 32, 201

Mossière, Géraldine, 217n3

MOVE bombing, 29, 201

"mulattos," 28, 34, 37, 41, 57

Mummy, Sister, 147

Munn, Keeble, 102

Muñoz, José Estséban, 68

myal, 194; ancestors and spirits in, 164; body unaffected by material reality in, 178; as complex, 83, 163–64; dancing, 174–75; and death, 171–72; *nkuyu*, 174, 176; as a *science* of attunement, 165; soul as multiple, 20–21, 164; as state of release from juridical realm, 22–23, 171–72; vulnerability to, 196. See also *kumina*; possession; Tambufest

"narratable self," 73

narration, 72–73

National Black Women's Health Project, 3

National Chief Takyi (Tacky) Day, 16

nationalisms, 15–16, 220n6; and folklore, 169–70

National Museum of Health and Medicine, 67

nation-state, 13–14, 66

Native Land Act of 1913 (South Africa), 66–67

nativist debates, 62

natural selection, 31, 63

Nazi Germany, 29, 43, 62, 64

Ndikung, Bonaventure Soh Bejeng, 6

"Negro in the New World" (Herskovits), 169

neoliberal dynamics, 24

Neto, Augustino, 219n22

Newell, W. W., 167

Newton, Melanie, 16
Nissenbaum, David, 79, 103, 106–7, 115–17, 157–59; on end of Coptic Church, 142–46; testimony of, 107–11
nkuyu, 174, 176
NoDAPL protests, 14
Nott, Josiah, 34
Nussbaum, Jake, 181–82
Nyabinghi drummers, 179

obeah practitioners, 163
Olivares, José de, 37
opacity, relational, 5
Operation Buccaneer III, 97
oral tradition, 14, 47, 177
Osborn, Frederick Henry, 64
Others, 6–7; "Age of Enlightenment" reports, 30–31; Christianity in opposition to, 31–32; race as mechanism for study of, 31; witchcraft as limit of understanding, 163
Otis Archives (National Museum of Health and Medicine), 67
ownership, 10, 13, 80

Palmié, Stephan, 19
pan-Africanism, 172
Panama, 134
Panton, Courtney, 188
past, as not past, 27–28
Patterson, P. J., 92–93
Peacemakers compound, 119
Pearson, Karl, 60
Penn, William, 58
Penn Museum (Philadelphia), 29, 64, 200–201; *Bearing Witness: Four Days in West Kingston*, 179
Pentecostals, 81, 217n3
People's National Party (PNP), 86, 89, 92, 119, 134–35
Pequot natives, dispossession and genocide of, 162
perception, as indeterminate, 20

performance, 217n48; African patterns, 76; in autobiographical narratives, 75; central to "giving-on-and-with," 22; as ephemeral, 69; possession as, 11; of sovereignty, 163; Tambufest as space of, 180
performance studies, 196–97
personhood, 211n20; African conceptualizations of, 20–21; co-constitution of with Holy Spirit, 217; possession as "constitutive other" for, 10; trace evidence of, 70
phenomenological approaches, 5, 18, 20–22, 203, 212n28
Pinnacle (Rastafarian commune), 89, 101, 104
Pioneer Fund, 29, 64–65, 216–17n42
plantation, 209n13; elaboration of life outside, 178; erasure of Afro-Indigenous solidarities, 16; and folklore, 169, 170; "Plantation America," 15; racial classifications West Indies, 65
Plato, 22
plural society theory, 66
"pluriverse," 21
political philosophy, post-Enlightenment, 10
polygenesis, 32, 34, 35, 59; persistence of approaches, 63–65; racial typology, 64
Popular Science Monthly, 63
possession, 211n21; border between body and land dissolved, 13; and border between ritual practice and (geo)political practice, 162; colonial memory enacted by, 162; as embodied phenomenon, 10–11; juridical and legal etymology of, 9–10, 164; as mode of redress and reclamation, 176; as performance, 11; and relation, 11; ritual, 161; spiritual and bodily reclamation and healing, 10–11; as substitute for sovereignty, 9–10; surrender to, 11. *See also* myal
Postnationalism Prefigured (Carnegie), 9
Powe, Joelle, 184, 186

Pratt, Mary Louise, 181
praxis, vulnerability of, 192–97
Preston, Jessie Fremont, 35
Preston, William, III, 35
Price-Mars, Jean, 169–70, 220n5, 221n7
prostate cancer, 190–91
Provine, William, 59, 216n37
psychological tests, 45–46, 56–57
Putnam, Carleton, 65

Quakers, 81
Quashie, Kevin, 18

"race crossing," 28; "degeneration," 34;
    "disharmonies," 40, 59, 60–61; hybrid-
    ity, problem of, 34–50, 51
Race Crossing in Jamaica (Davenport
    and Steggerda), 28–30, 166; autobio-
    graphical accounts of students not
    mentioned in, 67–69; autobiographies
    solicited, 45, 67–77; contemporary
    critiques of, 39; cosmopolitanism of
    research subjects, 47–48; criticisms
    of, 60–61; evidence not understood
    by researchers, 76–77; excess of data
    in, 50–54; genealogical pedigrees of
    subjects, 57–59, 69; inconsistencies in
    research, 39–40, 50; Jamaican partici-
    pants in study, 30–42; mental inferior-
    ity attributed to Blacks and Browns,
    59–60, 63; musical and numeric apti-
    tude results, 56–57; psychological tests,
    45–46, 56–57; results section, 50–63;
    sociological questions, 44–45; treat-
    ment of subjects, 48–50
Races of Europe, The (Coon), 64
racial classifications, 37–38; adjudication
    of race in United States, 30; colonial
    categories as, 33; craniology used to
    harden notion of, 32–33; Davenport's
    definition, 36; as folk heredity, 63;
    linguistic heritage of, 65–66; local
    cultural and class logics in, 38–39; as

mechanism of domination, 31; Scottish
    ancestry, 58, 72; in West Indies, 65–66
racial difference: assumptions about, 27;
    as innate, 27, 30–33; as problem of an-
    thropometric methods, 55–56
racial knowledge, Blackness as category
    of, 33
Rahaman, Farrah, 103–4, 184, 186
Rastafari, 78; as anarchism, 84; Coptics
    regarded as traffickers, 88–89; de-
    meaned by Coptics, 79, 90; "depro-
    gramming" strategy against, 90; gnosis
    of, 83–85; Holy Trinity of, 101; "I and
    I," 80, 152; inheritance of teachings,
    159–60; International Peacemakers,
    147, 152; as legitimate threat to state,
    131; and pan-African support, 90; Pin-
    nacle commune, 89, 101, 104; refusal of
    Western white supremacist norms, 83;
    and "schisms," 160; sonship, 84. *See also*
    Ethiopian Zion Coptic Church; ganja
Rather, Dan, 86
reading, art of, 203
Reagan, Ronald, 97, 140
recognition, logic of, 5, 7, 11, 13–14, 164
Red Thread Organization (Guyana), 9
Reilly, Thomas. *See* Brother Louv
    (Thomas Reilly)
relation: and autonomy, 8–9, 30; body as
    site of, 20; and myal, 166; poetics of, 5,
    11, 15; and possession, 11
repetition: surrender as, 11; "tidalectic"
    versus, 14–15
Requiem for a Nun (Faulkner), 27–28
Rhoden, Sydney, 37, 213n5
Ritch, Dawn, 87–88, 89, 153, 159
Robertson, Wilmot (pseudonym), 65
Rockefeller, John D., 40
Rockefeller Foundation, 29, 37, 214n8; In-
    ternational Health Board, 40
Roktowa arts space, 179, 182
Roquette-Pinto, Edgard, 61
Ryman, Cheryl, 172, 173, 175, 177